GOD AND THE ANGEL

Vivien Leigh and Laurence Olivier's
Tour De Force of Australia and New Zealand

Shiroma Perera-Nathan

M
MELBOURNE BOOKS

Dedication

For Joyce Attwood,
from one Melbourne fan to another.

Coming full circle serendipitously

———

For Ash

With whom anything is possible

Contents

9   *Introduction*

17   *Chapter 1*   TOWARDS THE PINNACLE SWAN SONG

27   *Chapter 2*   THE INVITATION

39   *Chapter 3*   VIVIEN LEIGH
                                   British Fashion Ambassador On The 1948 Old Vic Tour

51   *Chapter 4*   ON THE INDIGO SEA

63   *Chapter 5*   AUSTRALIA 1948
                                   The Land Of Clancy

69   *Chapter 6*   PERTH
                                   The Most Delightfully Isolated City In The World

87   *Chapter 7*   ADELAIDE
                                   Daliesque Tarndanya

105   *Chapter 8*   MELBOURNE
                                   Fandom From Fitzroy

127   *Chapter 9*   TASMANIA
                                   The Water Coloured Isle

139	*Chapter 10*	SURFERS *Paradise Unspoilt*
147	*Chapter 11*	SYDNEY *Where Larry Lost Vivien*
177	*Chapter 12*	BRISBANE *Farewell Australia*
191	*Chapter 13*	NEW ZEALAND *The Land Of The Long White Cloud*
213	*Chapter 14*	THE CURTAIN FALL

231 *Postscript*

236 *Endnotes*

243 *Bibliography*

244 *Index*

252 *Acknowledgements*

254 *The Author*

Introduction

A desire like a thousand windswept storms,
They courted lust like chasing its rain,
Clinging to a frivolous, yet all-consuming passion,
That cleared to a blossoming day,
Canopied by the mythical rainbow:
Only surpassed by blinding light of morrow,
Eclipsed by their jealous gloom, his status, her malady, mad ominous cloud,
Leaving their sketch on Australia's legendary landscape,
And Aotearoa's mural,
For mortals to dream of,
And that was their love … God and the Angel.

— Shiroma Perera-Nathan

In 1948, Laurence Olivier and Vivien Leigh, acting as actor ambassadors, led The Old Vic Theatre Company on a performance tour of Australia and New Zealand. It was a symbolic gesture by the British Government to thank both countries for their war efforts, underlined by political motives and the remnants of colonialism. Practically it was a way for the theatre to raise much-needed funds. The Old Vic represented the surviving spirit of Great Britain and with an internationally accepted and respected art form, it was a suitable gift. It also exemplified the appropriate 'British' influence on the two countries which had stood alongside her through her darkest days, however, post-war was drawn more to an American influence. Therefore, the company was also the vehicle through which Britain attempted to re-colonise her Dominions, to maintain and further her commercial, political and cultural interests.

The tour was one of many that deployed Shakespeare for British cultural diplomacy. This one was, however, the most influential and successful by an acting troupe bringing Shakespeare to the Antipodes; a type of highbrow culture and fan frenzy that had never been seen there before or since, due mainly to the Oliviers' star personas.

Olivier, the finest Shakespearean actor of his era with Vivien Leigh as his glamorous, world-famous, talented wife, made a stunning couple. Together they embodied for the British a sense of national pride – he the lyrical and she the visual. They were treated like royalty and indeed, by 1948, they were the undisputed King and Queen of the English stage. The public frenzy and anticipation started as soon as the press announced it. The Oliviers were the original global *celebrity couple* and the fever that ensued was compounded by the fact that, by 1948, they had almost mythological public personas; being beautiful, world-famous film stars, as well as accomplished and respected stage actors; a combination that has yet to be challenged today.

It was thought that Australia and New Zealand were treating the Oliviers, who were carrying the informal title of King and Queen of the British stage, as a dress rehearsal for the official visit of King George VI and Queen Elizabeth the following year. Newspapers wrote of nothing else. They were mobbed, invited to society balls, gave speeches, addressed Parliament, dined with leaders, lectured, and scouted for talent. They were also subjected to the same relentless intrusion that comes with stardom, being hounded by fans, media and the public – decades before the internet, the paparazzi and the enigma that was Princess Diana. Similar to this was the forced public image that needed to be maintained. Although the

Preceding spread, on left:
In Canberra. Credit: Kendra Bean Collection

Left:
Making a toast in possibly Sydney or Brisbane. Credit: Author's collection

Oliviers were still very much in love, they were also human and felt the pressures at times too much to cope with, reaching close to their breaking points.

Laurence Olivier spoke much to the press and at lectures, encouraging Australia to establish theatre schools to stop talent from leaving overseas. His speeches encouraged discussions in acting circles, prompting fresh ideas and thought. This encouraged other theatre companies to tour Australia and contributed to a Shakespearean boom in the 1950s.

The tour was a wonderful success financially; influential and fondly remembered by many. But it was also the beginning of the end of one of the greatest love stories of its day. The Olivier marriage, which had come at great personal cost (they had both abandoned their spouses and children to be together) never recovered from the stress, strain and exhaustion of the tour. Both suffered health issues, with Olivier needing knee surgery in New Zealand and Vivien, already stricken with tuberculosis (TB), constantly suffering colds. Her yet to be diagnosed bipolar disorder also contributed to mood swings and, at times, hyperactivity, adding further strain. It was also mid-way through the tour that Olivier was fired along with the other two directors of the Old Vic, John Burrell and Ralph Richardson by the Board of Governors, plunging him into what may today be called a mini mid-life crisis and depression. Olivier and Vivien kept this from the rest of the group in order to complete the tour in good spirits.

In Australia they met English-born, Australian actor Peter Finch, whom Olivier would go on to mentor and with whom Vivien would have an affair, causing irreparable damage to both the Olivier and Finch marriages. Olivier would later recall that he had in fact lost Vivien, the love of his life, his life force and inspiration, in Australia. He wrote in his autobiography, 'Somehow, somewhere on this tour I knew Vivien was lost to me. I, half-joking, would say at odd moments after we had got back home, "I *lorst* you in Australia".'[1]

Together they led the tour without letting their personal conflicts affect their professional duties. They always showed a united front to the cast; mentoring, supporting, entertaining and becoming surrogate parents when needed. During the nine months they toured, Olivier and Vivien occupied a very special place in their lives. So much so, that they affectionately referred to the couple as 'God and Angel'.

In 1994, the Australian National Library acquired what was most likely the personal album the Oliviers kept of the 1948 tour, containing close to 600 photos. (Note: the National Library confirms that it does not contain any

Left:
Posing at Scarborough Beach. Credit: Author's collection

information on the provenance of the album but it is titled – 'Athol Shmith Album Australia Tour 1948, Laurence Olivier & Vivien Leigh & Old Vic Co.' Louis Athol Shmith was a prominent photographer who took portraits of both Olivier and Vivien during the tour. It is possible that the album was gifted to Shmith by the Oliviers at some point).

The album provides a wonderful insight into the tour, showing a company that enjoyed a truly authentic visit to Australia and New Zealand. There are many landscape photos of their days out on picnics to beaches, people's homes and zoos. They are intimate, especially some of those of Vivien presumably taken by Olivier. They appear as studies and observations from afar, conveying a love expressed via the lens. The hundreds of casual photos cast a light on a side of the tour that is not conveyed in the myriad of newspaper articles, formal and press photos, video footage and even the excellent recount of the tour written by Garry O'Connor in his book, *Darlings of the Gods*.

The photographer 'assumed' to be Olivier in the landscape photos shows an appreciation for nature, farms, native flora, and a love of animals. These casual shots also capture the uniqueness of the two countries and provide an important timepiece of history because they show what Australia and New Zealand looked like in 1948, socially and demographically.

In September 2017, Sotheby's auctioned *The Vivien Leigh Collection*, of which Lot 211 – the Australia Lot – comprised a collection of books presented to them by Australian authors and a small album of photos taken on the tour, which lends further insight into Australian literary culture at the time and photographic scenery.

In these two albums, time has stopped for us, captured within the vision of the photographer, presumably Olivier, allowing us to travel back to 1948. In the blink of an eye, when the double image was recorded, we get to see what the photographer chose to focus on and also ask why it was singled out, giving us an understanding of the photographer himself.

Along with new archival material available for research, most notably the Laurence Olivier papers by The British Library, The Vivien Leigh Archive by the Victoria and Albert Museum and personal private collections, like Australian fan, Joyce Attwood's collection, the tour can be seen through a more personal and different lens to which it was viewed previously.

It was an astounding success both financially and artistically, capturing the public's imagination like no other theatre tour had done before or since, influencing the cultures of Australia and New Zealand, living long in the memories of those that formed the troupe, the audiences, fans and those lucky enough to have been touched by the experience in some way.

Along with the impact it had on Australia and New Zealand culturally, the tour lives on in a nostalgic sense in memories and also a new generation of fans and theatre buffs because of the fairy-tale aura that accompanied the tour due to it being led by two of last century's most glamourous, artistic and iconic couples. As Australian actor, writer and director Michael Blakemore, who as a young medical student was a lucky audience member, wrote in his memoir, 'There had never been a tour quite like it, and probably there never will be. In Laurence Olivier and Vivien Leigh were combined the theatre's most prestigious couple, Heathcliff and Scarlett O'Hara come down to earth.'[2]

It has been close to thirty-five years since the last and only compelling publication on the tour, Garry O'Connor's *Darlings of the Gods: One year in the lives of Laurence Olivier and Vivien Leigh*. In light of the new material available for research, a treasure trove of never-before published photos, a better understanding of history and its lessons, the medical conditions and dynamics of the Olivier marriage, it seems fitting to not only appreciate it through a fairer, modern, and visual perspective but also through an Australian context.

———

By reliving the tour now, we can look back with a privileged lens to take lessons from the past. Although it's primarily a story that attempts to nostalgically retrace Laurence Olivier and Vivien Leigh's footsteps during the tour, giving attention to long forgotten Australian and New Zealand personalities, this book will contain themes and references that do not reflect current understandings and must be read and understood in a historical context. This is because the ideals of the world in which they lived are now antiquated and may seem unrelatable or unfair to today's audiences and readers; a world that was steeped in 1940's patriarchal systems and colonialism.

In retelling this story, the author wishes to acknowledge Australia's First Nations Peoples — The First Australians, Traditional Owners and Custodians.

Below:
Booklet made for The Food for Britain appeal. Credit: Author's collection

Chapter 1

TOWARDS THE PINNACLE SWAN SONG

They say a swan loves only once and will
return to where its love was won to die.
Making its deathbed where it first made love,
it can forget it has withdrawn to die.
Are these tales true? In the dessert, where I live,
no swan has come, not a single one, to die.
But then they say that swans return to water,
in whose embrace life was begun, to die.
Open your arms, my dear, and slake my thirst:
the time has come for one more swan to die.*

* Part of poem *Swan Song* by Iranian poet Mehdi Hamidi Shirazi (1914–86) translated from Persian by Armen Davoudian.

Laurence Olivier, with his hair not quite back to his normal shade of brown after bleaching it for his film *Hamlet*, sat down for lunch with Reginald Pound close to departing on the nine-month Australasia tour for an interview. Olivier admitted to having welcomed the idea of the tour as timely, viewing it as a break from his close to eighteen-hour workdays and having had to resort to taking pills to keep himself awake.[1] Pound noted Olivier was already sleepy and sluggish at lunch, which didn't prove to him the tablets were working. In fact, he writes that he had trouble keeping Olivier interested and felt a sense of guilt, having had to occupy even that time with him.

The article describes a typical day for Olivier over the last ten months or so, prior to the tour commencing. He was on the home run with finishing his film *Hamlet* at Denham Studios, usually working twelve hours a day. The rest was spent answering masses of letters, contracts being discussed, new plays being visualised, considering films, making public appearances and to top it off, charity demands. He told Pound that the only day he had to watch films and relax was Sunday, when he and Vivien would sometimes fit in four or five films in one sitting.

Vivien Leigh had spent the winter of 1946 at their beloved country estate Notley in Buckinghamshire, recuperating from tuberculosis, renovating, gardening and falling in love with the estate that she had been so against buying. The tuberculosis had developed after a three-month stint at the Piccadilly, during a highly successful run of Thornton Wilder's *The Skin of Our Teeth*, in which she had finally come into her own, playing the siren through time, Sabina.

Preceding spread, on left: Getting onto the fateful flight at La Guardia. Credit: Greta Ritchie Collection

Below: Notley Abbey, Buckinghamshire, home of the Olivers in 1948, since 1944. An abbey Olivier fell in love with and Vivien called the only home she ever knew. Credit: Author's collection

Vivien had suffered from colds, coughs and ailments of the chest since she was a child. In fact, Stephen Galloway writes in *Truly Madly: Vivien Leigh and Laurence Olivier, The Romance of the Century,* that she might've actually had a bout of tuberculosis as a child.[2] The cough she developed while playing Sabina worsened and was accompanied by a recurring fever. With Olivier away on a victory tour with The Old Vic in Europe, even after an x-ray confirmed the tubercular patch on one lung, she continued to perform in *The Skin of Our Teeth*. She was only thirty-two, and – besides rest, sleep, healthy food, and potentially being confined to a sanatorium – there was no treatment available for tuberculosis.

During this time, Olivier's various correspondence and recordings show he was already exhausted. Throughout the tour, he wrote thirty-six letters to Vivien enquiring constantly about her health, missing her and conveying a sense of loving tenderness and care. In one he writes, 'I cannot live without you and I don't intend to bloody well try ever again … You are my inspiration, my hope, my whole hope, the oxygen in my blood.'[3]

Vivien, not wanting to worry Olivier while he was on tour, did not tell him about her illness and he only heard via the Lunts (Alfred Lunt and his wife Lynn Fontanne), when he met them in Paris. When he immediately called her from Paris, she still avoided telling him the full story. He wrote again 'Your sorrow is my worst fear … your life my life.'[4]

It was only after Olivier returned from the tour that she was forced to retire from the play. She then spent six weeks at the University College Hospital refusing to enter a sanatorium. In consolation, she agreed to stay at Notley, where she rested through the winter under the care of a nurse. Olivier was in London preparing for The Old Vic's new season and only returned to Notley and 'his girl' on Sundays. The 1946 season has often been claimed as what set Olivier apart in stature, while Vivien's career took a step back as she recuperated. Unfortunately, she would never fully recover.

After the recuperation period at Notley at the end of April 1946, Vivien accompanied Olivier, who by then had become part of the triumvirate in charge of The Old Vic Theatre alongside Ralph Richardson and John Burrell, on their six-week season in New York. Although not having any role, she used it as a time to catch up with old friends and be supportive of Olivier, who continued overworking. In trying to end the season on a high, with his usual acrobatic showmanship style, Olivier suffered the first of his onstage accidents, damaging a leg. At the end of the season, they both flew to Boston, where he was awarded an Honorary Degree at Tufts College; one of five he would receive and accept over the years from various institutions.

They returned back to England after surviving a near-death experience on a flight from La Guardia, when the engine caught on fire and an emergency landing occurred on an open field. The incident grounded a fleet of planes. At the time this traumatised both Olivier and Vivien and influenced the decision on how to proceed logistically on the tour, but surprisingly Olivier didn't mention it in his autobiography.

TOWARDS THE PINNACLE SWAN SONG

Below:
At Tufts College, Boston, where Olivier was awarded an Honorary Master of Arts Degree, June 16 1946. Credit: Greta Ritchie Collection

After returning, they had time to have a brief rest before Vivien started another season of *The Skin of Our Teeth* at the Piccadilly, although many felt she should have rested further. It was again a great success but she lost a lot of weight, giving evidence for her health remaining precarious. Olivier started his production of *King Lear*, directing *Skin*, administrating The Old Vic, and then on his film adaptation of *Hamlet*. It was still non-stop.

One may wonder why there was the need to work so much. Those who are driven and passionate about their careers tend to be workaholics, as Olivier and Vivien were. In hindsight however, their drive may have been too extreme. Some biographers point out that their expenses made it inevitable, living beyond their means. Olivier's salary from The Old Vic was £60 per week. He had to pay alimony to his first wife, Jill Esmond, of £3500 a year, and Notley was an expensive project to restore, especially with what Olivier had envisioned.

Why a seventeen-year-old Jean Simmons was cast as Ophelia in Olivier's film *Hamlet* and not Vivien is not known for certain. Many claim that after Vivien put in a gallant campaign for the role, she became deeply distressed when she was not chosen which, as a result, caused a rift within the Olivier marriage. Although there is evidence that she had communicated her intention of playing the role to Cecil Beaton, as he so diarised in early 1947, there is nothing to indicate the final decision had that much of an impact on their marriage. Strachan's comprehensive and well-researched biography of Vivien, *Dark Star*, supports this.[5]

There could have only been two deciders – either Olivier or Arthur Rank's backers. Galloway writes that Rank actually insisted on a younger woman and Olivier only put in a token protest but then relented.[6] Terry Coleman writes that Vivien was upset with the decision but she had happily joined in with all the planning, accompanying Olivier on a fully paid-for trip to Italy. She actively advised him on which characters to cut, helped him rehearse and was the only visitor permitted on the set. To assume Vivien was upset and jealous about the casting is to assume that she was fragile and insecure. It is also to assume that she didn't understand the vast age difference between seventeen and thirty-three. We don't know what might've gone through Vivien's psyche. It's safe to assume though that, somewhere in the back of her emotional recess, having a much younger version of herself (Simmons bore an uncanny resemblance and could easily have passed as her sister), playing opposite her husband in a role she herself had played at the height of their illicit affair, she felt the demoralising slap, even if ever so softly.

What would've caused her more grief was the inability to bring to life a role she very much identified with: *Anna Karenina*. The story of pursuing passionate love by committing adultery, and abandoning a child and husband, hit close to home. Vivien had left her first husband Leigh Holman and a young daughter in the middle of the night to be with Olivier, her secret lover of nearly two years. Vivien had loved Tolstoy's novel just like she had devoured *Gone with the Wind,* and it had all the ingredients of being another iconic role for her like Scarlett O'Hara had been in 1939.

The film was called a beautiful failure. It had a number of problems; casting, especially for the role of Vronsky to Kieron Moore with whom she had no chemistry; a dull and badly put together script; and costumes, although sumptuous, somehow overpowering the characters. This is not to say there weren't some beautifully filmed and poignantly memorable scenes, like Vivien glimpsing Vronsky for the first time through the fog-misted train windows, and the heart-wrenching finale. It is still a film worthy of a watch for there are various scenes where Vivien's ability to express a vast array of emotions on screen without a single word being said can be appreciated. Her disappointment was obvious and she conceded it had been a challenge: 'Anna Karenina is the most difficult role I have ever played. I had to bring to life her hidden feelings and deepest thoughts. I had to transform into flesh and blood her soul and mind … it was not so easy to do. I have tried my best.'[7]

Another major event leading up to the tour was Olivier's knighthood. It has been said that Vivien was jealous and annoyed with it, choosing to dress for the ceremony as if for a funeral. But she was very enthusiastic to take the title of Lady Olivier – something she didn't relinquish until her dying day. The outfit she picked to wear was a simple black suit with a hat that perfectly framed her face (evocative of another exciting time for her – signing the contract to *Gone with the Wind*). If one sees it as too understated, it may just have been to not overshadow Olivier in his moment of achievement. The 'funeral attire' criticism seems both unfair and sexist. For whatever reason, Olivier did not own a morning suit and ended up wearing a borrowed vest from Ralph Richardson and a coat from Anthony Bushell. Felix Barker (in an authorised biography of both Vivien and Olivier in 1953) writes that Olivier found a little comfort in owning the pants at least.[8]

By the close of 1947, Vivien started to show the first outward signs of what would become her lifelong battle – then manic depression, today bipolar disorder. Over the years, there had been indicative tremors startling those who bore witness but nothing that could not have been excused as hormonal changes, bad tantrums and the behaviour of a spoilt, beautiful woman. Noël Coward once assumed it may be alcohol induced. During the filming of *Anna Karenina*, there were incidents of odd behaviour, diarised by Cecil Beaton the costume designer, in his usual waspish style. These included concerns about the gloves she had to wear, and a rather strange reaction to the announcement of Olivier's knighthood. Biographers write that the presence of her mother, Gertrude, on the set indicated that all was not well. Alec Guinness, although not a close friend, was an observer from as far back as 1937, being Olivier's understudy during the Elsinore *Hamlet* season, during which time he said there were whispers of concern over Vivien's mental wellbeing.[9] Still, it's unfair to 'confirm' this from one diarist's account and the presence of her mother. Beaton was a character that often displayed a jealous, bitchy and mean streak even in his diarising. But the actors themselves knew while filming that Moore was badly miscast, including Moore himself, therefore predetermining the film's failure and adding to a negative environment.[10] The unhappy arena *Anna Karenina* was filmed in would certainly have contributed to an understandably depressive mood if Vivien was in that cycle of her disorder.

Apart from that possibility, she had not recovered fully from the TB – and she never would. Olivier's concern continued even though he was busy himself. He had insisted that she should not overwork. Sally Ann Howes, who played Kitty, remembered, 'She had been ill so her contract limited her time on the set to between eleven and four. Every time she stepped onto the set the telephone would ring and it would be Larry checking she was all right. Then at four, he'd ring again to make sure she didn't work any longer. I was seventeen and thought it very romantic.'[11]

Hence, when The Old Vic Tour of Australia and New Zealand had been proposed, an exhausted Olivier had toured New York with an array of roles with The Old Vic, just finished *Hamlet*, was being hailed as the greatest Shakespearean actor of his generation, and been knighted. Vivien had succeeded in claiming a role on stage for herself as Sabina in *The Skin of Our Teeth*, had barely recovered from a severe bout of TB, and completed a crushingly disappointing *Anna Karenina* through what might've been a depressive cycle in her yet to be diagnosed bipolar condition. She was still the more globally recognised film star out of the two, due to the enduring and iconic nature of her portrayal of Scarlett O'Hara in *Gone with the Wind* ten years earlier and the film's ongoing worldwide success. Romantically they still appeared very much in love, although like all relationships, feelings may have been hurt on and off and resentments lay dormant.

In this setting, the Oliviers – thinking the tour was well timed, giving them a chance to rest, to recover health-wise and reconnect personally – were instead heading into the most exhausting time of their careers. A tour that quite possibly was the swan song to the pinnacle of their romantic and professional life together.

Below: Olivier with Jean Simmons in *Hamlet* appears on the cover of *The Australasian Post* in time for its Australian premiere. Credit: Private Collection

Left:
Olivier with his hair coloured blonde for *Hamlet*, at Buckingham Palace to recieve his knighthood.
Credit: Greta Ritchie Collection

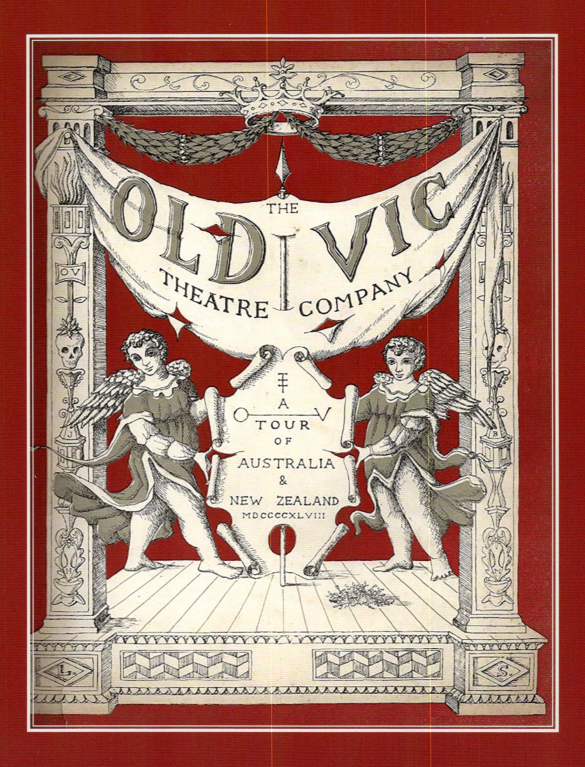

— *Chapter 2* —

THE INVITATION

Then the God and his Angel took flight,
From Mount Olympus' height,
Hebe, bearer of the cup,
Brought her promise to sup*

* A verse inspired by a poem found in *Papers of Peter Finch*, 1937–54, National Library of Australia NLA MS 7003.

The Old Vic Tour of Australia and New Zealand was, according to Felix Barker, the result of a suggestion by Sir Angus Gillan while on a tour of the countries himself after the war.¹ Gillan was then the Head of the Empire Division of the British Council. He had put it to Dan O'Connor, a New Zealander and concert impresario, that he should go to England to organise the visit of some companies, with the support of the British Council. O'Connor took that advice and duly secured the Boyd Neel Orchestra, the Ballet Rambert and The Old Vic Theatre Company. This was more than a mere suggestion – it was part of a bigger agenda. O'Connor was the go-between for the British Council, securing contracts and deals and the tours were the drivers of Britain's recolonisation attempt of the Dominions.

In 1934, the British Foreign Office created the British Council with the *official* ethos of supporting English education abroad, promoting British culture and fighting the rise of fascism. In 1940, King George VI granted the Office a Royal Charter for those purposes but after the war it was one of the vehicles through which Great Britain's new stage in post war recolonisation was driven. Recolonisation meant gravitating already settled colonies' social, cultural and commercial interests back to Britain and to engage them in projecting English culture to non-colonised nations. After the war, even with a considerable dissolution of Britain's South-East Asian Empire (Ceylon and Burma's independence, partition and independence of India and Pakistan), the Empire ideology was still important: to help pay off wartime debts to the United States, stop the

Preceding spread, on left: The cover of the official tour book. Credit: Author's collection

Left:
The Oliviers farewelled at Euston Station by High Commissioners for Australia and New Zealand. Credit: Author's collection

Left:
Majority of the tour group in Hobart, St John's Church, Richmond. Credit: Author's collection

threat of fascism and communism, and also curb the growing Americanisation of Australian and New Zealand societies.

Valerie Lawson wrote in *Dancing Under the Southern Skies; A history of Australian ballet* that the campaign seemed to have begun as far back as May 1944: a letter from the British Council representative to the British High Commissioner in Canberra expressed major concern that American books, films and music were making bigger strides in terms of influence than British.[2]

Britain was struggling to get her identity back in her post-war slump, and to understand her global role now that the Empire was crumbling and new world powers had emerged. Tours, especially when led by a 'celebrity power couple' personifying the 'British ideal', were a form of propaganda. James Lee Taylor in his thesis on 'Shakespeare, Decolonisation, and the Cold War' writes that although this kind of propaganda may ultimately fail to disguise weakness or the realities of decline, in the short term it can help economically project an image of strength and confidence.[3]

The cultural tours sponsored by the British Council were the most visible demonstration of this foreign policy initiative during those years. They decided on a soft strategy approach. A Council representative wrote to Secretary General in London, 'The Council's first approaches in Australia should be tactful. Any suggestion that the Council regarded Australia as a somewhat uneducated nephew in need of enlightenment would naturally be unfortunate.'[4] Starting with recruiting a network of Australians to support the campaign, the British Council then sent Charles Wilmot in January 1947 to Sydney as its first Australian representative. Wilmot told the awaiting press that the purpose of the British Council was to inform the 'rest of the world' about Britain's cultural and educational achievements.[5] In the next two years Australia would be bombarded with British cultural touring groups, starting with the Boyd Neel Orchestra and then the Ballet Rambert.

Today, the Council's website describes itself as a council that builds connections, understanding and trust between people in the UK and other countries through arts and culture, education, and the English language.

The Old Vic tour was the next coup. In its official tour program booklet, The Old Vic is described as a British institution. Established in 1818 by former Surrey Theatre Managers James King and Daniel Dunn and John Thomas Serres, the King's marine painter, it was called the Royal Coburg Theatre. It went through many more managers and names over the years and then, as the Royal Victoria Hall, it came under Emma Cons' management between 1880 and 1912. Charles Wilmot wrote, in the program's foreword, that Cons converted it into a place where the poor from London's south of the river went for refreshments and recreation. By then it was already known as The Old Vic. But it was under Lilian Bayliss, Cons' niece, who took over after her death, that it really became a world-celebrated home for Shakespeare and good drama.

Dame Sybil Thorndike wrote an article titled 'Of Pioneering' in July 1949, in which she said The Old Vic of the day was very different to the one she had joined.[6] Then it had been a group of young unknown actors under Bayliss who placed no importance on publicity and preferred word of mouth from one patron to a friend. Bayliss didn't give much credence to critics and never gave them any free seats. But Thorndike wrote that The Old Vic was always pioneering and had become grander in operation, with world-famous distinguished actors, actresses and ambitious undertakings like the 1948 tour. She thought Olivier's performance of *Richard III* was electric and astonishing and Vivien's in *The Skin of Our Teeth* beautiful and brilliant.

The Old Vic was severely damaged in the Blitz but continued to be involved in the war effort by touring and taking Shakespeare, ballet, and opera to those suffering wartime toil through the years 1940 to 1943. In 1944, the company got re-established in London with Ralph Richardson and Laurence Olivier performing mostly at the New Theatre (now the Noël Coward Theatre).

Therefore, in 1948, the British Council felt that The Old Vic was an appropriate representation of the British spirit – 'a characteristic contribution to an art universally practiced and esteemed which maintains the highest traditions and standards of a great calling.'[7]

Further, Wilmot writes, 'We are proud of the Old Vic. It has arisen from the very heart of the British people, sustained and encouraged by them. It belongs to them. They are glad of this opportunity of sharing it now with their Australian and New Zealand fellow members of the Commonwealth from whom they received so much during these dark years.'[8]

The powers at The Old Vic at the time, notably Lord Esher, who had interest in the British Council too (he was a member of The Old Vic Governors as well as Chairman of the British Council's Drama Advisory Committee) and secretary of The Old Vic Governors, Tyrone Guthrie, thought that by The Old Vic aligning itself with Britain's new path of cultural diplomacy, it would help garner big Government funding, which it did during the tour.[9]

Below:
A page from a booklet published in 1948 for the Theatre Royal in Hobart.
Credit: Author's collection

American film producer, Samuel Goldwyn, asked Laurence Olivier, 'Why are you, the greatest actor in the world, taking a touring company to Australia of all places?'[10] Olivier, in his memoir, wrote that when he was approached by the Council to head the tour with Vivien, he accepted the invitation with pleasure. It would not only secure a good pay cheque for him and Vivien, but would allow him an opportunity to create a stronger Old Vic, which had been struggling to exist independently since the war, and which had recently been approached by the National Theatre to combine interests.[11] These reasons must've outweighed the negatives as he was giving up four film contracts, a comedy for Vivien and also taking a substantial cut in his pay. Whatever his personal reasons were, Olivier and Vivien were very patriotic and held nationalistic views. This was the norm after the war and, whichever side of politics one stood on, England always came first. They would therefore have had no qualms in leading the tour.

Their star power was a crucial ingredient for the mission and it was likely that they were fully aware of the fact. Olivier had a grand vision of this being the first step in creating a little Empire, even stating he was embarking on a grand twelve-year plan and that when he got back to England, The Old Vic would be decent enough to be worthy of being called one of the National Theatre companies.[12]

Even though Australia and New Zealand were at the other end of the world, *'Down Under'*, Laurence Olivier and Vivien Leigh were still household names. Michael Blakemore, a teenager in 1948 Sydney, shows the nature of their fame in his memoir:

> *On screens all over Sydney I'd seen their eyes, as big as headlamps, mist with feeling; I'd seen them laugh, kiss and lament in monochrome and in colour. [...] stars whose two-dimensional image had been amongst the first to spread across the world like a virus. [...] this acting elite held sway in both mediums. [...] They were famous, rich, lacquered in glamour and magically skilled.*[13]

As their roles demanded, they were more than mere stars and actors. They were expected to do more than just act. As actor ambassadors sponsored by the British Council, they would have to attend civic receptions, do interviews, make speeches and broadcasts, and everything else that a royal visit might have entailed; representing and personifying everything that was *British*.

The company that Olivier picked were mainly young talent with a handful of mature and experienced actors, many of whom had worked with Olivier and Vivien before and were friends. Couples included George Relph and Mercia Swinburne, Terence Morgan and Georgina Jumel, and Peter Cushing and Helen Beck. In Cushing's autobiography, he recalled telling Olivier that his only concern about the tour was being apart from Helen. Their love would be one of the sincerest to have existed. Olivier must've sensed Cushing's desperation and, with a kiss to his forehead, had said the war had caused too many separations so Helen was welcomed to join.[14] Cushing and Terence Morgan had already co-starred in Olivier's *Hamlet*.

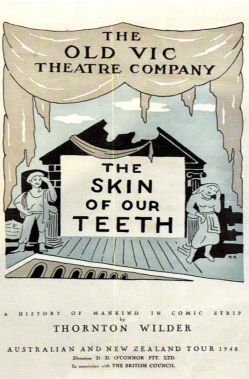
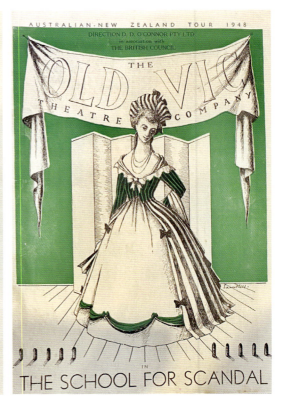

Left:
Theatre program for *Richard III*.

Middle:
Theatre program for *The Skin of Our Teeth*.

Right:
Cover of *The School for Scandal* theatre program.

Credit: Author's collection

The remaining cast included Dan Cunningham, Eileen Beldon, Thomas Heathcote, Michael Redington, John Barnard, Bernard Mereford, James Bailey, Hugh Stewart, Oliver Hunter, Robert Beaumont, George Cooper, Tony Gavin, Derrick Penley and Denis Lehrer. The ladies in waiting were Anne McGrath, Meg Maxwell, Peggy Simpson and Jane Shirley whose mother Angela Baddeley would act small parts and help out.

Olivier decided on a repertoire of three plays to perform. *Richard III* was a forgone conclusion, having already toured Europe in 1945, and Olivier's performance being so highly hailed and received. It was expected to be the performance that Australians and New Zealanders most wanted to see from him. After six years of a hiatus of sorts from the stage, Olivier's interpretation of *Richard III* took him into the realm of theatre immortality almost instantly. John Mills, Olivier's contemporary and good friend, remembered being summoned by Olivier to see him, but warned him to prepare for a dismal performance – 'So I went and had two double brandies. The curtain went up, on came his lordship, and said, "Now is the winter of our discontent ..." and the whole theatre froze. It was the performance of a lifetime.'[15]

If one play was to showcase Olivier, another would need to showcase Vivien who, at this time, was actually a bigger draw card than Olivier in Australia and New Zealand (because of her Hollywood star power from *Gone with the Wind*). The play was an obvious pick but was risky and unlikely to be approved by the Council.

Thornton Wilder's folk story of mankind, *The Skin of Our Teeth*, provided a unique vehicle for Vivien in the role of Sabina to showcase her natural mercurial vitality and comedic timing. Olivier had already directed her as Sabina in 1947 and the press agreed it was her best performance to date on stage, and one he was also very proud of. He seemed desperate during that time to have the press critically recognise Vivien, to the point of even chastising critic James Agate for arriving late after intermission to his seat at one performance.[16] Despite this, Agate's review was very favourable and one that's been quoted many times. 'Through it, all, lovely to look at, flitted and fluttered Miss Leigh's hired girl, Sabina, an enchanting piece of nonsense-cum-allure, half dabchick and half dragonfly.'

Thornton Wilder himself was very impressed with Vivien's performance and wrote to Olivier after seeing a Liverpool performance: 'Vivien has quite definitely, beyond all doubt, established herself as a seriously considered actress from every point of view.'[17] And after seeing a London rehearsal wrote again, 'I saw and felt the menace hanging over the house ... Vivien unrolls a continuous stream of fascinating art, clear and yet subtle, unforgettable – and I dream with joy about the Sabina of Act III.'[18]

There's no doubt that many professional relationships experience tinges of jealousy and, at times, ego tugs of war. However, accusations of Olivier's overt envy towards Vivien and him purposely trying to ruin her career seem extremely unfair, considering he went out of his way to find a play to showcase her and balance the three plays out evenly – 'talent'-wise, that is. The British Council and the Governors of The Old Vic had to be convinced about *The Skin of Our Teeth*, as it was American (nothing British about it), modern, controversial, somewhat confusing, and therefore the riskiest choice for an Australian and New Zealand audience – especially seeing they were not regular theatregoers and considered naïve in that sense. But Olivier was adamant about having it for Vivien and eventually, he got what he wanted.

The third play he picked was to have equal roles for both him and Vivien. He picked the comedy of manners, *The School for Scandal* by Richard Sheridan, which they had not done before. Costumes and sets were to be designed by Cecil Beaton and in typical Beaton ingenuity, the sets were designed as back cloths and drops providing easy shipment for touring but still maintaining the ambience of an eighteenth-century playhouse.

The company rehearsed through January 1947 and were originally meant to have set off in autumn of the same year but didn't. According to Olivier, after the war, it was only by February 1948 that a ship was found to transport the whole company. However, it has also been suggested that Olivier deliberately put off the voyage due to delays in his filming of *Hamlet*.[19]

Regardless of why the tour didn't start at the time originally planned, the advance party consisting of three actors, a scenic artist, a property master, a master carpenter, an electrician, the stage, assistant stage, and company managers left on February 6th, 1948, on SS *Moreton Bay*, sleeping four to a cabin.[20]

On February 14th, Valentine's Day, on what was described as a grey morning, the Oliviers boarded their boat train at Euston Station. They'd only had a few hours of sleep after an extravagant and 'intimate' going away party for seventy-odd friends at their small London home, Durham Cottage, the night before. Vivien, an ardent cat lover, was most affected by having to leave her beloved Siamese, New, behind. The reception at the station would be a preview of the welcome and hype they would receive at every city they called on during the course of the tour.

They spent a good hour on platform thirteen recording for BBC news, posing for nearly fifty cameramen, listening to speeches by the High Commissioners to Australia and New Zealand, Mr Beasley and Mr WJ Jordan, and signing autographs for masses of weeping fans. Police struggled to keep the crowd cordoned. Flowers, scraps of paper and autograph books were thrown at the couple by what newspapers described as Bobby Soxers, shouting, 'Goodbye and good luck.'

One article quoted Olivier as saying, 'I hope Australian audiences will be receptive to Shakespeare, but whether they will be receptive to our interpretation of him, I don't know.'[21] Vivien, noted as wearing the new length fur coat over a brown herring-bone tweed suit and a pea green hat, said, 'I want to see the Koala bears in Australia. The trouble is that I know I shall fall in love with them and want to bring some back.'[22]

The Evening Standard that same night reported it was expected The Old Vic Company would advise the Australian Government on the development of the theatre, particularly amateur theatre. Apparently, a Government committee had already begun investigating and would defer any decisions until they had met Olivier.

Papers in Australia had already begun

reporting on the impending tour as early as November 1947. There was public outcry when talk of Tasmania being excluded from the tour was discussed. The civic leaders of each State had been advised by The British Council of the tour's purpose and they had already started preparing. Barker wrote in the first approved biography, *The Oliviers*, in 1953 that the States most likely wanted to outdo each other, contributing to what would become a social marathon.[23]

James Lee Taylor in his thesis on 'Shakespeare, Decolonisation, and the Cold War' claims that the British Council was aware that there may be objections to their establishment of a network in Australia because of the pressing political needs of Britain and in order to divert attention whilst they did so, advance publicity for the tour was used as a cover.[24] Taylor quotes an internal report by the committee set up to advise the British Council on relations with the external territories of Australia as hoping that the tour's preparation (i.e., the advance press) would 'appear to justify' the British Council's 'presence and also help to allay any suspicions that […] [we are] there to push any political propaganda under the guise of cultural activity.'[25]

The tone, attention, expectations, the impact the tour needed to have on Australia and New Zealand, and even the frenzy that would accompany the Oliviers had been pre-determined even before they set sail. The tour that fatefully set out on Valentine's Day was also the tour that Olivier claimed lost him the love of his life, Vivien.

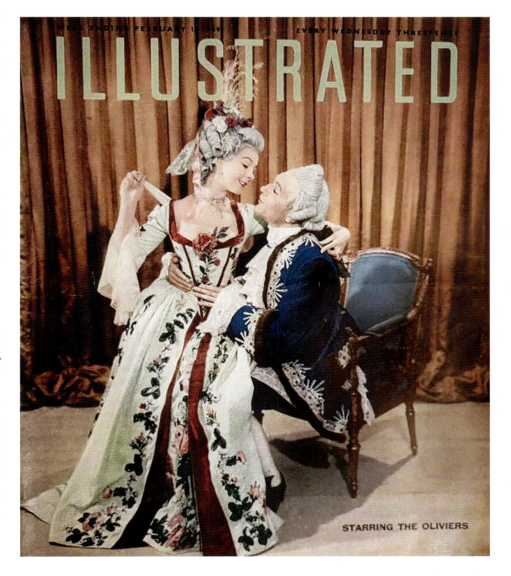

Below:
The Oliviers on the cover of *Illustrated* magazine in *The School for Scandal*. Credit: Alicia Powell Collection

Chapter 3

VIVIEN LEIGH

BRITISH FASHION AMBASSADOR ON THE 1948 OLD VIC TOUR

Only England could have produced her. She was the perfect English rose. When the door opened and she was there, she was so terribly good-looking. She had such an exquisite unreality about her.*

* Former *Vogue* editor in chief and style guru Diana Vreeland on Vivien Leigh. Reference http://vivandlarry.com/vivien-leigh/vivien-leigh-as-a-style-icon/ Vivien Leigh as a Style Icon, April 20, 2011 Date accessed 20 June 2023.

Vivien was never a fashion icon in the traditional sense like Audrey Hepburn, Twiggy and Jean Shrimpton, but by 1948 she had the perfect attributes to be a fashion ambassador for The Old Vic Tour. As 2017 Sotheby's Vivien Leigh Estate Auction showed, Vivien was a woman of tremendous taste, style and intelligence, and had a discerning eye for detail. The items auctioned included artwork, jewellery, dresses, books, furniture and homewares; testament to those qualities. Harriet Quick wrote:

Beautiful means different things in different times but what remains true over and above the changing tides of fashion is appropriateness, sensitivity to colours, proportions, textures and a sense of self. Leigh, who loved dress up as a young child in India, acutely understood the power of clothes and the subtle nuances of details.[1]

Furthermore, by 1948, she was formally Lady Olivier, and had inadvertently perfected her part as 'Queen' in theatre's royal coupledom with her husband Sir Laurence Olivier. Combined with her purposeful evolution and her unofficial ambassadorship of European luxury goods (having been drawn to high-end luxury labels), Keith Lodwick – former curator at the Victoria and Albert Museum, London – noted that she was ready for the role even before the tour started.[2] Additionally, considering couture represented a big part of Europe's economy – in the late '40s in France, for example, it was one-third of the nation's GDP – the role was certainly more important than she was given credit for.

The Mail, in the Women's Interest section of 1948, informally announced this role in a piece titled 'Vivvy – Dresses by Britain': 'Lady Olivier, better known as Vivien Leigh to world theatre

Preceding spread, on left: At an official function. Credit: Author's collection

Left:
Two months before departure, Vivien wearing a Matilda Etches design for Britsh *Vogue* was photographed by Clifford Coffin. Credit: Author's collection

audiences, and as "Vivvy" to her friends, will be an unofficial ambassador for British fashions during her Australian tour.'[3] It went on to say how the tour wardrobe was carefully picked to use British materials and styles. Vivien herself picked London-based designers Hardy Amies and Matilda Etches.

It's important to understand why the role, although unofficial, was relevant to the purposes of the tour. The Old Vic Tour was sponsored by the British Council. Created in 1934, its function was to support English education abroad, promote British culture, and fight the rise of fascism. In 1940, the Council was granted a Royal Charter to promote British culture. As part of British language, Shakespeare was well-suited, so Olivier's insistence on having American folklore play, *The Skin of Our Teeth* – a vehicle for Vivien to shine on her own – was a hard-fought battle.

The tour was the ultimate grand imperial gesture on behalf of Britain to Australia and New Zealand, who had helped in the war efforts. Olivier and Vivien personified the British ideal, not only through the English language via theatre performance, but as Australian Steve Vizard wrote in *Beyond the Stage*:

> ... more than theatrical performance, his very presence enunciates the history, identity and authority of Britain. Olivier is perfected in every detail. In his dress, speech, movement, manner, he is the composed, lacquered and manicured representation of British pomp, civility, love of ritual and benevolent governance, the traits which have seen Britain tame, claim and order not only their own islands, but an Empire, a world.[4]

Unfortunately, in his creative brainstorming, Vizard assumes only Olivier was given the part, and did not consider it was a joint Olivier-Vivien leadership of the tour. Their partnership was not just in marriage, but also in profession, representing British culture together.

A specific example worth mentioning here to further illustrate the appropriateness of Vivien as an ambassador of not only fashion of Britain but also language is an interview Vivien had in 1948 with Bill Strutton, an Australian screenwriter and novelist. The vast majority of critics and biographers paid exclusive attention to Olivier when it came to speech and vocals, which overshadowed Vivien during their marriage. This seems unfair now, but understandable given the sexism of the times and Olivier's acting status. It's true Vivien's voice was slight and had trouble carrying in large theatres, but for speeches, radio, films and commercials, it was perfect: 'To talk to Vivien Leigh is to have a lesson in classic English. Years of concentrated training have given her voice a bell-like clarity that is, if anything too perfect and precise for every day speech. Her pure, highly "produced" voice screens her character like a cloak.'[5]

To return to her Fashion Ambassadorial role, Vivien's pick of the two designers was a very well-thought-out decision. Designer Matilda Etches was known in the '40s for her innovative styles, often incorporating thoughtful sculpted detailing. She had already toured Australia in 1946 to promote Ziker Asher prints to Australian buyers and was a perfect choice by Vivien. With no formal training and education, she was a self-taught genius, forced to set up her own business as no-one was willing to employ her with no formal qualification. She had an unorthodox method of draping material straight onto a model and cutting the material pattern then and there. Innovative and out of the box – 'Her clothes philosophy is for updated simplicity, for an elegance which relies on cut rather than trimming and above all for comfort: this last, an unusual and very welcome viewpoint.'[6]

Etches provided nine designs that were simple and based primarily on the new look, including two boleros made from Brussels lace, in black and white, each fastened at the front with a cabbage rose (to wear with evening gowns), with fitted, three-quarter length sleeves; her signature contribution.

Hardy Amies was a designer for Lachasse for seven years before opening his own business in Saville Rowe after the war. *British Vogue* in 1948 described him as, 'Sensitively attuned to the undertones of advanced fashion, he incorporates its newest impulses in his clothes. His designs are vigorous – progressive – up to the minute – characteristic of the man himself. His aim is to dress the "*English Lady*," with her roots in the country and her playground in town.'[7] Amies seemed to have developed a good understanding of Vivien's requirements and his designs as *Vogue* affirms were representative of the English female.

Amies gave names to all of his nine designs, including, Primavera, Furbelow, Crackerjack, Betty Martin, After Six, and Cosy. 'Furbelow' was the dress Vivien is pictured wearing in Cape Town, which was a cocktail dress that had a wide sunray pleated skirt and scooped neckline, edged with pleating to form sleeves. Amies' 1948 styles featured a swirl of a thousand and one pleats in skirts and peplums with tiny waists, which Vivien knew suited her figure very well. Even at that first port of call, reporters honed in on her dress, noting that Vivien had all the essentials of the 'New Look', which she wholeheartedly supported. They even noted in detail her outfit worn for shopping the next day: 'Lady Olivier wore a light brown worsted costume, with rounded shoulders, short tuxedo lapels and accentuated hipline. The skirt was straight and slim. Her accessories were all brown, except for her lime green cloche hat, trimmed with brown corded ribbon and veiling.'[8]

In February 1947, designer Christian Dior had revolutionised fashion trends when his debut collection featured a never-before-seen look, making it known as the 'New Look' – an iconic reference to Dior – from then onwards. It is epitomised by the legendary 'Tailleur Bar' (the 'Bar Suit'), featuring a jacket made of ivory silk shantung and a voluminous black skirt made with yards of material which was still restricted in post-wartime. The line featured rounded shoulders, a cinched waist, exaggerated padded hips, and skirts draped in opulent yards of material. Although called the 'New Look', it was actually inspired by Dior's nostalgia for Belle Epoque fashion of the late 1800s.

The New Look was not welcomed by everyone, though. Feminists of the day felt it was a regressive trend, inspired from a bygone time, putting women back in cinched waists which emulated corsets, and the length was again long. Coco Chanel – a designer who, after World War One, popularised a sleek, casual and sporty style

Left:
Wearing the lavender Hardy Amies suit at the Adelaide Civic Reception.
Credit: Courtesy of Judith Koop from Joyce Attwood Collection

Right:
At the Food for Britain rally at the Exhibition Grounds.
Credit: Author's collection

– commented, 'Dior doesn't dress women, he upholsters them!'[9] But as history has shown, it's irrefutable that Dior was a visionary who, with this launch, revitalised not only an ailing postwar French fashion industry, but changed the way women dressed around the world. People during and after the war were used to a pragmatic and functional wardrobe, and Dior's collection was certainly not that; his look was one of glamour, prosperity and extravagance. Regardless of the critics, we cannot deny that Dior, with that first collection, introduced a look that influenced fashion globally, and from there, established a fashion house with a relevant legacy even today.

Vivien was initially not supportive of the trend herself, as it felt wasteful in a time when thrift had been engrained in the English psyche. However, as it gained instant popularity amongst all classes, she soon realised it was a welcome change from the dowdiness of wartime fashion. For Vivien to change her initial disapproval and decide to promote it on the tour shows a person discerning in her decisions and not afraid to change her mind.

Two months before the tour, Vivien finalised her wardrobe and had already been photographed wearing a slate-grey Etches design for *British Vogue*. It featured a folded bodice, and a deep V-neck that sloped over the shoulders in pleats. The hat, like most of the hats taken on tour, was designed by Madame Pavy, of Pissot et Pavy. In January 1948, three weeks before she was due to leave, the special correspondent for the *Sydney Morning Herald* noted that Vivien was spending a lot of time in salons still having fittings, having given considerable thought to her clothes, hurrying through lunch without her constant cat companion New.[10] She had given preference to the New Look and knew which current trends suited her, especially those with simple lines. Besides those eighteen designs provided by her chosen designers, she contemplated picking one each from the houses of Victor Stiebel, Bianca Mosca and Angele Delanghe: all London-based fashion designers. The push for British designs and textiles had already begun.

In Australia, too, even before the tour commenced it seemed the promotion had started. The *Australian Women's Weekly*, in February 1948, commented on how Vivien had been converted to the New Look in her choice of wardrobe for the tour and that it was particularly designed for train travel.[11] English company Coleman and Sons were chosen to produce all the material for her coats and skirts, and apparently did so in lightweight wool – suitable for Australia's autumn and winter.

Although lightweight, they ended up being too thick for Perth; their first city on the tour. As it happened, they arrived in Perth in the midst of an unusual heat wave. Olivier remarked as he disembarked to reporters, 'My first plan is to go and buy a suit – the lightest I can find.'[12] Vivien, a few days later, noted that even her morning dresses (made of British cotton) were heavier than the more common American cottons and were therefore unsuitable for Perth. Some of her silk evening dresses were also heavy and she hoped that the other States would be cooler to wear them.

Media posed all the professional questions relating to acting, the choice of plays, Shakespeare and even politics to Olivier. Typical of the sexism at the times but appropriate to her role as fashion ambassador, Vivien was scrutinised on her wardrobe. They noted she was perfectly attired to suit her slim figure, even detailing what was on her hood and jewels she had in her hair. For a reception that first week, Vivien wore what she said was the only cool frock in her wardrobe – a sprigged muslin – and commented again that even her morning frocks of silks and cottons were too heavy for the current Perth weather.

Vivien spent much of her time in Australia promoting her British wardrobe. When interviewed by Karara for *The West Australian* on her attire for the tour, Vivien stated that, with few exceptions, her private wardrobe was all-British. This led Karara to write that Lady Olivier must surely be regarded as an ambassadress for English fabrics and London designers: "'I prefer to wear British-made clothes as much as I can,' she said. 'Our fashions have improved tremendously recently and I think they now can hold their own with any in the world.'"[13] The article noted that Vivien had brought with her fourteen evening gowns, fourteen afternoon dresses and ten suits, and a large number of hats, shoes and exquisite accessories.

The Adelaide Civic Reception in April was a magnificent affair held at the Town Hall, where the 'political' objective of the tour was obvious. The whole troupe were welcomed by the Acting Lord Mayor and the State's Premier. All the 1300 seats in the hall were occupied and hundreds lined the streets outside to catch a glimpse of the couple. The event was to aid the Food for Britain Appeal and promote being British.

Vivien appropriately picked the fabulous Amies model of English blue lavender with a white design print, a full skirt, and a tight jacket that nipped her small waist. She wore a small white hat banded in black velvet with a black spotted veil that tied around the chin. When she rose to acknowledge the speech, the audience gave her a warm ovation.

At Melbourne's press conference, Vivien picked a gun-metal blue Amies suit. They noted in detail everything she wore:

> *Her large-brimmed picture hat with a fine veil, which was stretched beneath her chin. Heel-less and toe-peeper shoes, a large black handbag finished with a gold mount, and black suede gloves, were her accessories. She wore a narrow fur stole and her adornments were gold earrings, a chunky gold piece of period jewellery, pinned to the bodice of her frock, and a small gold bracelet.*[14]

Her hat was by Simone Mirman; a French-born, London-based milliner, who was supplying hats to Hardy Amies and then, in 1952, became the designer for the British Royal Family. An example of Vivien's impeccable attention to detail and taste was the brooch; described as the chunky gold piece of period jewellery that was actually an eighteenth-century Spanish cornucopia of rubies, pearls, emeralds and diamonds set in gold. It was a brooch she had spied in an antique shop and had wanted for a long time, and Olivier bought it as a surprise first-night gift.

Politically and legally, Australia followed the British models, but fashion during the '40s was

Left:
Vivien poses in the same hat and outfit which she did for *British Vogue* in late 1947, photographed by Clifford Coffin, but this time for Melbourne photographer John Warlow. Credit: Author's collection

Right:
Possibly in the Canary Islands in an Etches design. Credit: Athol Shmith, 1948 – Australian Tour 1948, Laurence Olivier and Vivien Leigh and The Old Vic Company, Bib ID 3044576. Credit: National Library of Australia

influenced by American pop culture, having had many Americans stationed in Australia during World War Two. Jeans were a big trend that influenced work and leisure. Clothes rationing, along with rationing of other necessities, had started in May 1942 for Australia; intended to manage impending shortages, curb inflation, reduce spending, and ensure a more equitable distribution of goods. Material was scarce and people preferred to mend and make do. The media encouraged multi-purpose clothes and made suggestions on making old clothes new with alterations. Housewives were encouraged to do their bit for the war effort by making do. Women also entered the workforce during the war to help fill the gap left with men away at war – around 200,000 women entered the workforce, doing jobs that were normally done by men. Clothing reflected this new role.

For Australia, rationing was never as severe as it was in Britain and America, but clothing rationing was only abolished in June 1948 – five and half months into The Old Vic Tour. In July 1948, the high-end department store David Jones presented fifty Dior designs at a gala dinner. It was a significant moment for Australian fashion, as it was the first time designs by Dior were seen outside of Paris.

In July, Vivien was able to shine on her own – without the shadow of Olivier over her – when she attended the Killara Camelia Show to raise funds again for the Food for Britain Appeal. A crowd of approximately 8000, trying to catch a glimpse of her, caused a minor riot, wrecking a display of rare and valuable camellias in the process. Vivien's outfit for the day aroused much fashion interest, as newspapers noted. She looked radiant in a floor-length fur coat over a black silk dress. She wore a powder-pink felt hat flower trimmed with a spotted black veil and matching pink gloves.

New Zealand relied exclusively on designs imported from Europe before the 1940s. Being so isolated geographically, the war severely impacted the movement of goods, services and information into the country. With clothes rationing and fashion news from Paris limited, a number of local designers like Trilby Yates and Ninette Gowns managed to start up businesses to provide an alternative. A big part of their business was inspired by the American servicemen stationed there, much like in Australia, and many designs were given American names like the 'Yankee Jacket' or 'American Stroller Coat'. New Zealanders were encouraged, as in Australia, to be prudent, buy wisely and less, and make do with what was there. Even the manufacture of clothing was controlled and certain methods, like tucking and pleats, were banned.

It was onto this scene fashion-wise that Vivien entered with her carefully picked British wardrobe. The year was also significant to Australasian fashion. Dior's New Look – styles and an extravagance that had not been available to the vast majority of Australasian women. With the excitement of seeing world-famous husband and wife actors and theatre like they'd never experienced, the vision of an undeniably ethereally beautiful Vivien in a fabulous British wardrobe was an image that would be etched into memories of that generation for decades to come.

Vivien and Olivier represented the embodiment of British imperial virtue, not only in theatre but also visually. This highbrow culture and the British feminine luxury Vivien represented was something Australasia had never experienced before. Australia, grappling with a post-war identity crisis and the 'cultural cringe' (an inferiority complex of the country's culture), welcomed it with awe and reverence after the dreariness of the war and nearly a decade of being attired in the Government-enforced 'austerity suit' – a short, straight skirt and a jacket with no more than two pockets and four buttons.[15]

The *Weekly News*, from Auckland in September, noted that Vivien looked like a miniature painting, wearing a simple black accordion-pleated frock for a civic reception under a mink coat with wide kimono sleeves. Vivien endorsed the New Look, but in a less exaggerated form, to appear, it seems, not to be overtly extravagant. Although the timing of the New Look may have been slightly inappropriate; during a period when the English were still used to coupons and rationing, the piece notes that she thought it was a welcome change. Vivien again, as expected, goes further to endorse English designers and says she herself prefers English designers – in particular, Hardy Amies and Victor Stiebel.[16]

In return, Vivien gave Australian fashion a boost and attention, too. While in Auckland she mentioned Australian woollens being easy to buy and that she had bought them as presents. When they returned to England, she wore a beige hat bought from a young Sydney milliner, John Pickworth. Pickworth designed a wool georgette hat that could be worn in three different ways and was said to have been worn by Vivien and Hedda Hopper. At the party put on by the Old Vic in their honour, the next day, she wore a black suit which she had also bought in Sydney.[17]

Vivien Leigh is not classified as a fashion icon, but she should be. Her lifelong interest in fashion was not frivolous or superficial. Her movie roles set fashion trends and influenced dress designs internationally. She modelled and aligned herself with high-end luxury brands for years. Her unquestionable style, taste, and elegance was a consciously formulated personal image which, if looked at from the success of her estate sales in recent years, was a successful one. Vivien's role as a British Fashion Ambassador, although unofficial, was extremely important. In order to promote British industry, her textiles and designers were exclusively British. As assigned by the sponsorship of the British Council, not only did she showcase British style, culture, language, speech, and theatre, but she also visually personified the quintessential *English rose* on a tour that had a lasting impact on a whole post-war generation, and the social and cultural environment of Australasia.

Chapter 4

ON THE INDIGO SEA

*They spoke in whispers
of the indigo sea,
of Orion shining on her velvet face
of winds crashing on steel.
The places she would take them
that she only saw and knew**

* Verse inspired by an entry in Laurence Olivier's Tour Journal, Shiroma Perera-Nathan.

Once onboard the SS *Corinthic*, a 15,000-tonne refrigerated cargo ship, carrying one hundred passengers and forty from the tour, the Oliviers were photographed in their suite, surrounded by masses of flowers. Olivier started writing in his deep maroon leather-bound journal that night. The gold-leafed diary, which had been a well-wisher's gift, had gilt lettering on the cover – 'My Trip Abroad' – and would've provided a comprehensive first-hand insight into the tour if he had continued to use it throughout. He started off enthusiastically and in his typical detailed wordy recounting style, with dustings of his well-known wit, sarcasm and even drawings. He wrote:

Many sweet fans and many sweet flash bulbs. Liverpool about 3. Masses of flowers on board, about 100 wires, books from Jamie [Hamilton] of course. About 4.15 tugs pushed us out and round. Cecil [Tennant] and Dorothy [Welford] waving from gantry on landing stage until we were nearly mid-channel. Beautiful boat and very comfy. Unpacked for the night, dinner alone together in cabin. Baba not eating much. Went for a walk by myself wearing duffel coat. Poured bath, but went to bed without it. Read Logan Pearsall Smith's 'English Aphorisms' for a while, before turning out light.[1]

Baba was a term of endearment for Vivien, which was how he referred to her in his diary entries throughout this tour.

It was winter when they set off and the seas were the colour of gunmetal, ironically a favourite colour for some of the clothes Vivien had picked

Preceding spread, on left: Vivien at wheel of Corinthic. Credit: Athol Shmith, 1948 – Australian Tour 1948, Laurence Olivier and Vivien Leigh and The Old Vic Company, Bib ID 3044576. Credit: National Library of Australia

Left:
A postcard Elsie Beyer sent of the Corinthic on the trip to Australia. Credit: Author's collection

for the tour. Icy winds came blustering onto the decks as the ship started its journey. It was a restless night and continued to be so on the second night, too. Vivien at one time resorted to taking a sleeping tablet to help her deafen out the banging and creaking caused by the thrashing winds.

They unpacked over the next few days, inspecting the ship, and walking on the decks but preferring to have their meetings, catch-ups and meals inside their cabin. That didn't last long, for they decided to join the others at the captain's table for their meals and other areas for entertainment and rehearsals.

Elsie Beyer, during the course of the tour, sent detailed reports to Cecil Tennant, the Oliviers' agent and great friend. On February 23rd, she reported that Olivier and Vivien were in fine health and spirits. She had never seen an actors group getting up so early to be on deck by 7am to exercise before breakfast and then rehearse in the morning. After morning rehearsals, the rest of the day would be spent playing games and swimming in the rigged-up canvas pool, sun baking, tennis, and watching fish and sharks. Then they would have afternoon rehearsals before dinner and various night games like bingo and gin rummy. Beyer wrote, '… you can't keep them out of the public rooms, the Dining Saloon, the games deck, sundry cabins … They are adored by everybody and have made an enormous hit and voted the best mixers ever.'[2]

There was plenty of drinking, too. The Oliviers – unable to stay off the wagon as they had planned – preferred Black Russians during the day, wine and champagne with lunch, and dinner with night caps of brandy or port in their cabin. Even

CHAPTER 4

Top left:
Strolling on the high seas.

Top right:
Vivien looking out to sea.

Middle left:
The dawn of a new day onboard.

Middle right:
Vivien, George and Peggy possibly in Las Palmas.

Bottom left:
Olivier and Vivien on board.

Bottom right:
Olivier diving into the canvas pool.

Photos credit: Athol Shmith, 1948 – Australian Tour 1948, Laurence Olivier and Vivien Leigh and The Old Vic Company, Bib ID 3044576. Credit: National Library of Australia

ON THE INDIGO SEA

Top left:
L to R George Relph, David Kentish, Mercia Swinburne, Vivien, Terence Morgan, Georgina Jumel

Top middle:
Vivien at wheel of Corinthic

Top right:
Olivier and Dan Cunningham coming back on board with bananas

Middle:
Vivien and unidentified male playing volleyball on board

Bottom left:
Albatross.

Bottom right:
Vivien wearing the big straw hat bought in Las Palmas

Photos credit: Athol Shmith. 1948, Australian tour 1948, Laurence Olivier and Vivien Leigh and the Old Vic Company Bib ID 3044576. National Library of Australia

CHAPTER 4

Top left:
George Relph, Vivien and Mercia on the high seas.

Top right:
Games on board.

Middle left:
Peggy, Mercia and Vivien possibly in Las Palmas in the open air cab.

Middle:
Vivien relaxing next to Dan Cunningham with binoculars.

Bottom:
Olivier and Vivien relaxing on board.

Photos credit: Athol Shmith, 1948 – Australian Tour 1948, Laurence Olivier and Vivien Leigh and The Old Vic Company, Bib ID 3044576. Credit: National Library of Australia

the preferred dessert, *crème de menthe*, was laced with alcohol. Drinking played a large part in their socialising, lifestyle and the acting environment in general, but in hindsight, the consumption could definitely be seen as excessive and one can only imagine the harm it must've had on Vivien's already precarious health and later mental illness, combined with her prescribed medication. What one must bear in mind, like the many photos that capture life on board that month, is that it is indicative of a different time; the people living in these times did not have a full understanding of the consequences of their consumptions and actions. In later years, both Vivien and Olivier tried many times to give up alcohol but never with long-term success. It seemed to have been their preferred poison.

However, one of the reasons Olivier had picked a sea voyage was because just over a year beforehand, they had escaped near death when their Pan American Constellation flight they were on had an emergency landing after an engine had caught fire mid-flight. He also felt that it would benefit Vivien's health to relax in the sea air and the photos show her doing just that on the sun decks, reading and playing.

The *Australian Women's Weekly* article on 21st February, 1948 reported that Olivier was rehearsing his group on the decks of the ship, and Vivien ironically said the tour would be a welcome relief from her busy twelve-hour filming routine. It also went onto a very detailed description of the 'New Look' wardrobe Vivien had picked for the tour; as discussed in depth in Chapter 3.

It was also on board during the month-long voyage that Olivier felt the first pangs of pain in his right toe which would be misdiagnosed by the ship's doctor as *not* being gout, when it was. He bathed it in warm water to try and soothe it but seemed frustrated a lot of the time, getting stiff necks, unbearable headaches and disrupted sleep. On good days they managed to have afternoon naps and Vivien would massage him. The toe pain would nag him on and off throughout the tour, on top of the knee injury he would later sustain in Sydney.

Olivier had settled on the dining room as the space for rehearsals. They would rehearse daily in the morning, allow tables to be put back for lunch service and then do further rehearsals in the afternoon. His diary notes in detail and insightfully, on the seventh day, February 21st he was rehearsing *The School for Scandal* and finding it somewhat frustrating. This entry shows a typical day on board but also Olivier's genius mindset when rehearsing and studying a play. He rehearsed first to check for all the words. They started at 10:30 and packed up the dining room for lunch at 11:45 and back to it at 2:45 until tea. He found it hard to get his thoughts together. It eluded him and gave him no peace.

> *I think the first scene must be every director's Waterloo. Of all authors' dialogue, it seems to me, Sheridan's indicates the least movement where it seems to require most. Where it is human it comes instantly alive and presents no difficulty, where it is artificial it seems rehearsed (sp) in death unable to burst it cerements, and, to prevent the*

audience dying as stiff as our ancestors in 1780, has to have arbitrary choreography thrust upon it. How are the two to be married? I can only think by the spirit and vitality of the playing.[3]

The ship sailed past Cape Verde Islands and they sighted North Africa that day.

The first days onboard had been cold and taunted by harsh winds. Their first stop was warmer. They arrived in Las Palmas in the early morning to the magical sight of tiny lights dotted all on the edge of the land and into the mountains. They spent the day sightseeing and shopping. Olivier, Vivien, Mercia Swinburne, Peggy Simpson, George Relph and Elsie Beyer took an open-air cab, painted in a horrendous colour (according to Olivier), into town, where they shopped and drank two bottles of the local wine – which were thankfully iced – but they had a drab view at the Parcque Hotel. Olivier thought Las Palmas had a certain charm but lacked the picturesqueness he imagined would come with a name like the Canary Islands. They went in the same cab into the mountains through hair-raising bends to lunch at a beautiful restaurant surrounded by flowers where they downed two further bottles and were treated very nicely by the owners, who put on their best service having recognised the guests. The weather suddenly turned as they returned down the mountain; the ladies were given the men's coats for warmth. Before getting back on board at the quay, they were overcome by haggling marketers and succumbed to the purchase of unwanted merchandise including big straw hats.

On most nights Olivier walked the decks before retiring. One particular night seemed especially memorable and beautiful. The chalcedony sea had turned into a dark velvet shade of indigo and upon looking at the night sky he noted the appearance of the constellation Orion. When he went back to his cabin, Vivien read him passages from 'Ah Trivia' before they turned the lights off.

They spent a great deal of time reading and writing. Olivier started on the foreword to *The Skin of Our Teeth* program as Wilder had requested. He also planned well in advance for The Old Vic repertory upon return to London and, after reading *The Wild Duck* by Ibsen, felt it would be another ideal vehicle for Vivien; far from trying to jeopardise her career, he was constantly looking for ways to enhance it.

There were nights Vivien would stay up very late playing games with the other members of the troupe, dancing and chatting, while Olivier retired to their room exhausted, in pain and overthinking plans for the upcoming tour. This would become a running theme in their marriage, and her bipolar condition during a high phase would have exacerbated the need to be constantly active. Even before her condition was diagnosed, her mother Gertrude Hartley remembered her needing very little sleep as a baby and after marriage to Leigh Holman with a newly born baby she would often be partying into the small hours of the morning. Many guests at Notley would remember times they simply could not keep up with her. On this gruelling tour with so many commitments and obligations, Vivien's

Top:
From L to R Ivor Novello, Olivier, Zena Dare, Olive Gilbert, Gwen Ffrangcon-Davies, Vivien, Robert Andrews and Vanessa Lee in Cape Town. Credit: Greta Ritchie Collection

Bottom:
At a party held at the High Commission, where they were photographed with 3 children, Cape Town. Credit: Athol Shmith, 1948 – Australian Tour 1948, Laurence Olivier and Vivien Leigh and The Old Vic Company, Bib ID 3044576. Credit: National Library of Australia

CHAPTER 4

Below:
The group on board the *Corinthic*. Credit: Author's collection

unquenchable energy would begin to affect Olivier professionally for the first time.

On Sunday morning, February 22nd, they sat on the deck watching flying fish and hammerhead sharks. By noon they had passed Sierra Leone. Vivien and Olivier had still not perfected the quarrel scene in *The School for Scandal*, which annoyed him. That afternoon the annoyance was cast aside at the sight of more sharks.

The ship docked at Cape Town on the afternoon of March 1st and the company had their second trip ashore, spending two days sight-seeing and attending an official dinner. They were met onboard first by the press. Olivier's diary entry is again very detailed. This time his irritation with the press and being interviewed is obvious and they had not even arrived in Australia to the full onslaught.

After rehearsing the Clarence scenes in *Richard III* in the morning, everyone stood on the deck waiting for Table Mountain to come into view. Unfortunately, it was covered with mist; annoying those who were looking forward to taking photos. Flowers, fruit and cables started to flood their cabin, but Olivier seemed pre-occupied and more worried about the press party waiting for them as they docked. He didn't have much to say to the press and oddly, in turn, the press had little to say back. Gwen Ffrangcon-Davies, Ivor Novello, Bobbie Andrews, and Vanessa Lee arrived to welcome them. 'Baba looking v. lovely in New Look black and white. Ivor's car took us to the Alhambra to see Perchance to Dream.'[4] They found Ivor's performance highly enjoyable. As they entered the theatre in darkness, the audience became aware of them and stood to give them a clap and cheer. Elsie Beyer who had entered with them felt it was like being around royalty, such was the overwhelming reception.

Perchance to Dream was Ivor Novello's latest West End Musical that just happened to be playing in Cape Town when they docked. He was considered the most successful British composer of musicals at the time and the crew enjoyed the show and meeting old friends. During their two-day stopover they did not manage to see the famous top of Table Mountain, as fog covered it the whole time – 'tablecloth'. They shopped at the department stores, posted food parcels back home, ate a duck curry as an aphrodisiac, drank wine, danced at a club called 'The Gay Adventure', drove around the coast, did a broadcast and attended a party at the High Commission house which gave them a preview to what was to come; being treated as true ambassadors. Amusingly, Olivier thought the Afrikaans accent the oddest he had ever heard and wrote for once in this life, the two days had managed to tire even Vivien.

They set sail out of Table Bay on March 3rd, a radiant day but straight into the turbulent waters of their final stretch, the Cape Rollers. It was a rough couple of days before the calmer indigo Indian Ocean started to roll around them and, like a sign from above, albatrosses and the smell of gum trees accompanied the *Corinthic* towards Fremantle.

Chapter 5

AUSTRALIA 1948

THE LAND OF CLANCY

And the bush hath friends to meet him, and their kindly voices greet him
In the murmur of the breezes and the river on its bars,
And he sees the vision splendid of the sunlit plains extended,
And at night the wondrous glory of the everlasting stars.*

* A.B 'Banjo' Paterson, Verse 4 of *Clancy of the Overflow.*

One of Vivien's best friends at school had been an Australian, and having learnt Banjo Paterson's poem 'Clancy of the Overflow' by heart at a young age, she had always wanted to visit Australia. She was the more read, travelled and worldly of the Oliviers and this showed in her interests and social interactions. The company had also learnt 'Waltzing Matilda' on the ship, most likely at her insistence. They would be bewildered to find that they knew the words better than Australians themselves by the time they arrived.

Australians had been looking forward to a real royal tour by King George and his daughters Princesses Elizabeth and Margaret in the spring of 1949, but this never eventuated. As the tour drew closer, the King's ill health became a major concern, and it was apparent that it would preclude the visit. In announcing the cancellation, Australia's then-Prime Minister, Ben Chifley, said about his communication with the United Kingdom, '… although we in Australia would not have the privilege of having their Majesties and Princess Margaret with us as planned, that was of a very secondary consideration when compared with the King's well-being.'[1]

The Old Vic Tour which was viewed by many Australians as a dress rehearsal for the actual Royal Tour, never got overshadowed by one, with the tour leaders Olivier and Vivien unwittingly taking on the roles of King and Queen, albeit even if it was merely the theatre they ruled over. After another cancellation of a planned Royal visit in 1952, due to the death of King George VI, only in 1954 did Princess Elizabeth and Prince Philip manage to complete one, then as Queen Elizabeth II and

Duke of Edinburgh. By then The Old Vic Tour was firmly imprinted in the public's imagination.

There has always been a kinship, economically and culturally, between Australia and New Zealand, despite their being politically separate entities. The two countries served as the primary goods supplier for Britain in the world economy and the kinship extended to the price given at well below market prices. An opinion poll in 1947 found that 65 per cent of Australians preferred to keep their British nationality rather than a separate one, leading a future Prime Minister, Robert Menzies, to say '… the boundaries of Great Britain are not on the Kentish coast but at Cape York and Invercargill.'[2]

However, this was not to say there were no unresolved hostilities. The Second World War brought home to Australia that it could not rely on Britain alone for security. With the fall of British-held Singapore in 1942, the bombing of Darwin, the discovery of two Japanese submarines in Sydney Harbour, and eventually the bombing of Pearl Harbour, it was obvious that Australia needed to align itself more with the US for protection, leading Prime Minister John Curtin to state that it should be allowed to 'turn to America free of any pangs as to our traditional links with the United Kingdom.'[3] This was not accepted by Winston Churchill who held stubbornly onto outdated imperialist views even after the war had ended.

The Cold War brought with it major concerns over security and Soviet infiltration in Australia and it was under British guidance that the Australian Security Intelligence Organisation (ASIO) was established in July of 1948. Under these threats, Britain wanted to engage Australia as a partner in projecting British culture to non-settled colonies, specifically in South-East Asia.

When the tour started in February 1948, the memories of the Great Depression and war were still very fresh for many Australians. The 1930s had seen millions of people unemployed or working drastically reduced hours, and wages at an all-time low. Although the situation improved by the late '30s, it was only in 1945 that Australia introduced sickness and unemployment benefits and transformed itself after the ravages of the Depression and the Second World War into a social welfare state.

In order to coordinate the war effort and the recovery afterwards, the federal Government took over many financial and social responsibilities from the States.

Demographically Australia had started an immigration drive around 1945, under the notion of 'populate or perish' that emerged after the Second World War and a large non-British immigration movement began to transform Australian society.

When Japan bombed Darwin in 1942, Australia experienced a vulnerability it had never felt before and when the war ended, the Government began to look at policies to populate and increase defences. Arthur Calwell, Australia's first Immigration Minister, said in a speech in 1945, 'The door to Australia will always be open within limits to our existing legislation to the people from various dominions, United States of America, and from European continental countries.'[4]

Preceding spread, on left: Landscape 1948 taken by presumbly Olivier. Credit: Author's collection

Left:
Kangaroos delighted the Oliviers.

Right:
Australia, landscape 1948.

Photos credit: Author's collection

In the theatre scene, Australia had witnessed a few Shakespearean performances throughout the decades, with the first in 1800 at the John Sidway's Theatre, Sydney. It was a performance of *Henry IV* whose actor is unable to be deciphered from the only poster that has survived.[5] Being such a young country, Australians believed the best Shakespearean actors had to come from overseas. After Englishman Herbert Beerbohm Tree toured in the early 1900s, a fervour was aroused, which led a local businessman to form a provincial Shakespearean company in time for the 300th anniversary of Shakespeare's death. Many amateur productions were put on in subsequent years and theatres grew in numbers. The most influential and acclaimed tour would be The Old Vic Tour in 1948.

Australia has had a very big trade union culture, although from mid-1950 onwards there has been a slow and long decline in workforce memberships. But in 1948, after compulsory arbitration was enforced to promote mediation in workforce conflicts, union support and membership was at its peak.[6] Union culture was engrained in Australia's large working-class society, with social, cultural and even educational events being organised via union membership. Australia's class structure had not changed either, with two-thirds of the population being employed in the blue-collar sectors consistently between 1891 and 1947. In 1948, 64.9 per cent of the workforce had union membership.

Actors' Equity had already started to protest with the Tivoli Theatre Management in Sydney back in January 1948, when it was announced that Tivoli had been offered the Sydney season of

The Old Vic tour. Actors' Equity insisted that if The Old Vic played there, there should be no job loss to the local actors employed by Tivoli. They threatened to find a way to stop The Old Vic and also the Ballet Rambert, both sponsored by the British Council, from performing in any of the theatres in Sydney unless at least 25 per cent of the local artists were employed by the productions or found alternative theatres to work in.

On the 6th of January 1948, the *Sydney Morning Herald* reported on this dispute, clearly defining each side's point. In their defence, Tivoli management (via its Managing Director David Martin) said that Tivoli had a legal obligation to allow them to perform, having signed an agreement a year prior with Kerridge-Odeon Theatres with one condition being that the Tivoli would be made available to British companies. Interestingly English film magnate, J. Arthur Rank, owned a half interest in over one hundred theatres of this chain.

However, the shows continued as planned as Walter Humphries, the Theatrical Manager for the British Council, confirmed in the *Adelaide Mail* on Saturday 7th February, all members coming to Australia were Equity members and on Equity contracts.[7]

Politically in 1948, The Australian Labor Party under Prime Minister Ben Chifley formed the Government. Australia was and has been a bi-partisan party system in that only two parties have dominated politics at any given time; Labor and the Coalition (composed of the Liberal and National Party). The Labor Party was created by the trade unions and its constitution defines itself as a democratic socialist party thereby associating itself with the labour and working-class movement. While initially supporting the White Australia Policy (the barring of non-European migration), it was under Ben Chifley that a major immigration policy shift happened, and the welfare state came into being. Chifley is often regarded as Australia's best Treasurer, having responsibly managed the country out of wartime depression and hardship. When Olivier was introduced to Chifley in Canberra, he noted he was 'amiable, very, if protected by an armour plating of political misterioso.'[8]

Chapter 6

PERTH

THE MOST DELIGHTFULLY ISOLATED CITY IN THE WORLD

Whether she be near or whether she be far I wish the winds to the Sabina …*

* A line of poetry Vivien wrote to christen a boat *Sabina* in Perth.

The coastal city of Perth, Western Australia's capital, is commonly referred to as the most isolated city in the world. On one side is the far-reaching Indian Ocean and to the other, a vast land space from where the nearest city, Adelaide is 2500 kilometres away by road. It stands on the traditional lands of the Whadjuk Noongar peoples, Indigenous cultures that have lived there for over 40,000 years.

In the 1940s, Perth had an unmistakable city centre that focused around St Georges Terrace and low-rise buildings with a distinctive unique charm being mostly made from sandstone. Its charm and character also came from its unmistakable association with the river, positioned in close proximity to King's Park, a heritage of over 1000 acres of land for the public.

Perth had been occupied by American troops during the war and therefore was heavily influenced by American culture. Its people were mostly white (90 per cent having British background), due to the Indigenous peoples being segregated into the rural areas and the by-product of a White Australia Policy. Perth was cleaner than Melbourne and Sydney because it didn't have big manufacturing areas, so there was no pollution or slum-like areas. In the early years of federation, Perth was predominately a sleepy country town reliant on agriculture. The change into the small but elegant 'country'-style city it was in 1948 came slowly after the discovery of gold and other mineral booms.

The American journalist HR Knickerbocker wrote in a cablegram to the *Chicago Sun* in 1942, 'This delightful city of Perth shows a curious

PERTH

Preceding spread, on left:
Arriving in Fremantle.

Left:
Perth from King's Park from a booklet on the city in 1948.

Photos credit: Author's collection

Below:
Arriving in Fremantle. Credit: Author's collection

mixture of equanimity and war-madness.'[1] Like The Old Vic Company would do a few years later, but after the war, he compared it to England and then in ending wrote:

Perth is undoubtedly the least fairly advertised of any city of its kind on earth. Its modern stream lined residences, its American-styled shops, and its maze of scenic water ways and parks make one of the loveliest cities in the southern hemisphere. Perth's only trouble is that it is so incredibly far from everywhere else.[2]

The *Corinthic* officially arrived in Fremantle, Perth, early on Monday March 15th. Olivier rose at 7am not feeling very well and gave himself an hour to get ready to meet the onslaught of the press. Along with the press came immigration officers, a doctor, a banker to check the finances of the crew, and of course the British Council representatives. Peter Cushing remembered, 'Anchored outside Fremantle Harbour, awaiting high tide, we felt embalmed by its intensity, and a humid off-shore breeze, laden with the acrid, oily perfume of Eucalyptus trees, added to this discomfort.'[3]

Newspapers the next day wrote of how lovely the couple were in the midst of the barrage of questions, crowds and uncomfortable heat. Endearingly, Olivier started by expressing a desire to learn as much as possible about Australia, the people and nature. 'We know practically nothing about Australia,' he said. 'We want to see the country. We want to see every kind of animal or bird there is. Black swans, for instance; why aren't there any here? Where are they, anyway?'[4]

Olivier and Vivien, although stylishly attired, found the material of their outfits was too thick and unsuitable for Perth's rare heatwave that year – even in the morning – leading Olivier to remark, 'My first plan is to go and buy a suit – the lightest I can find.'[5] Vivien, looking ravishing in a light brown, speckled 'new look' suit, revealed that her first school friend had been Australian and ever since she had always wanted to visit Australia.[6] The Oliviers, as expected from anyone preparing for their ambassadorial roles, had read about Australian history on the trip and the words and music to 'Waltzing Matilda'. Their first priority as actors was to perform well and provide entertainment through their plays and therefore they actually expected little time for ex-curricular activities. They had diligently rehearsed six days a week onboard and told the press how seriously they took their profession. Olivier spent a while explaining that, although he appreciated how film gave an actor a medium by which to be self-critical, his first love has been and will be the stage – even though directing a film was very interesting. Vivien, dazzling with a corsage of fragrant frangipani pinned to her lapel, spoke of there being plenty of scope for both film and stage, and that she enjoyed a bit of both.

Their first interaction with the Australian press and public was very positive. They charmed them with their patience, knowledge, beauty, enthusiasm and composure in the face of a barrage of questions, cameras, crowds and stifling heat, with their only concern being the unsuitability of their attire. The Oliviers had arrived and were an instant hit.

Left:
Vivien with Joseph Totterdale, Mayor of Perth. Credit: Author's collection

Right:
With the Vice Chancellor of the University of Western Australia. Credit: Westpix/Seven West Media

The advance party from the tour had arrived a few weeks before the official one, had also been given a wonderful reception, and now were reunited with the rest of the crew. O'Connor mentions that Marie Donaldson from Christchurch, New Zealand, was engaged to look for accommodation for the tour members nine months beforehand.[7] Being accommodated by hosts seemed to be the way to go for many of the minor stars, and that was hard enough as a lot of people couldn't understand an actor's hours of living. Offers for Olivier and Vivien were boundless – which was as expected.

The Oliviers were driven to their apartment block at 16 Bellevue, overlooking the Swan River to the east and King's Park to the west. The French windows would welcome a pleasant breeze in the afternoon. Although they wanted privacy, it didn't stop Vivien, a natural 'people person' from making friends with the neighbours. Fifteen-year-old Barbara Atherton, living next door when the Oliviers moved in, remembered how Vivien would hang clothes out every morning and chat to her mother over the fence. She would also hand her bunches of flowers from the performance the night before as she just had far too many to accommodate in her place and theatre. She remembered Vivien as displaying a youthful, friendly approachability in her character as opposed to a grumpy and limping Olivier with a leg problem.[8] Of course Olivier had started with toe pain on the journey to Australia and this worsened after finding his shoes for *School for Scandal* had been made too small.

Michael Redington, one of the youngest members of the tour and someone who would go on to be involved in TV production and later become a successful stage producer, remembered in 1982 on a radio segment in Australia that, after the rationing they had experienced in Britain, the group was overjoyed by the food on arrival in Perth: fat steaks with poached eggs on top, served with glasses of milk.[9] Although some members were given the top floor of Bellevue according to Barbara, the others were settled in private homes and average motels across various suburbs of Perth.

Peter Cushing and his wife Helen unpacked and went for a stroll in what they thought was a cool breeze but was still a heatwave compared to England. Sitting down on the grass in the park, they realised what they thought was moving earth was a swarm of beetles under them and quickly went back to their room, dropping a trail of beetles as they walked.[10]

Lunch was served at the iconic Esplanade Hotel with British Council representatives and tour organiser Dan O'Connor whom, according to Garry O'Connor, the group warmed to instantly.[11] They then went to inspect the Capitol Theatre where they would be performing *The School for Scandal*. They were extremely disappointed; with little dressing space, far too big, and bound to produce acoustic nightmares. The Capitol designed by George Temple-Poole, opened in 1929, at 10 William Street, with a seating capacity of 2250 and was meant to hold civic functions and be a cinema, but that particular role didn't prove successful for a city with a small population. Unfortunately for the tour, as Olivier noted on first inspection, an oversight of its design was there was limited backstage room for live theatre, in particular dressing rooms. He and Vivien endeared themselves even more to the troupe (by now they were being referred to as the God and the Angel), by insisting they make do with screened-off sections on each side of the theatre and letting the others take the six dressing rooms. Switchboard facilities and acoustics were also a major hurdle but having brought their own lighting board, some aspects were thankfully improvable.

The Capitol Theatre was one of the many buildings of significance that Perth lost over the years before heritage-saving legislation was passed. In 1966, entrepreneur and later Mayor of the city, Thomas Wardle bought it, the same year that Bob Dylan performed in it. Wardle sold it only two years later in 1968 for more than he bought it and soon after it was demolished to make way for office buildings. Its teardrop chandelier now hangs in Melbourne's Princess Theatre and the Rudolph Valentino bust that was in its foyer was placed in the WA Performing Arts Museum. According to Ross Thorne in *Picture Palace Architecture in Australia*, it should never have been demolished, despite its shortcomings, because it had a unique architecture and its decorations were the essence of real artworks. For example, instead of moulded plaster, the architects decided to use paint. 'The flat wall, square column faces and ceiling panels were vividly decorated in patterns, panels and leafy murals. The lounge foyer displays curvilinear patterns and stylized plant forms in an art nouveau style still struggling to escape from Victorian clutter.'[12]

The Oliviers' exhausting first day in Perth ended with a pleasant sunset drive down to Scarborough Beach, where a black swan flew over them much to Olivier's delight! The black swan has much significance in the Australian culture, both to the Europeans and its Indigenous peoples. In European culture, stemming from Roman times, the black swan was a reference to something that was rare and therefore a metaphor. Only in 1697 was one first sighted and recorded by Dutch explorer Willem de Vlamingh, who then named the western part of Perth's river – Swan River. To Australia's Indigenous peoples, the black swan is a part of their history and lore. The people of Nyungar (southwestern Australia) were referred to as the black swan group, from lore that said their ancestors were once black swans that transformed to men. There is also a Dreamtime story about two brothers who turned into white swans to defend an attack, who in turn were helped by black crows and replaced their torn features with their own, making them black. The black swan is the official State emblem of Western Australia and is depicted on its flag and coat of arms.

Ironically, Olivier expected to sleep well that night but didn't, for the Perth mosquitos, like the insistent fans and press from then onwards, had other ideas. The itching only subsided after he got up and bathed the large lumps that had formed from the bites in ammonia.

Despite having poor sleep, Olivier managed to get through another extremely draining day. After a short run through at the theatre in the morning, and a broadcast with the ABC at 1pm, he and Vivien had afternoon tea at 4pm with Lieutenant-Governor Sir James Mitchell and his partner. They then rushed to a 5pm cocktail party at the Esplanade Hotel, where he wrote he

Top:
Speaking to the players of *Oedipus Rex*.

Bottom:
Waiting for the box office to open to get tickets.

Photos credit: Westpix/Seven West Media

shook hands with all of Perth, ending with dinner with a professor and his wife at Perth University before watching a performance by students of *Oedipus*. At the end of which, close to 11pm, they still managed to greet and shake hands with the queue of people outside the theatre waiting to buy tickets. On this day, Vivien wore the only cool frock she had in her collection made of sprigged muslin with a flower brooch at her chest, one that would be a favourite all her life.

The open-air production of the Greek tragedy *Oedipus Rex,* by the University's Dramatic Society, had been in its beautiful Sunken Gardens Amphitheatre. The cast had a young Neville Teede, the president of the Dramatic Society and who after the war was studying under the Commonwealth Reconstruction Training Scheme. Teede would go on to become a lecturer and an actor. In the '50s he would also act with The Old Vic in London before returning to Perth in 1956. The Oliviers were very impressed with the production, leading them to encourage further development of theatre in the University. Vivien thought the Sunken Garden was the most beautiful open-air theatre she had ever seen. The tradition would go on, and the Sunken Garden would be the location of many more performances over the years and in 2008, it celebrated its Diamond Jubilee, with some of the original cast members of that 1948 production attending.[13] Today it's also a popular setting for weddings and photography. The University obviously left quite an impression on Olivier as he remembered to send a telegram to congratulate them on the opening of the New Fortune Theatre in 1964.

The Friday before the premiere, March 19th, the weather was so hot they only managed one dress rehearsal. Olivier was still not happy with the makeup for Sir Peter, thinking now it made him too young. His foot was also getting more and more painful. They had been working until the early hours with no breaks, with even Vivien sewing and ironing costumes. On Wednesday night there had been a downpour and the wardrobe staff had to bail out water from the dressing rooms. The hours they were putting in were surprising to those with Australian Equity as they did not receive any extra pay for the hours they were working. Australia's union culture was just as shocking to the English team.

Long queues started to form as soon as bookings were opened. Newspaper photos show people queuing for hours (some even sleeping on the pavements) and determined to get seats. Although to modern readers this may seem rather normal (frenzied online buying for popular concert tickets crashing selling sites or people sleeping outside ticket stalls for days on end before the web), this was the first time Perth – in fact, *Australia* – had ever reacted in such an excited way. Perth had not had a professional acting tour for twelve years, let alone one headed by theatre royalty of the day. The Oliviers obligingly greeted and spoke to fans on a number of occasions that week. O'Connor included an insightful quote from a M.W Jarvis:

Our schoolboy son – then aged fourteen – went into the city at 4pm … as number 5 in the queue. At 6pm my wife and niece relieved our

Left:
Vivien at the University of Western Australia with Winthrop Hall in the background.

Right:
At University of Western Australia

Photos credit: William John (Jack) Lorimer

> son in spot number 5 until 9pm. By this time the queue was half the length of the next street. I took over number 5 at 9pm – equipped with Thermos, stool and rug. It was quite a jovial line of people and a cause of much amusement to evening people in the city. About midnight when theatre people and strollers had mostly wended their way homeward a large car pulled alongside the head of the queue and we all gasped as we identified who had alighted from the car. Sir Laurence Olivier and Vivien Leigh. They came across and spoke with great interest and pleasure to up about spot 7 or 8. Sir Laurence shook hands with me. The rest of the night passed so quickly.[14]

Opening night that Saturday, despite the heat and humidity, a late arriving Sir James Mitchell (State Governor of the time), the inaudibility of the theatre, and an unrecognisable Olivier in make-up, was an astounding success. The audience exceeded 2000 and were mostly dressed in evening attire oddly in extremes; some in furs and others in summer dresses. Police and officials controlled the crowd and patrons were welcomed with doormen opening the doors of the cars as they arrived. A crowd on the opposite side of the road had gathered to watch the unfolding of the most glamorous event Perth had probably ever seen.

The *Sunday Times* the next day went into great detail about the fashions of the audience. Women were dressed lavishly and the men wore summer suits and some in tails:

> Piled high coifs, silky flowing tresses, the New Look in eye-catching bouffant skirts, the uneven hemline so popular overseas at the moment. There were debs in cool off-the-shoulder whites; smart young matrons svelte and groomed; lovely women in models. Popular was the Ballerina with its varied bodice lines and cool low necks. Many gowns were brilliantly beaded and sequined. White was popular while all black held its place amid the array of fresh new shades.[15]

Mrs RW Hefti's (wife of the American consul) dress probably would've won best dress if there had been an award that night and received a special mention in the article 'Billowing skirt of lilac organza was hand-painted with a design of violet orchids'. It was the equivalent of a modern-day red-carpet event and the article reads like the commentary that follows from the hosts and interviewers outside.

In contrast to the theatregoers, the Oliviers arrived discreetly and dressed lightly – Vivien in a light floral dress and Olivier in an open-necked white shirt with his sleeves rolled up. Michael Redington noticed a calm and friendly Olivier that night (surprising as he was obviously in pain; he wrote in his journal that his foot was very painful) and seemed in awe of the two principal performances.[16] The audience stood to sing 'God Save the King' and two stewards from either side of the stage walked in time to the music to light the footlights and the show began. Throughout the ensuing performance, alarm grew when only certain sections of the audience seemed to be reacting. It quickly became apparent that the other sections were experiencing an acoustical gap.

In the end, Olivier gave a nice speech in which he made sure to mention Western Australia's Sheffield Shield win (Australian domestic first-class cricket competition) and embarrassingly got presented a wreath before Vivien. Afterwards, the cast had drinks in the opulent foyer which was enjoyed by everyone.

Raymond Bowers writing for the *Sunday Times* the following morning started with, 'Old Vic came to the Capitol last night with an unforgettable flourish. It was a performance the artistry of which unerringly tripped the tightrope of perfection.' *The West Australian* review headline on Monday was, '"School for Scandal" Acclaimed'. Olivier went unnoticed on his first entrance, looking very middle-aged with overdone make-up, cloaked in a large coat and hat, limping onto the stage, but his performance was acknowledged as admirable and masterful. Vivien upon first entrance was instantly recognisable and received enormous applause at first sight:

> *But when we come to Miss Leigh, we finally drop a word that here would be libel. Here we can do no other than become lyrical in simile, for this Lady Teazle is indeed as a piece of entrancing music, a lyrical poem floated on the tones of a lovely voice, soft and melting.*[17]

Together Olivier and Vivien displayed between them, wrote Bowers, so implicit a timing, so mutual a give and take of nuance and point, that it was a joint triumph. This was what Olivier had wanted in picking *The School for Scandal:* a play to showcase both their talents. Together they were poetry in motion.

The supporting cast members also received triumphant feedback, in particular Peter Cushing. 'And the brilliance of the rest of the cast was by no means extinguished by principals who acted in combination. For the sheer genius of pose, Peter Cushing's Joseph Surface was almost balletic in its aptitude'; 'Terence Morgan, as Charles, shaded all but the principals.'[18]

Cecil Beaton's scenery and stylisation were pointed out as an effective keynote of the production and reminiscent of mezzo-tint book illustrations. This was obvious from the very start of the play with the footmen resplendently dressed and illuminating the stage with the lighting of certain sections of the stage with their candles as was needed for each of the five acts. Drops would rise with a tap on the door in time with the music and then the interior of the walk inside the interior of the house.

It appeared that the biggest issue – and admitted by all, including a frustrated Olivier – were the acoustics, which were therefore looked at as soon as possible. Tests were carried out on Monday and the audibility problems were fast fixed by the joint efforts of the engineering department of the Postmaster General's Office, specialists from the University and another local company.

Brent Bellon was a sixteen-year-old student at Perth Modern School in 1948. The upper classes were taken by bus to attend one performance and to this day, he can remember Olivier's rich cultured voice and how the hairs on the back of his neck were aroused by it.[19]

Meanwhile Adelaide, the second Australian city on their tour, had opened bookings, with an all-night queue of 500 which at one time numbered 1000.[20]

Armed with portable radios, torches, books, and flasks of coffee, more than 300 people waited in a queue that stretched for two city blocks tonight for preferential bookings which open tomorrow for the Oliviers' Old Vic season. Some who had placed chairs in the queue at noon today, 19 hours before the booking office opened, had made small camps with collapsible chairs, rugs, sandwiches and thermos flasks.[21]

Their second week in Perth went just as fast if not faster than the first. On Tuesday 23rd March, they called on the Lord Mayor at the Council Chambers and there were on-lookers lined up on the street. The crowd outside surrounded their car, ignoring the police preventing them from getting out. It was a scary moment. When the police finally managed to push them away, they exited into sweltering heat. Elsie Beyer reported that they were very much taken by the charming Mayor, Joseph Totterdale. Hailing from Lancashire, he still had an accent. Elsie wrote that he did a marvellous speech to which Olivier and Vivien replied. Champagne flowed and he presented to Vivien a book on Western Australian wildflowers, with details of the presentation and a signed photo inside.

They also addressed a packed Winthrop Hall at the University where the students were allowed to ask questions. Olivier gave a lecture on 'Poetry in Drama'. The special visit was captured by a young twenty-three-year-old student at the time, William John (Jack) Lorimer, a member of the University Dramatic Society using his Carl Zeiss Contax camera. Jack would graduate with a Bachelor of Science Degree at the same ceremony as Bob Hawke – the future Prime Minister of Australia. Jack's images are now a part of the UWA Pictorial Archive Collection.

Olivier wryly but proudly noted that Vivien made a few delightful speeches herself on these occasions, and although she fussed about them because of nerves, he sensed she was beginning to like it. He thought if he had tried to oblige when she complained, she would have seized the mike and made it even more bewitching. She said that day, 'There are many advantages of being married … one of them is that your husband does all the talking on occasions like this.'[22]

A lovely Sunday picnic was organised where the group sailed up Swan River. Photos show them on the banks of the river swimming and laughing. Vivien christened a boat *Sabina* at Claremont Yacht Club; a day Olivier wrote descriptively about:

After lunch Baba christened a new boat 'whether she be near or whether she be far I wish the winds to the Sabina' The beer bottle bounced the first time, but she made it the second with great danger to her face varying the poem a little. I steered a good deal of the time during the next leg of the voyage … We hitched all boats to the pier and most of us braved the jellyfish … fantastic sunset.[23]

In Perth, Olivier saw several people about his foot, including masseurs and a doctor but nothing worked. Vivien went to see kangaroos on her own at the Perth Zoo and there was an amusing luncheon by the Reeler's Fraternity of Western Australia. Despite the whole company attending,

Left:
Vivien christens a boat *Sabina*.

Right:
On board a yacht taking a rare nap.

Photos credit: Athol Shmith, 1948 – Australian Tour 1948, Laurence Olivier and Vivien Leigh and The Old Vic Company, Bib ID 3044576. Credit: National Library of Australia

CHAPTER 6

Left:
At Scarborough Beach.
Credit: Author's collection

no-one knew what or who the Reelers were. Olivier made do with an improvised speech that purposely went over their heads. The only thing he noted of worth was the good beer and only when the Reeler members started singing their anthem did the company realise it was a film society.

Olivier and Vivien also organised a daring midnight bathing party for the company at Scarborough Beach. Beyer wrote:

> *We arrived at the beach and there wasn't a soul about. I really do think the bus driver thought we were 'mad dogs and Englishmen' because most of the company including Larry and Vivien immediately undressed and into the water they went. Floodlighting is a very good idea because it does enable you to see just how far out the water is and whether there are any rocks. Those of us who didn't bathe got the supper ready and when the others came out of the water and dressed again, we all set to and had a most wonderful feed and plenty of wine and beer. Then all sorts of games were played until about a quarter past one when the lights went out.*[24]

On the last Saturday, the 27th, having rashly promised to be professionally photographed at the beach, Olivier wrote:

> *Norman drove us to a quiet one near Scarborough v beautiful but v rough and treacherous looking sea. We posed in a few agonising positions and then jumped in. Poor Mr. Watson had stayed over all week to get these rather ravishing pictures. Feet were badly burnt by roasting sand on way back to car.*[25]

Their pain and Mr Watson's patience were worth it because these photos are some of the most stunning of the tour.

Their time in Perth was a breathtaking success. Having only played *School for Scandal*, in Perth they had been able to concentrate and stay focused on one play. One lady had flown all the way from Darwin to see them and was featured in the newspapers. At the last performance on Tuesday 30th March, Olivier gave a witty speech expressing gratitude to Perth and the audience for their kindness and reception. 'We have all got indigestion at the thought of leaving you. You have spoilt us – you have given us a bonzer time.'[26]

On the day they left, Vivien insisted on having one last swim at Scarborough beach first thing in the morning. They didn't end up swimming but just basked in the brilliant West Australian sun. After their last performance, the audience had no intention of leaving until they saw them off and a large unmovable crowd blocked the roads outside the theatre. They gave them a riotous send-off as the buses taking the cast to the airport were mobbed. When the Oliviers appeared, police motorcycles had to pave a path for their taxi to leave. The Oliviers and their team had enchanted the most isolated city in the world and left a lifelong impression in two very short weeks.

— *Chapter 7* —

ADELAIDE
DALIESQUE TARNDANYA

The Adelaide hills undulating and the Adelaide hills may look bare
But the temperate woodlands have a natural beauty in the Countryside around Belair
These hills have been sketched by great artists and these hills have inspired poets to rhyme
And these hills they were old in the days of the dinosaurs long before the Historic Dreamtime.*

* Stanza of 'The Adelaide Hills', Francis Duggan.

Adelaide, the Garden City, also the City of Churches named after Queen Adelaide, consort to King William IV, was founded in 1836. The capital city of the State of South Australia, it was the only city in Australia that was not settled by convicts and carried a proud history of only being settled by free British, explaining the staunch colonialist attitude of its residents in 1948. It was also proud of its town planning, designed by Colonel William Light, giving consideration to the aesthetic and commercial needs of a city. The city centre was designed around the River Torrens in an area that was originally occupied by the Kaurna people, and in their language called Tarndanya. Light's city design was in the grid layout today known as 'Light's Vision'. Surrounded by parks and big boulevards, its design is now listed as a national heritage. One attempt at reconciliation after the devastating impact colonisation had on the Kaurna people is a commitment by Governments to rename and include Kaurna names for local places.

The tendency back in that time for white Adelaideans to feel more superior and aligned to the British, being free settlers, was quite evident during the tour. Speeches by the Lord Mayor at their first formal presentation are laced with colonial and racist rhetoric. To understand this in the context of the times we must look at the Australian psyche during this period. In 1950, Australian writer A.A. Phillips referred to the term 'cultural cringe' to describe Australia's conflict with their self-identity from its convict history. This conflict led to the obsession of thinking the measure of greatness was anything 'English' and

Preceding spread, on left: *The Skin of Our Teeth.* Credit: Alicia Powell Collection

Left:
Arriving at Parafield Airport.
Credit: Author's collection

Right:
From the Sotheby's 2017 Vivien Leigh Estate catalogue. Hans Heysen's *Ambleside Pastoral.* Credit: Author's collection

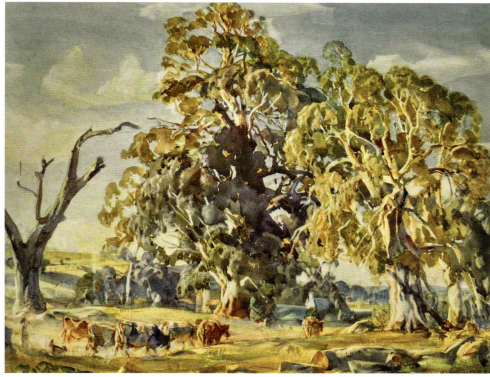

nothing of their own was ever going to be worthy – an inferiority complex, specifically in relation to literature and art; acting of course falling under arts.

On their overnight flight to Adelaide, O'Connor mentions that the group were awoken by a vision of Vivien, fairy-like in a pale blue negligée, exclaiming the sunrise over a magnificent sight of the near perfectly straight Perth-Adelaide train tracks across the dessert.[1] Stretching across the Nullarbor Plain, it served as the only freight passage between Western Australia and the eastern States and has the longest section of completely straight train tracks in the world. Vivien had been deeply disappointed that the trip had not been by train to fully appreciate it. When the flight arrived in Adelaide, in the early hours of the morning, there was still a throng of fans to welcome them as they made their way to their suite at the historic South Australia Hotel, where they were greeted with dozens of bouquets and a room that had French windows opening out onto a delightful terrace, much to Vivien's approval.

The South Australia Hotel is an example of a historic building that lost its life during a time when preserving iconic buildings relevant to a city's rich history was not a priority. The hotel was built in 1894 and progressed well business-wise, being well located next to the railway station and innovative for the time, having luxurious rooms, twenty-four-hour service, hot and cold water, and eventually even air conditioning. The beautiful dining room, seating close to 200 guests, entertained Adelaide's most illustrious. In the 1920s, it was neglected for a while, before being bought in 1934 by a female hotelier extraordinaire, Louisa O'Brien, who immediately overhauled it back into an even bigger success. The South Australia Hotel for the next thirty years or so was one of the best in the world. Louis Cotton, fondly referred to as Lewy, was its unforgettable head waiter from the start to the end. He was known to refuse entry to any man regardless of social standing if they didn't wear a tie. The hotel would entertain such notables as Marlene Dietrich, Anna Pavlova, Noël Coward and – the highlight of 1964 – The Beatles. Not only was The South a centre of social life but it was also a huge part of Adelaide's community life. In 1939, during a catastrophic bushfire season, the Blue Room was offered to firemen as a place of rest and in the Second World War it housed American forces.

Louisa O'Brien was also a philanthropist. She gave the hotel over to many charitable causes during her time and was awarded a Member of the Order of the British Empire (MBE) in 1948. When she passed away in the hotel in 1957, the reins went to her daughter who was by then fully trained to take over. Sadly, Adelaide would lose this significant hotel with over a hundred-year history in 1971 when Ansett Transport Industries bought it and bulldozed it to the ground. A rather generic-looking Ansett Gateway Hotel took its place and today it's the Stamford Plaza. The South Australia Hotel is still remembered fondly and missed by those in love with nostalgia and history. When we consider that it was once compared to Singapore's Raffles in nostalgic significance (which is still much loved and well preserved), the loss to Adelaide is even more momentous.

Top:
The South Australia Hotel, 1940. Credit: State Library of South Australia, B-23785

Bottom:
Theatre Royal. Credit: State Library of South Australia, B-2910 P80

The Oliviers went straight into their British ambassadorial roles and worked with no real rest. A press conference was held at noon where the customary photos were taken. Then a visit to the Governor of South Australia after a quick lunch. Olivier insisted on an hour break to take Vivien for a drive around the city, and up to Light's lookout to see the view. Vivien thought Adelaide was very beautiful. They managed a small rest before an early dinner and then they went to see the theatre they'd play at: Theatre Royal. They worked until past midnight. It was lucky that the theatre was only a short distance from the hotel.

When the Oliviers returned to England at the end of the year, they commented that most of the theatres in Australia and New Zealand were too large for their performances. They liked the smaller ones, especially the one in Hobart, but their favourite was noted to be Adelaide's Theatre Royal.[2] Built in Hindley Street in 1878 to replace the original theatre built in 1868, it was designed by Melbourne architect George R. Johnson and was simple in design. The theatre was balanced in size, with well thought-out details which included Corinthian pillars and concisely sectioned off areas over three levels. It was improved on two further occasions; first in 1884 and second in 1914.

The theatre was bought by Adelaide's department store Miller Anderson and Company and ultimately demolished in 1962 to make way for a multi-level car park, giving literal meaning to the lyrics of Joni Mitchell's 'Big Yellow Taxi' in 1970: 'They paved paradise and put up a parking lot.'

There is no doubt where the Oliviers would've stood in regard to their favourite Australian theatre being pulled down, especially Vivien. In 1957, she would campaign and protest heavily to save London's St James Theatre from demolition. In a foreword to a book about theatre, she described it as a 'memorial or obituary volume', personifying the theatre as having been the victim of 'murder' and of the 'apathy and levity with which our generation disposes of London's landmarks'.[3]

Adelaide's population in 1948 was less than 500,000. Close to 3000 waited outside the theatre just to see the audience attend, and the Oliviers arrive on the gala opening night of *Richard III*. Adelaide resident, Australian actor, critic, columnist and radio personality Peter Goers, was born in 1956, eight years after the tour. During his childhood, he never met anyone who had not seen a show during that Adelaide stint.[4] Memories were cherished and remembered frequently, especially that of the antique chair Olivier sat on that gave way, in response to which – with both athleticism and comedic timing – he jumped up and flicked the broken wood into the fireplace, amazing everyone at the press conference.

Ray Oberman was five years old in Adelaide in 1948 but he recalled how the shows lived long in the memories of his parents.[5] They continued to talk about the performances with glowing comments and memories throughout their lives. He himself values their *Richard III* theatre program, signed by both Olivier and Vivien, very much.

Michael Redington, who stayed with a distinguished Adelaide doctor during the Adelaide run, remembered its first night well. The doctor who had come to see it would not stop talking about it. He had not seen acting like it before and could not get over Olivier's voice as Richard.

Left:
At press conference. Credit: Author's collection

Right:
At the Adelaide Civic reception. Credit: Courtesy of Judith Koop from the Joyce Attwood Collection

This is a recurring memory for many; Olivier's *voice*. 'A great triumph,' is how the *Advertiser* critic C.R Jury described opening night. 'To see Olivier act Shakespeare anywhere is an experience that contributes to the best part of one's mind. To see the Old Vic in action is a matter of vicarious pride.'[6]

Lyn Sharp was in her first year of high school at Unley High School. She had no chance of getting a ticket for any of the shows. Every seat had been sold. She remembered the build-up had started months prior so there was an electric anticipation by the city.[7] Her connection to Olivier is strong, with family members having been in theatre and acting circles. After seeing him in *Hamlet* in that year, she became an ardent Olivier fan.

Lyn's cousin Ralph Peterson, a writer and actor, was married to Betty Lucas – an actress too. Lyn remembered Olivier had noticed her talent and encouraged her to leave Australia for England, which she did, only returning in 1965 to give birth to cinematographer Joel Peterson.

Olivier's connection didn't stop there, for Lyn's *husband's* cousin was Meredith Kinmont, who married an actor with The Old Vic, Paul Daneman. The Danemans would dine with Olivier and his third wife Joan Plowright in Brighton when Daneman filmed *Oh What a Lovely War* in 1969 with Olivier, and to this day they are memories that are recounted often when Meredith visits family.

Interestingly, Meredith Kinmont is the daughter of Joan Kinmont, writer and poet who presented to the Oliviers a copy of her very successful book of poetry, *This, My Son*, when they were in Adelaide. This book found its way back to Melbourne and the author of this book, as it was a part of the Australia Lot in the 2017 *Vivien Leigh Collection*.

Perth had seen the best of the company. Even by Adelaide, they were beginning to tire. The Adelaide Civic Reception was described as the drollest, the most obvious for its overt pro-colonist rhetoric. The main 'political' objective of the tour; being the promotion of Britain; was obvious in the Food for Britain Appeal. After the war, Britain was compelled to appeal for food from her Commonwealth allies. Australian cities donated through what is now known as Lord Mayor's Charitable Fund.

The importance of being British and promoting all things British was obvious in the Acting Lord Mayor, Sir Lavington Bonython's speech that night: overtly Empire-dedicated with pro-colonial idealism, he said:

> *Sir Laurence Olivier and Lady Olivier have come to us through the courtesy of the British Council, a body that is doing much to foster good relations between different parts of the world, more particularly in an effort to bring the various parts of the Empire into closer touch. We are proud of the fact that our guests are British, for we in this State are proud to be British and want to remain so to the end.*[8]

The second week in Adelaide was devoted to *Skin of Our Teeth* and therefore Vivien. It was preceded the Sunday before by a freak storm. In the early hours of Sunday April 11th, on what was expected to be a normal autumn day, a hurricane

Top:
At the University of Adelaide. L to R Vice Chancellor Professor McKellar Stewart, Vivien, Sir William Mitchell, Olivier, unidentified person and Diana Lorking at far end.

Bottom:
At the University of Adelaide.

Photos credit: Author's collection

hit Adelaide. It was the worst storm in living memory for many. The city and surrounding suburbs suffered widespread damage along with the entire south coast. Glenelg's jetty was washed away. Only the kiosk and aquarium remained. Hundreds that had queued and camped to buy tickets went scattering for shelter on the Saturday night in preparation for the rain.

However, the storm had no effect on Vivien's performance as she had greatly improved since the London run. As Sabina, the femme fatale – an archetype that reappears in various characters throughout the history of the human race – her ability to switch moods mid-air, mercurial intelligence, and provocative and impish sexiness made it a perfect role for Vivien. But it was as Olivier described the 'Picasso' of the plays. With its unconventional vaudeville presentation, it divided the Australian audience. Some were perplexed and bewildered, not sure what to make of it, and some others just hated it.

James Clarke wrote to the editor of the *Advertiser*:

> *Having witnessed* The Skin of Our Teeth, *I can quite understand the difficulty of many people in trying to give a coherent interpretation of it. The play reminds one of a visitor to an art gallery, looking perplexedly at a surrealist picture asking a nearby person the meaning of it, receiving the reply, 'Don't ask me. I'm only the artist.'*

Mary Armitage wrote favourably but still noted a certain frustration that it is a play that dazzles and bedevils and is enormously exciting, stimulating and different – even if the difference is sometimes too self-consciously naïve and the public scene shifting, rehearsing and other jiggery pokery does occasionally exacerbate you.[10] Olivier wrote in his journal that there were 'rude letters' about the play but didn't elaborate, going on to describe his excitement from a trip to see albino kangaroos instead. He still wasn't happy with his part Antrobus but thought that Vivien was wonderful – better than ever!

At the last performance, Vivien had insisted Olivier give a long speech and, in trying to explain and to somewhat justify the choice of the play he said, 'A picture gallery must have its Rembrandts and its Henry Moores – an allusion as to why a play like *The Skin of Our Teeth* was in our repertory.'[11]

They visited The University of Adelaide in the second week. Student Diana Lorking had queued for hours the previous night for a ticket. She was tired the next morning and studied in the library. When she looked up, she was amazed to see Laurence Olivier and Vivien Leigh walk in.[12] It made the night-long waiting more worth it.

On one social outing, the Oliviers visited the charming property Carrick Hill. Overlooking the city on a romantic hill, the estate was the building project of society couple Edward Hayward and Ursula Barr Smith, a marriage between two of Adelaide's wealthiest families. The land on which Carrick Hill was built was the wedding gift from Ursula's father. During their year-long European honeymoon, the pair acquired many items that would be shipped to build the manor, including panelling, windows and even the staircase from Beaudesert Hall in Staffordshire before its demolition.

Left:
Carrick Hill. Credit: State Library of South Australia B-44852

The unconventional and eclectic Haywoods hosted many notables, artists, writers, and eccentrics of all kinds in what was described as an intoxicating and heady atmosphere. They entertained lavishly, with good wine, food and dancing. For the Oliviers, it would've been a reminder of their beloved country home back in Buckinghamshire, Notley, where a similar atmosphere presided. Thankfully, today it's an example of a historical mansion that has survived with its original contents and gardens intact and a must-see for any visitor who wants to take a step back in time. Although financially helped by the State Government, its survival and maintenance wouldn't exist without its volunteers and the Friends of Carrick Hill fundraising.

After an impressive visit to the University, where they spoke to the Student Theatre Group – an audience of close to 4000 – the company had the pleasure of visiting a winery, being big wine appreciators. Vivien could've taken the connoisseur title, having learnt about grape varieties in school while in Germany and having toured many French vineyards. Once when they were in Los Angeles to do *Gone with the Wind* retakes, they had bought with them six crates of French wines, which unfortunately were confiscated from them – California being a wine-producing state.

Adelaide, over the years, had become known for its wines; especially the picturesque Barossa Valley named after Barossa in Spain, settled by the British and Germans in 1842 which has a distinct

Left:
Vivien and Mercia at possibly Stonyfell Winery. Credit: Author's collection

culture and style that is still the same today. Income came mostly from wheat, wool and wine but by the 1890s, Adelaide became one of the biggest producers of wine in Australia. At Stonyfell's Vineyard, they watched the crushings and had a lot explained to them. Stonyfell was bought back in 1859 in Langhorne Creek and named after the stony slopes, called 'fells', in England. They especially liked the sherry and were devastated when a gifted crate smashed when opening the car door back in the city.

After returning to England in November, during an interview for a representative of the *Herald*, Vivien and Olivier remembered Australian wine. Vivien even asked, 'Why don't we see more of those wonderful wines of yours? They're absolutely fine! I believe they are bottled and drunk too soon after arrival here, but they're certainly wonderful.' Olivier responded, 'Yes indeed. They're among the finest we've ever tasted. There should be more of them here.'[13]

Another visit that seemed to have impressed the Oliviers was the home of one of Australia's most famous landscape artists, Hans Heysen. The Cedars sit just outside of Hahndorf in the Adelaide Hills and is a unique and charming property. Heysen was a German-born immigrant with humble beginnings. His love of art started at a young age and, with lessons, he eventually exhibited his work enough to get noticed and sponsored by prominent Adelaide citizens to study in Paris. When he returned from his European training and travelling through Italy, his successful exhibition in Melbourne in 1912 made him renowned. With that money, he bought the colonial home, set amongst thirty-six acres. It was a landscape of cattle, eucalyptus, pine, gum and cedar trees; the same trees he studied, painted, conserved and gave him critical acclaim, a body of work that was honoured by a knighthood in 1957.

At Cedars with his wife Sallie, Heysen raised their eight children, including famed artist daughter Nora: 'Graced by pines but not hemmed in by them, within a call of the house but far enough to shut out the lap and ripple of its domestic tides … not a place on Earth more finely attuned to the spirit of the artist it was to serve.'[14] The Heysens were well-known for their warm hospitality at Cedars, entertaining the likes of luminaries like Dame Nellie Melba, Helen Keller, Anna Pavlova and of course Olivier and Vivien in their unimposing and humble home; similar to the artist who inhabited it for fifty-five years.

The Oliviers, like the others who visited, made Cedars worthy of mention. With its floors covered in rare and beautiful rugs, the house and the hosts were warm and welcoming. Olivier and Vivien were so mesmerised that they performed a Shakespeare scene for their hosts. But it wasn't impressive enough for Lady Heysen to part with one of her massive teacups that Vivien asked for. Like when Anna Pavlova had begged for the painting over the dining room mantlepiece the year before, Lady Heysen wasn't relenting.

Vivien in her spare time during the tour would shop for furnishings for Notley, including curtain material. She would also get cuttings of trees, ferns and gum trees in particular for its massive gardens. Whilst visiting Cedars, she fell in love with Heysen's art just like everyone else did

CHAPTER 7

Left:
Changing a flat tyre in Campbellfield on their way to Melbourne.

Right:
Looking at the map on their way to Melbourne with presumably the chauffuer.

Photo credit: Athol Shmith, 1948 – Australian Tour 1948, Laurence Olivier and Vivien Leigh and The Old Vic Company, Bib ID 3044576. Credit: National Library of Australia

Left:
Postcard of Jen's Hotel, Mount Gambier, 1948.
Credit: Author's collection

and bought a watercolour of *Ambleside Pastoral*, depicting cattle grazing amongst the grandeur of his beloved gum trees. This painting was auctioned in the *Vivien Leigh Collection* by Sotheby's in 2017. It is not hard to imagine that one of the gum trees that were shipped and planted at Notley from the tour came from Cedars itself.

Cedars has been open to the public since 1994 and is still furnished and decorated as it was in 1948, maintained by the Hans Heysen Trust since 2016 by his grandson Peter. Hans' art studio still stands on the hill's ridge, graced by ancient gum trees over 600 years old and inside it, his painting material and last work on the easel sits as if time has stood still.

They left Adelaide on April 18th for Melbourne for an eight-week season performing all three plays. Vivien and Olivier decided to drive on their own while the rest of the team took a midnight train. Vivien wrote a beautifully descriptive letter to Hugh Beaumont back in London:

We drove ... through the most wonderful country imaginable, the first bit so Dali-esque as to be incredible – great shallow blue lakes surrounded by glistening white sand, black and white branches of trees sticking out of the water and birds of every kind and description everywhere. Then through great forests to Mt Gambier where we spent the night in a very strange hotel. The midnight clock struck eighteen and the fire alarm was sent off every two hours just to see if the poor old thing was all right (and that we knew it). A lot of marsupials tramped about on the roof and bang on each other's doors. Not very restful, but different.[15]

CHAPTER 7

Top:
One of the small coloured photographs of the Mount Gambier lakes in the Oliviers' personal snap shot album. Credit: Author's collection

Bottom left:
Adam Lindsay Gordon memorial obelisk. Credit: Athol Shmith 1948 – Australian Tour 1948, Laurence Olivier and Vivien Leigh and The Old Vic Company, Bib ID 3044576. Credit: National Library of Australia

Bottom right:
Browne's & Valley Lakes, Mount Gambier, as they were in 1948 taken by presumably Olivier. Credit: Author's collection

The strange hotel described was Mount Gambier's Jen's Hotel, which still operates today. Olivier wrote that they saw the famous blue lakes but oddly writes not the real ones. Mini postcards, not actual photographs, exist in their personal album of the lakes so maybe they didn't get to see them up close. From their suite, they could see the fountain that Captain Robert Gardiner had presented to the town.

They took time to view the childhood home of Captain Gardiner's grandchild – none other than their great friend, Robert Helpmann who was born in Mount Gambier in 1909. Helpmann, a dancer, choreographer, and artistic director was probably more Vivien's friend than Olivier's. His family had moved to Adelaide when he was five and his mother encouraged the stage at a young age. In London in the '30s, he became very successful with the Vic-Wells Ballet and starred in Olivier's *Henry V* and 1948's *The Red Shoes,* which he also choreographed. One of the most accurate descriptions of him was by Ninette de Valois: '… talented, enthusiastic, extremely intelligent, witty, cute as a monkey, quick as a squirrel … on the debit side, academically backward, technically weak … too busy having a good time'.[16] It's easy to see why Vivien gravitated towards him. In 1965 he was named Australian of the Year and appointed co-Artistic Director along with Peggy Van Praagh of the Australian ballet. He was also the first Australian performing artist to be given a State funeral at St Andrews Cathedral, Sydney. A bust of him by John Dowie is kept in the Adelaide Festival Centre.

They also made it a point to visit the memorial obelisk to poet Adam Lindsay Gordon, erected at the spot he made a leap on horseback over an old post and rail guard fence, onto a ledge overlooking the Blue Lake. Olivier photographed it artistically. Gordon was the first Australian poet to have his work recognised internationally and the first to use Australian idioms in his work. He savoured everything he saw, smelt and felt while he rode his horse, setting them down into poetry. South Australia's landscape, fauna, starry nights, beaches and environment fascinated him. He is the only Australian who is commemorated with a bust in Poet's Corner, Westminster Abbey.

As they drove towards Melbourne the next day, Olivier wrote descriptively, 'Then on through really wonderful pasture country, brown hills of dry grass cut by cypress windbreaks. Always high mountains in the distance and always cream, dirty ochre and black dairy cattle in the foreground.'[17]

— *Chapter 8* —

MELBOURNE

FANDOM FROM FITZROY

I would ride as never a man has ridden
In your sleepy swirling surges hidden,
To gulfs foreshadowed, through straits forbidden,
*Where no light wearies and no love wanes.**

* Adam Lindsay Gordon. Part of last stanza 'The Swimmer'.

Melbourne: a city built from scratch, started illegally when sheep farmers from Tasmania crossed the Bass Strait in search of new pasture. Starting on the banks of the meandering river of mists and shadows – as the Yarra was known to its traditional owners – it grew during the urbanisation surge in the nineteenth century and boomed during the Gold Rush in the 1850s. It was the gateway to the hinterland, the land of the people of the Woi Wurrung and Boon Wurrung language groups; the traditional owners. Under colonisation, it became known as 'Paris of the Antipodes' being the *cultural* centre of Australia, as it is today – an international city with a melting pot of cultures, quaint bustling laneways, brimming with trams, old buildings, a vibrant café culture, a sporting epi-centre – a jewel in the southern hemisphere.

O'Connor wrote after the generous hospitality of Perth and Adelaide that Melbourne was out to 'get' these 'darlings of the gods', but Olivier's humility won everyone over.[1] Melbournians, like Sydneysiders, thought themselves more culturally advanced than those from Perth and Adelaide and so the team felt a bigger need to impress and prove themselves. It also appears the press were given forewarning from their peers in America and England that Olivier was difficult to interview and was reserved. There was already a preconceived bias.

The Oliviers checked in to the Windsor Hotel and then attended their biggest press conference to date – with Vivien looking particularly elegant and chic – at the Menzies Hotel. The press' preconceived bias was soon overturned. The papers devoted pages to Vivien the next day, capturing all her beautiful facial expressions. Even Olivier noted in his journal that, 'V. carried the wretched

Preceding spread, on left:
Vivien amongst the ferns.
Credit: Athol Shmith, 1948
– Australian Tour 1948,
Laurence Olivier and Vivien
Leigh and The Old Vic
Company, Bib ID 3044576.
Credit: National Library of
Australia

Below:
The Windsor Hotel in 1948.
Credit: Author's collection

Left:
Victorian Parliament Building from the top floor balcony of Windsor Hotel, 1948.

Right:
Looking out towards St Patrick's Cathedral from The Windsor Hotel top balcony, 1948.

Photos credit: Author's collection

thing off with superlative charm, starting by breaking up the formality of the arranged chairs and having us all mill around.' His hesitancy and disdain for the press as they had suspected showed as he described it as 'wretched' and a 'weary hour and a half'.[2] Weary and wretched as Olivier was unprepared, nor did he understand Australia's conflicted relationship with Britain after the stresses of war: on one hand feverish enthusiasm and reverence (compounded by the *cultural cringe*) for everything British, and on the other a mistrust and ambivalence, having been left to defend herself and turn to a new world leader for protection– America. This unresolved hostility and doubt would explain questions put to Olivier by the press, starting off with, 'Now that Britain is finished …' which incensed and ignited a naïve and patriotic Olivier.[3]

The following day, the articles were not as hard as they anticipated with many wonderful write-ups. F. Keith Manzie wrote that he expected a 'highbrow' and formal Olivier but was pleasantly surprised at how agreeable and easy to talk to he was. 'Well, that is how I found Laurence Olivier and his wife – approachable, pleasant people. Soon many Victorians will meet them – across footlights, doing the jobs they know so well and it is to be hoped, in the highways and byways, as citizens like ourselves.'[4]

Another piece for *The Argus* was titled 'The Oliviers Are As Charming As You Hoped They'd Be'. It wrote, 'They are two very, very charming people, natural, patient – they must have answered hundreds of questions from a vast horde of press men and women for well over an hour yesterday afternoon – good looking, interested in others, as well as themselves. And above all, deeply sincere about their work.'

Vivien said that they loved to collect books and already they had been gifted many about Australia to take home. The road trip from Adelaide had shown them how truly beautiful Australia was. 'We don't mind how many we get. We love Australia and we are deeply interested in it. Our motor trip from Adelaide yesterday was a revelation to us of how beautiful your country is.'[5]

An unfortunate incident that caused some embarrassment and resentment was the exclusion of Melbourne's radio representatives from this conference without a real excuse. Famous radio personality of the time, Norm Banks – who had received prior approval from the Council to attend – was told he was not welcome at the entrance. When it was referred to Dan O'Connor, the excuse given was that due to prior incidents in Adelaide, it was decided that only the press would be included. However, this did not appease the broadcasting circle, who felt they had been unjustly discriminated against and Banks was left humiliated.

Another example of the awful trend that beset Australia in the name of progress in the '70s was the demolition of the incredible Menzies Hotel, where this press conference took place. Melbourne's architecture was influenced greatly by the Gold Rush years of the 1850s and, as most things that eventuate from outlandish money making, tended to be ostentatious. The Menzies was built in 1867 to accommodate the Duke of Edinburgh's visit and was the city's first grand hotel. On the ground floor was a Moorish-inspired hall and a 'winter garden' with Indian rugs, and ceilings adorned with ornate nymphs.

The Menzies, along with many grand hotels from this era, was not considered modern enough without the American-style contemporary amenities that travellers preferred; another way American culture was starting to influence Australia. Its contents were auctioned off in 1968 and within a year it was demolished to make way for the bland BHP office block. Victorian opulence was considered old-fashioned and out of date.

Melbourne went through nearly two decades of a demolition phase, so much so that the demolition company, 'Whelan the Wrecker', became infamous when signs placed on Victorian buildings with 'Whelan the Wrecker is Here' led to urban myths and even a song.

It was only after more and more beloved landmarks of old Melbourne came tumbling down in the name of progress, that there was a call for the preservation of the remaining few, and the National Trust of Victoria was formed in 1956. Unfortunately, it was only in 1974 that legislation was passed to formally protect heritage buildings, but by then of course too late.

One hotel that was spared and manages to still survive today was where the Oliviers chose to stay during the Melbourne stint. The Windsor Hotel, referred to as Melbourne's Duchess of Spring Street, is Australia's last remaining hotel of the nineteenth century, built in European style. The Windsor pre-dates the Savoy in London, The Plaza and Waldorf Astoria in New York, the Ritz in Paris, and Raffles in Singapore. Built in 1883 by shipping magnate George Nipper, it was named

Left:
At the Melbourne press conference. Credit: News Ltd/Newspix, News Corp Australia

Right:
Fifteen-year-old Richard Laver presenting a flower to Vivien. Credit: Private collection

the Grand Hotel and designed by renowned architect Charles Webb. It instantly became a famous Melbourne fixture, even hosting the final drafting session of the Australian constitution in 1898. When it changed hands in 1920, the name changed to The Windsor in honour of the British royal family.

If a hotel's endowment to its city is made by the guests, memorable staff, its place in history and the stories that resonate through it, the Windsor would rank in the top ten in the world. In its over 138-year-old history, with its old-world charm, it has seen hundreds of notable people come and go and survived many handovers and demolition attempts.

In 1916, the hotel converted some of its suites into six apartments, to make up for the lack of travellers coming through because of the war, which were leased to semi-permanent residents. In February of 1948, Flat 3 was occupied by Mrs Mercer's family for three weeks to allow her to attend her debutante ball.

> *On the day of my coming-out dance, when my dress had been delivered and was hanging in the hall, my mother answered the phone and was asked by the manager if he could bring someone up to look at the flat. My mother agreed and so up came the man planning the Olivier's tour. He inspected the flat and said it would suit beautifully: then he noticed my dress in the hall and admired that too.*[6]

These flats were phased out in a 1980s renovation and were incorporated into what is now the Victorian Suites. Flat 3, where the Oliviers stayed, would be what is now the Royal Suite. In 1961, when Vivien toured Australia and New Zealand on her own, with her then-partner Jack Merivale, in what seems a painful need to relive the nostalgia of the '48 tour, she insisted on having the same suite.

There is a lovely story told by Christopher J. Spicer in his book *Duchess: The Story of the Windsor Hotel,* of how the then-fifteen-year-old bellboy Richard Laver carried the couple's luggage into the elevator and endeared himself to them. Olivier had asked him, 'Who are you?', to which young Richard had answered cheekily, 'I'm Richard the Third.' 'No,' said Olivier. 'I'd say you were Richard the Second.'[7] Richard would deliver the papers to their room every afternoon and recalled Vivien in bed resting and inviting him to sit at the foot to have a chat. The Oliviers on many occasions asked him to accompany them on their outings as a guide. It's said upon their departure they asked Richard to join their company, but of course, how would a fifteen-year-old leave his home; even for the world-famous Oliviers?

The Windsor left a lasting impression on Laver's family. Some sixty-six years after the tour, in 2014, Laver's mother Ivy Laver turned 101 and was granted a cheque for back-paid rent on her housing commission flat. Citizens in Victoria, after turning one hundred, received rent-free housing. Mrs Ivy Laver decided she would spend the money taking her family to a Windsor Hotel high tea. She made it a point to tell the interviewer of *The Age* who reported on it that her son Richard Laver (by then deceased) had worked for the Windsor in the late '40s.[8]

As in Adelaide, the crowds had camped out over a day before tickets were released on Collins Street. Glenn's Newsagency were the booking agents. A coupon system was initiated for the centre and back stalls. As the weeks went on, the queues got worse until the Council was inundated with complaints from ratepayers. They protested that the camping was undesirable, creating debris, and hampering normal foot traffic. It got so bad that by May, police were called in to break up competing queues from forming and setting some order.[9]

The Princess Theatre was originally an equestrian amphitheatre near the time of Melbourne's foundation. As with many of the classical buildings in Melbourne, it was built after the gold boom in the 1850s, and in 1857 it opened as The Princess Theatre and Opera House. The theatre went through many changes of hands, refurbishments and renovations over the years. In 1890, Austin Brereton wrote for the *London Theatre Magazine*:

I have never been in a more beautiful or perfect theatre than the Princess. Indeed, I will make bold to say that with respect to the graceful design of its interior and the comfort and cleanliness of its stage and dressing rooms, it has no equal in London. The building which is practically isolated has spacious luxurious entrances and every convenience for the public.... everywhere there is an air of thoughtfulness, ease, cleanliness and comfort that was foreign to me in the matter of theatres until I visited this one.[10]

From 1942 to 1947, The Princess was owned by Garnet H. Carroll and served solely as a cinema through the war years. In 1948 it reverted back to a live theatre for the tour. The Old Vic Tour would influence and revitalise the theatre scene and the coming decades – the '50s and '60s – has been commonly referred to as the golden age of Melbourne theatre. This saw it permanently restored to a live theatre.

The Princess, along with the Windsor, has been lucky to survive the demolition era. In 1973, the theatre was listed by the National Trust; although this didn't stop times where it deteriorated and was ignored, needing fresh investors and further refurbishments. Since the 1990s, though, it's established itself as Australia's musical theatre home.

The tour opened the Melbourne season with *The School for Scandal* on the 20th of April in what was described as a thrilling atmosphere. The audience were dressed in their finest as a guard of honour was accidently created by the many sightseers who had braved the rain to see the couple and also the lavishly dressed attendees. Olivier received four curtain calls after the performance and said, 'Thank you for your most brave and generous attendance and for your extremely warm and generous applause. We do not feel it was justified, but thanks for it. It is a greater joy to us to play host for once and say to the people of Melbourne, "Welcome to the Old Vic".'[11]

In general, the reviews were favourable, although one noted that it was not Australia's most memorable drama experience. *The Age*'s headline was 'Old Vic's First Night Triumph': 'The first

Top:
Girl's sleeping outside Glenn's Newsagency. Credit: News Ltd/Newspix, News Corp Australia

Bottom:
Vivien being presented with souvenir scarf. Credit: Museum of Applied Science

offering of The Old Vic Company in Melbourne provided us with one of the great theatre nights, with two famous artists whose screen images only were known to us, superb staging and direction and décor of brilliant artistry in stage design by Cecil Beaton.'[12]

The next day they attended a British Council luncheon at the Menzies where 200 invitations were given to meet the Oliviers socially. A souvenir scarf was presented to Vivien, commemorating the tour. Produced by Melbourne-based design company, Prestige Ltd, it had hand-stencilled designs of the theatre and various characters played by Olivier. Designed by Prestige's Nan Gooderham, it was influenced by the company's style which had shifted towards a European-inspired design aesthetic after the war, especially in its textiles, under the artistic direction of Gerard Herbst. Prestige also adopted a Staatliches Bauhaus ideology towards their textile designs, allowing individual artistic interpretation in their mass-produced fabric designs to compete with overseas imports. Another beautiful and nostalgic example of this is the scarf titled 'Fantasy in Collins St' designed by William Salmon, depicting a busy Melbourne streetscape evoking a definite Paris vibe.[13]

On the 23rd, Vivien dressed in a tartan wool frock gifted by the wool industry of England was given eight pairs of double bed blankets by Australia's own Wool Board in apricot and pale blue. It was a gift made by the contribution of 100,000 Australian wool growers. The reception again was held at the Menzies and indicated the reciprocal promotion of industries.

In their never-ending ambassadorial obligations, the most honourable but possibly, in hindsight, inappropriate – being just actors – was the Oliviers' required presence at ANZAC Day celebrations in Australia's capital, Canberra. They flew in on the 10:30 flight and went straight to lunch with the Governor-General, William McKell and his family at Yarralumla, Government House. The official residence of the Governor-General since 1927, its name coming from Arralumna, meaning echo, Australia's Government House sits on Canberra's most historic pastoral plains. Originally the house of a sheep station of 40,000 acres owned by Frederick Campbell, it was bought by the Commonwealth Government in 1913; after which extensive work began to make it suitable for an official residence. Today it is thankfully heritage listed – although only sitting on fifty-four acres, the residence serves as the administration centre for the employees who support the role of the Governor-General. Olivier was impressed with the residence, taking a casual photo from the Vista Lawn view.

After lunch, they participated in the ceremony at the War Memorial of which some footage survives and Vivien sits next to Prime Minister Ben Chifley, at times looking slightly uncomfortable. They were driven up to Mount Ainslie to see a picture-perfect view of the city that they thought was very well-planned, something that is commonly observed about Australia's capital.

After returning from the drive, they were introduced to the Cabinet and their wives. Olivier was bombarded with political questions, which he

Left:
At the British Council's reception at Menzies Hotel, the Oliviers met singer/stage star Gladys Moncrieff, Coral Browne an Australian actress revisiting from London and renowned Australian pianist Eileen Joyce. Credit: Author's collection

Right:
Vivien at the Wool Board Presentation. Credit: Alicia Powell Collection

CHAPTER 8

Left:
Arriving in Canberra. Credit: Esperanza Alcastle Collection

Top:
Government House, Canberra. Credit: Athol Shmith, 1948 – Australian Tour 1948, Laurence Olivier and Vivien Leigh and The Old Vic Company, Bib ID 3044576. Credit: National Library of Australia

Bottom:
Vivien trying out the president's chair in the Legislative Council chamber at Parliament House. Sir Clifden Eager and his daughter Muriel look on. Credit: Private Collection

must have felt apprehensive and out of place to answer. 'Tell us, Sir Laurence, now that Britain's finished, how will the Empire be divided up?'[14]

Back at Yarraluma, they had dinner while getting more and more nervous about the speeches they had to make at the night's Food for Britain Appeal at the Capitol Theatre. When they arrived, their nerves were even more aggravated upon seeing the set-up. 'I have never known a more alarming set-up including the Albert Hall wartime stuff. Arc lights, two movie news cameras, four microphones, 2000 people. Baba looked wonderful in pale lime green, and a blood red rose at her waist.'[15] Vivien was so nervous that she hesitated halfway through her speech and put her hand to her brow. Luckily Olivier was sitting close by and was able to lean forward and give her a prompt. She finished with sonnet 116. Olivier was even more petrified, leaving out a section of his speech, but he got through.

Although the day had been nerve-wracking and uncomfortable, the room they were given to spend the night in at Yarralumla had a beautiful view and after a few nightcaps, they were thankfully able to get some sleep.

On the flight back the next morning, they learned Oliviers' speech had been cut short by the ABC, with listeners so irate that they wrote letters to the press. One might wonder if it had anything to do with his overly nationalistic tone and his insistence that Britain did not want pity from Australia with the food parcels.

One cannot help but feel a sense of unfairness at the tremendous pressure the Oliviers must have been under – not only having to perform in their shows, but also at such ceremonies, which in all due respect, they were ill-trained for. It's telling to note that Olivier's writing in his journal after that entry started to peter out. Arriving back, instead of resting, they went straight into the opening night of *Richard III*.

It was another gala night with the attendees lavishly dressed, some dripping in jewels and fur. The atmosphere was electric. One account said they didn't care what the audience was wearing as they were mesmerised by Olivier: 'For all I cared, the audience could have worn gum boots and mackintoshes. Every atom of my awareness was gripped by Laurence Olivier's acting. Strange to sit through something so fearfully alive that until the final curtain, I hardly realized it was Shakespeare!' On Vivien, this delightful description was mentioned; bearing in mind it was a token role, as this play was Olivier's vehicle: 'Vivien Leigh looked incredibly lovely, the pure oval of her face framed in a filmy white headdress with a pearl tipped golden coronet. She was a stained-glass window come to life. She was the perfection of beauty walking in a modern world.'[16]

Another headlined 'Olivier excels in Richard III' and continued, 'The quality of Sir Laurence Olivier's *Richard III*, in The Old Vic's staging of vitality, gusto, and verve in a style resilient, integral, direct.'[17] In another:

> In Shakespeare's *Richard III*, the second play in The Old Vic Company's repertoire at The Princess Theatre, Sir Laurence Olivier revealed his qualities as a great tragedian, just as The School for Scandal showed him as a master of

character comedy. With sure and subtle touches, he built up the character of misshapen and villainous Richard into a figure of truly terrifying malignancy.[18]

Olivier's annoyance at the audience's coughing which closed off whole dialogues at the opening of *The Skin of Our Teeth* the week prior was not exaggerated, as even reviews mentioned it happening again: 'Mr. Peter Cushing had to compete with the Princess' now notorious chorus of coughers, who also smothered Elizabeth's farewell apostrophe to the Tower.'[19]

However, Olivier felt it was his flattest performance and became despondent. The strain of endless public engagements, the exhaustion that followed, the pressure to perform, the expectation to answer a barrage of questions at every event, and the falseness of having to put on the 'public' face to uphold the legend of the Oliviers, had begun to show. It started with the nerves, then irritation with the person closest to him, and then – as happens with such stress – the physical ailments. Many years later when Olivier had left Vivien for Joan Plowright and wanted to embark on a new life, he wrote to Vivien that he had become bored with the legend of the Oliviers and to let him go. A legend that had first started to become tiring on the 1948 tour with its relentless pressure.

Vivien missed five performances, falling sick with bronchitis. Olivier also missed several with a bad throat. They were replaced with competent understudies but the audience must have surely felt robbed. O'Connor wrote how the parties, late nights, ceremonial commitments and obvious physical exhaustion began to show to the extent that the Tour Manager, Elsie Beyer, became overly concerned and somewhat overbearing in trying to curtail the fun and drinking she felt was the cause. This became an annoyance, especially to Vivien, and both she and Olivier seriously considered firing her.[20] Vivien, whose never-ending energy had her nicknamed Miss Vitamin B in the press – not needing much sleep since birth and her love for a good time even through illness (most likely exacerbated by a yet-to-be diagnosed bipolar disorder) – did not appreciate this matriarchal attempt to constrain them. Beyer's reports and letters to Cecil Tennant back in England show a motherly concern that unfortunately went unappreciated by her fun-loving de-facto children. Olivier was more forgiving and just ignored her. He also started to delegate most of her duties to others.

There were further reasons for the exasperation and disagreeable temperament that crept in during this time. An attempt by Olivier to be light-hearted and humorous by using Australian slang was not appreciated by the press. At a luncheon given by the Victorian Premier and Cabinet, he was lost for words when called to do a speech yet again. He had not wanted to repeat himself in front of the same people and said, 'You have all been absolute beauts. And we've had a bonzer time here.'[21] Olivier wrote to John Burrell back in London about his embarrassment and the constant mention of it in the press from then onwards. They seemed confused as to if he had made an insult or not. Olivier would not have known nor understood the Australian *cultural cringe* mentality back then.

Then came the opening night of *The Skin of Our Teeth* and although most of the reviews were favourable, confusion ensued. Phrases such as haphazard, crazy, wasting talent, and strange being used to describe it. One woman went as far as to say, 'You know if any local outfit tried to put on a crazy play like this, they'd probably be booed out of town'[22] – thus implying that they were only forgiving of such an atrocious play because it was *the Oliviers* performing. Another contingent, obviously suffering from a bout of *cultural cringe,* wondered if the play was trying to mock their intelligence and if it had indeed gone over their heads. Were they that unsophisticated and stupid? For the first time, the appropriateness of an 'American' play in the repertoire of a partly British taxpayer subsided tour was also questioned.

The continuous call for public appearances reached a climax in Melbourne with a stirring speech on May 9th when Olivier addressed 3000 young students at the Empire Youth Rally at the Town Hall reciting Princess Elizabeth's twenty-first birthday declaration. This was followed by a trip to Flinders' Naval Depot.

In May, despite the exhaustion, ill health, irritations and the oncoming winter, there were a few reasons to celebrate. Special birthdays for one.

A private event that was remembered fondly by Michael Redington was the celebration of his twenty-first birthday on May 17th at the home of renowned Melbourne photographer Athol Shmith. Chico Marx, who was performing at the same time in Melbourne, entertained the entire company by performing his whole show to them at the party. On Margaret Throsby's radio segment for ABC in 1982, Redington remembered, 'In the home of Athol Shmith, his home, his family, his mother. We had the most marvellous party. The Oliviers came, the entire company came. Chico Marx sat in the middle of the floor on the piano and went for 30 or 40 minutes performing his act. Could anyone have had a better birthday?'[23]

Athol Shmith was a renowned Melbourne-based photographer, working for J.C Williamson, who were theatrical producers in 1948 and he was commissioned to photograph all their performances. Vivien, as she had a habit of doing with those that worked with her, developed a wonderful rapport with him and commissioned some personal portraits during their Melbourne stay. She liked one in particular, which was gifted to her mother as a reminder of her time in Australia; the original of which hangs in the National Gallery of Victoria. Athol, whose finesse was in lighting, recalled many years later the method he had used for it:

> *It was taken in my Collins St studio and is a good example of the effects that can be achieved through the use of various lights – in this case, glow lighting with a boom on the hair and a background halo. It is a combination of lights that I still enjoy using today.*[24]

Of Olivier, Athol said, 'In my opinion, Olivier is the greatest English-speaking actor of the twentieth century. In private he was extremely natural with no theatrical gestures, and a pleasure to photograph.'[25]

Athol is remembered for the sense of Hollywood glamour and romanticism he brought

Left:
Dan Cunningham, Vivien, Dick Watney, Olivier, Cecil Tennant and Titus the Alsatian.

Right:
Vivien with Titus the Alsatian.

Photos credit: Athol Shmith, 1948 – Australian Tour 1948, Laurence Olivier and Vivien Leigh and The Old Vic Company, Bib ID 3044576. Credit: National Library of Australia

to his art. The technical accomplishments and sophistication of images such as the ones of Olivier and Vivien made him one of Melbourne's premier fashion and portrait-takers for a long time. It is interesting to note that the official and personal tour album kept by the Oliviers and which is now at the National Library of Australia, is indexed as the 'Athol Shmith' album. Without any information about the provenance of the album, it may have been gifted to Athol at some point.

Another day that seemed to have been especially memorable was a drive to Healesville, where on the way they visited Dick Watney and his wife Lorna at their delightful home in Lilydale. Dan Cunningham had spent time with them prior and hadn't stopped with the praises. Watney was a car racer who lent them one of his cars during the tour. Vivien and Olivier got along with the couple like a house on fire. Their dogs, a white Alsatian named Titus and a corgi named George took a particular liking to the guests. Many photographs were taken of them frolicking in the vast gardens, playing with the dogs and eating.

The Watneys recommended a drive to Mount Donna Buang, which was mesmerising. They parked and walked up to the summit leisurely. The day was crisp and the mountain air was refreshing. Vivien kept her fur on, intrigued with the fauna. They climbed the tower at the top for panoramic views of Victoria. They were particularly fascinated with the ferns. Olivier noted that they were only found fossilised in other parts of the world. His photos of Vivien on that walk are peculiarly haunting, especially the one of her walking alone taken from behind. There seems to be an observance by the photographer from afar like many of the casual shots he was to take of her. That day they also visited Healesville Sanctuary where they saw emus, an evasive platypus, kangaroos, and lyrebirds. On the way back they stopped again at the Watney's and ended a glorious day, getting back to the hotel very late.

Like the haunting nature of the photos, oddly this was the last 'detailed' entry Olivier was to make in his journal. The last one on May 4th about the Actors' Equity reception where he talked for an hour and had pictures taken with Chico Marx was only three short blunt sentences. Tellingly, he wrote as his last, 'Got very tired of it.'

Olivier's own forty-first birthday fell on May 22nd and the owner of The Princess Theatre, Garnet Carroll, gave a party in his honour in his home for the entire company. They presented him with an antique ashtray as their gift to him. O'Connor wrote that the party continued until 6am the next morning; exhausting indeed![26]

One of the city's most prominent families, the Myers, were supposed to host the Oliviers in their just-as-famous mansion 'Cranlana' in Toorak. Mrs Sidney Myer told the press that she wanted to host a supper party with dancing afterwards for her friends to meet the Oliviers. Cranlana, hidden behind ornate, architecturally designed gates, has what can be called one of the finest gardens in Melbourne; with its sprawling lawns, clipped conifers, a beautiful sunken garden, water features, and Italian marble statues. It is still the Myer family home. But Vivien was feeling sick and cancelled last minute along with all the others. It was just too much.

Opposite:
Vivien walking up possibly Mount Donna Buang. Credit: Athol Shmith, 1948 – Australian Tour 1948, Laurence Olivier and Vivien Leigh and The Old Vic Company, Bib ID 3044576. Credit: National Library of Australia

Left:
Joyce with her dog Rudy and bicycle in North Fitzroy.
Credit: Courtesy of Judith Koop

Despite the misgivings and exhaustion, Melbourne managed to produce one of the most memorable and lasting fan impressions on the Oliviers, particularly Vivien. Amongst the hundreds that had lined Collins Street to buy tickets that year, was twenty-five-year-old Joyce Attwood from North Fitzroy. Joyce's respectful love for the theatre, the Oliviers, and later Vivien, is a touching story that would resonate for many decades until the present day, including this book and its author.

Her life did not begin happily, having been abandoned alone in a cot by her mother when she left her father. Joyce grew up not knowing or ever seeing her mother again. As life would have it, she was blessed to have had an exceptionally close extended family. Grandmother Mary Ann Attwood and her father provided baby Joyce with a stable and loving environment at 164 McKean Street, a house that would be her home all her life.

It's poignant to appreciate as an Australian that Joyce's fan connection and love for Vivien would become more pronounced after the Oliviers divorced in 1960.

Vivien, who toured Australia again with The Old Vic in 1961 – this time without Olivier – enjoyed several afternoon teas with Joyce at the Windsor. That year, she even made a point to visit them at their home personally as Mary Ann had become too frail to travel.

Joyce sent birthday wishes to Olivier in 1950, and his responding letter included fond reminiscing on how touched he had been by the audience's kindness at The Princess Theatre in 1948.

Chapter 9

TASMANIA

THE WATER COLOURED ISLE

This is a beautiful, beautiful little place. It's a little gem. It's absolutely a museum piece.*

* ABC Media abc.net.au Laurence Olivier: Hobart, 1948. Date accessed 7th October 2021.

As if the gods had sensed the Oliviers' need for a more relaxed and restful environment after Melbourne, Tasmania's short one-week interlude provided just that. Like a pendant hanging off the east coast, Tasmania is the island State of Australia. Hobart, its capital, sits under the shadow of an unimposing Mount Wellington, quaint and picturesque on the estuary of the Derwent River. Legend says, before colonisation, it was surrounded by forests full of wildlife and that one could walk across the backs of whales to the other side of the harbour. It had been settled by Europeans in 1803 as a penal settlement and has an evocative and haunting convict history. The Indigenous community, members of the mounenneener tribe who had inhabited Tasmania for thousands of years prior to colonisation, were nearly all wiped out within a thirty-odd year conflict and diseases to which they had no immunity.

Tasmania – to its Indigenous inhabitants, Lutruwita – is landscape-wise the most geographically diverse of Australia's states, with a much cooler climate; closer to that of New Zealand. In the past, many referred to it as 'Southern England' in its climate and landscape and for many of the Old Vic group, it felt like coming home.

Michael Redington described it to O'Connor while staying at the Wrest Point Hotel, where the view of Mount Wellington, Kunanyi, was paramount …

The actual peak was above the clouds, so we saw these waves of clouds and the sun brilliantly shining on us, a lovely sight. But just under the clouds, we had this most wonderful view, hills and lakes and we could see for miles and miles, everywhere is so lovely and green, so much like England.[1]

Preceding spread, on left: Cecil Tennant, Vivien and possibly chauffeur picnicing on the edges of Lake St Clair. Credit: Athol Shmith, 1948 – Australian Tour 1948, Laurence Olivier and Vivien Leigh and The Old Vic Company, Bib ID 3044576. Credit: National Library of Australia

Left:
A postcard of Wrest Point in 1948. Credit: Author's collection

Arriving late on the evening of June 13th from a flight at Essendon Airport, where close to 200 ladies broke through a cordon of officials to get autographs and send the couple off with streamers, the Oliviers drove straight to the theatre before heading to the Wrest Point Riviera Hotel. It was Australia's first luxury resort hotel set on a picturesque river. From this point, Hobart's harbour and city could be seen in panoramic beauty. The hotel had spacious lawns, flower gardens, a tennis court and a saltwater swimming pool. In 1970 a complete remodel started with the commencement of the seventeen-storey hotel tower with a casino. Australia's first casino opened in 1973 in a bid to attract more tourists to Tasmania. The hotel looks nothing like the art deco building it was in 1948, but the stunning vantage location has not changed, making Wrest Point one of the most recognisable buildings in Australia.

The old section still exists, connected by a walkway with small changes to its façade. The rooms where the Oliviers stayed are now the Derwent reception room. As of 2023, most of the building is undergoing interior renovations, but the art deco ambience of how it must have been in 1948 still exists. Photos of Vivien, taken again presumably by an observing Olivier on the

Left:
Vivien on the grounds of Wrest Point Hotel.

Right:
Vivien can be seen in second floor window possibly their room at Wrest Point Hotel.

Photos credit: Athol Shmith, 1948 – Australian Tour 1948, Laurence Olivier and Vivien Leigh and The Old Vic Company, Bib ID 3044576. Credit: National Library of Australia

grounds, at the foreshore point, and eerily sitting in their room from the window outside; provide a haunting comparison.

Olivier seemed eager to see the theatre, as he always did, and was more than impressed. The press conference later back at the hotel was very low-key and surprisingly enjoyable. The press weren't intrusive and acted like normal, pleasant people.

The gala opening night the next day with *School for Scandal* was again attended by a glamorously dressed audience, with every type of fur coat imaginable over their gowns for warmth. The performance itself was greatly received. *The Mercury* the next day headlined 'Spontaneous Acclaim for the Old Vic Show at Hobart': 'Probably the most spontaneous display of emotion the Theatre Royal has experienced in its 100-year history was seen at the conclusion of The Old Vic Theatre Company's opening performance … As the final curtain dropped, cheers, stamping of feet and thunderous clapping broke out. Call after call was taken.'[2]

The Theatre Royal touched a special place in Olivier's heart. He had been informed that it was under threat of closing beforehand. After the curtain call, he made a specific appeal for its retention.

> 'We appreciate playing in it,' he said, 'not only because it is a beautiful little theatre. It is more than that. Your parents and grandparents have sat here as audiences. Our parents and grandparents have sat here as audiences. Our

Left:
Hobart Harbour. Credit: Athol Shmith, 1948 – Australian Tour 1948, Laurence Olivier and Vivien Leigh and The Old Vic Company, Bib ID 3044576. Credit: National Library of Australia

Right:
At the Wrest Point foreshore. Credit: Author's collection

parents and grandparents have acted on this stage. In the 111 years it has been played in, it has built up an atmosphere, and the secret of the atmosphere is antiquity. You cannot have one without the other.'[3]

The Theatre Royal had a colourful start. Opening in 1837, it found its home amongst brothels, factories and working-class cottages. It even had a sleazy tavern underneath the auditorium and during performances intoxicated commoners along with prostitutes would get into the pit, annoying the gentry sitting in the boxes. Despite that, it was a charming theatre with perfect acoustics. Over the years it was refurbished and saved from demolition many times, its most notable defender being Olivier. He pleaded even during an ABC interview broadcast from the dressing room of the theatre:

Do not build a National Theatre yet … see to it that you do not lose any of the theatres you have now. Do not let them be turned over into warehouses. Do not let them be pulled down for any reason whatever … Please keep the theatre alive … This is a beautiful, beautiful little place. It's a little gem. It's absolutely a museum piece. It's most delightful. There has been expressed to me some concern about its future.[4]

In 1948, while the Oliviers were in Tasmania, a booklet chronicling the history of the Theatre Royal with memories and statements from various high profiles was produced. One was from the

Top:
At the Hobart press conference.

Bottom:
Vivien and Mrs R O Harris, Mayoress at the Town Hall.

Photos credit: Author's collection

British Council's representative in Australia, CH Wilmot. Australia incidentally was the only country to have employed a representative. The statement expressed how proud the Council was to have teamed with The Old Vic to bring to Tasmania Britain's top-quality theatre and wished Hobart's Theatre Royal much success for the future, encouraging as was Olivier in its preservation. It also included a portrait of the Oliviers with their signatures.

In 1949, plans for a National Theatre were legalised through an Act of Parliament whose requirement partly was to acquire the Theatre Royal for preservation. In 1951, upon hearing of this, Olivier sent a telegram sending the best of wishes and expressing his delight about the developments. Then in 1986, in a letter addressed to Ian Satchwell, Executive Director of the Tasmanian Theatre Trust in a request for a caption (for whatever reason) about the theatre, he wrote, 'The Theatre Royal, Hobart, is a gem of a place, and how well I remember it. It must be the oldest theatre in Australasia, and it should be most highly regarded for its ancestry as well as its acoustic qualities and generous atmosphere of charm.'

Before arriving in Hobart, the Oliviers had insisted on having no official civic ceremony. They were both still recovering from their respective ailments. They did approve an informal reception at the Town Hall allowing the aldermen and their wives to meet them without the strain of a formal affair.

Their agent Cecil Tennant; a friend and mentor more than anything; had come from London for the premiere of Olivier's *Hamlet* at the Atheneum Theatre, Melbourne and also accompanied them to Hobart. Together, they managed to have a few days of sight-seeing.

On 15th June, they went for a long car drive to see the Central Highlands and strolled around the rugged wilderness of Lake Saint Clair, picnicking on its banks and taking in the breathtaking beauty of Australia's largest freshwater lake, going so far in to be able to view Mount Ida. They came back very late that night. It was Elsie Beyer's birthday the next day. She wrote in her account of the day:

Just after 2 o'clock they took me out in a car and we drove to the top of Mount Wellington. It was a beautiful day, but again bitterly cold and you could hardly stand on your feet when you got to the top of the mountain because of the thick snow and ice. However, it was very, very nice and one got a wonderful view of the country.[5]

Cecil Tennant hugged a shivering Vivien wrapped in a woollen blanket and Olivier took photos of the incredible view over Hobart from its summit. The Tasmanian press noted how grateful theatre lovers were for the chance to see a masterpiece of the English theatre played by whom they considered England's greatest actors. 'The consummate artistry of the players and the meticulous attention to every phase of the art of the theatre combine to bring to Hobart audiences really great theatre. A new generation has grown up since any professional company remotely approaching the Old Vic's standard has visited Tasmania.'[6] Indeed, for The Old Vic to have included the smallest Australian State, an isolated

Top left:
Vivien, Cecil and Elsie at Mount Wellington, June 16; Elsie's birthday. Credit: Athol Shmith, 1948 – Australian Tour 1948, Laurence Olivier and Vivien Leigh and The Old Vic Company, Bib ID 3044576. Credit: National Library of Australia

Top right:
Mount Ida, Lake St Clair. Credit: Author's collection

Bottom:
Some of the group in Hobart, on Richmond Bridge. Credit: Author's collection

Left:
Theatre Royal as it is today.
Credit: Author's collection

island at that, was an honour – one not usually included in tours even today.

After their pleasant week in Hobart, it was decided that everyone would have a much-needed holiday before the Sydney season. Some decided to stay in Tasmania while others headed straight to Sydney. The Oliviers, along with Tennant, Cunningham and Roger Ramsdale, had decided they needed and preferred warmer weather and flew to Broad Beach after Vivien's ambitious idea of the Great Barrier Reef was vetoed.

The Water Coloured Isle's Theatre Royal remains a memorial to a past long gone, but echoes of the luminaries who performed their art and took bows can be heard through its walls. Olivier's clear voice resonates from 1948, urging its preservation. Carol Freeman, a long-time resident of Hobart, theatre lover and now tour guide, distinctly remembers it was this recording of Olivier's voice that prompted her life-long interest in theatre.[7] The Theatre Royal went through many refurbishments over the years, including a devastating fire in 1984 which saw it close to destroyed for good. But it has survived the ravages of time, criticism and disaster.

If we are to take lessons from the past and learn how a city should protect its history respectfully, the Theatre Royal in Hobart is the perfect example. The building, as it is today, is preserved well, supported and attached to a new state-of-the-art world class structure in the Hedberg building. The Friends of the Theatre actively work in preserving its history and importance to Tasmania's performing arts and social culture. It's modern in technology and appearance, but tasteful in its inclusion of the past and present whilst simultaneously acknowledging the Muwinina and Palawa peoples on whose land the buildings stand.

There is one photo of Vivien and Olivier taken by a member of the press in its dressing room. The oak leaf wallpaper, visible on the back wall, was only discovered in 1985 during further works, along with four other layers over a century old. It was how that dressing room area was able to be identified. Although it's now disused, with sandstone crumbling walls and uneven floors, hidden underneath in the back of the theatre like a bomb shelter, tour guides always include a visit to this room; a portal back to 1948, with the voice that epically romanced the spoken word filling its air.

Left:
The Oliviers in their dressing room at Theatre Royal with the oak leaf wall paper on the back wall. Credit: Author's collection

Chapter 10

SURFERS
PARADISE UNSPOILT

The Interlude

The Oliviers flew to Surfers Paradise via Sydney and then into Brisbane. They were accompanied by Cecil Tennant, Dan Cunningham and Roger Ramsdale. O'Connor, in *Darlings of the Gods,* alludes strongly of a possible affair between Vivien and Cunningham during this time although no-one on the tour admitted to it afterwards and he does not cite how and by whom the rumour started. Only Olivier, in his biography, writes about Vivien's flirtations with a company member – during what seems to have been the journey home, when he was incapacitated after knee surgery in New Zealand – which left him embarrassed. Olivier does not pinpoint anyone in particular. But if that had been the case, it seems odd of Olivier to want to holiday with the man his wife was supposedly having an affair with, especially within an intimate group of five. It's unfortunate that the usual narrative on where and how the Olivier marriage started to crumble is based solely on Olivier's autobiography, one with errors and written with impatience towards the end of his life when memory was starting to fail him.

Surfers, as Australians call it, is a coastal resort seventy-five kilometres south of Brisbane. The strip forming Surfers lies between the Nerang River and the beach. The group booked themselves into Surfers Paradise Hotel but soon realised that they were not going to be left alone by the press or the fans, who even climbed balconies to get a glimpse of them. Olivier resorted to wearing sunglasses and a hat to disguise himself as he tried to venture out. It all became too much and one night it was decided that they would go stay

Preceding spread, on left: Vivien at sunrise. Colourised by Victor Mascaro.

All photos in this chapter credit: Athol Shmith, 1948 – Australian Tour 1948, Laurence Olivier and Vivien Leigh and The Old Vic Company, Bib ID 3044576. Credit: National Library of Australia

CHAPTER 10

with Dan Cunningham, who had rented a small beach cottage in Broadbeach, ten minutes away but hidden; far from prying eyes on the edge of the beach.

Broad Beach in 1948 was a backwater and not an inch of what it eventually became. The first high rise was only built in 1959, and after the war, this area of the coast had become the place to buy and sell land. It was only after 1950 that development eventually started and it became the ultimate beachside resort.

Candid personal photos taken of the five of them during those few days of bliss are some of the most glorious of the tour. They show the five of them sleeping on the beach, playing, acting, eating, swimming and resting. The simple timber beach cabin was the perfect hide-away and get-away they had needed.

In 1977 Olivier was in Newport filming *The Betsy*. Vivien had passed away in 1967, ten years earlier. Without a prompt from his interviewer, Olivier remembered this little holiday specifically, almost longingly, and instantly how beautiful Vivien had been. He was chatting with Australia's beloved television journalist, Ray Martin, whilst strolling through the beautiful gardens of Rosecliff.[1]

As Broad Beach had been in 1948, it was their unspoilt paradise if only for a few days and obviously left a lasting, evocative memory, recalled by the leading protagonist of the 1948 Old Vic Tour story twenty-nine years later.

Below:
Vivien on presumably a Surfers Paradise beach.
Credit: Kendra Bean Collection

Chapter 11

SYDNEY

WHERE LARRY LOST VIVIEN

Somehow, somewhere on this tour I knew Vivien was lost to me. I, half-joking, would say at odd moments after we had got back home, 'I lorst you in Australia.'*

* Laurence Olivier, *Confessions of An Actor*, Weidenfeld & Nicolson, 1982, pg. 168.

S ydney, the oldest European-settled city of Australia, named after British Home Secretary Lord Sydney, was and is still Australia's commercial and dynamic epicentre. Home to the Eora peoples for over 50,000 years (Eora meaning 'from this place'), it was only settled eighteen years after HMS *Endeavour* docked in 1770 at Botany Bay.

In 1948, only one of Sydney's most recognisable structures existed – the Sydney Harbour Bridge – and not the most iconic image Sydney is now known for – the Sydney Opera House – which was only opened in 1973. The bridge must not have been that impressive but still remembered by Vivien when she tried to recall where their flat was, as she replied at the press conference; 'It's across a big bridge, but I don't suppose I'll ever know where it is as I travel to and fro by car.'[1] She found Sydney a stimulating city, its bays and beaches particularly exquisite.

Arriving for their Sydney season, both Vivien and Olivier stressed that they were going to curb their social commitments. Even though they were appreciative of the hospitality, it was putting a considerable strain on everyone physically. Some days, on top of two performances, they would have to visit hospitals and attend civic duties, besides the many private invitations they received. Olivier described it as a shocking state of affairs. It was a no-win situation; especially for Vivien, who had suffered from a weak chest and precarious health since childhood. Her lifestyle, which included smoking and drinking excessively, would not have helped – nor did her still-undiagnosed bipolar disorder, causing manic periods which exacerbated her insomnia and drained her energy.

Preceding spread, on left: At the press conference at Usher's Hotel looking perplexed at the questions thrown at them. Credit: NAA: SP1011/1, 3605 (ABC publicity photos)

Left:
Syndey Harbour and Bridge 1948. Credit: Author's collection

Right:
Over the Harbour Bridge. Credit: Athol Shmith, 1948 – Australian Tour 1948, Laurence Olivier and Vivien Leigh and The Old Vic Company, Bib ID 3044576. Credit: National Library of Australia

At the Sydney press conference, she stressed that her doctor had specifically insisted on her curbing social engagements for the rest of the tour.

Elsie Beyer had found them a flat in Cremorne that, despite having a lovely view of the harbour, was too far from the city and more importantly didn't have hot water. So, they moved into the Australia Hotel. The Australia Hotel was completed in 1891 and boasted its first-ever guest Sarah Bernhardt. Its luxurious interior was renowned. With Italian marble pillars, an enormous mahogany staircase, chandeliers and an extravagant bar and winter garden, it was probably the most well-known hotel in Australia for decades. The description in *The Sydney Morning Herald* at its opening gives an indication of the craftsmanship and opulence it became known for.

The grand staircase leading to the first floor is of marble, the steps of white Sicilian, and that used for the handrail and balusters of deep Rouge and Dove, from the Belgian quarries. By it, we reach the main corridor, 16 feet wide, massive with Doric columns, and richly lighted, like the staircase by windows of stained-glass.[2]

An unusual and memorable tradition of Australia's patrons in the following years was to flip coins into four chandeliers in its long bar with the money collected donated to charity.

A notable regular included the Oliviers' good friend Robert Helpmann, who had a permanent apartment reserved for him and also Marlene Dietrich. A refurbishment and extension in the '30s ensured it was the place to be seen until well into the '60s. In 2017, the Museum of Sydney

Left:
Vivien leaving the Tivoli after opening night for a party in an unusal black velvet hood. Credit: NAA:SP1011/1, 3605 (ABC publicity photos)

had an exhibition titled 'Demolished Sydney' in which the fate of The Australia was shown. There were extravagant menu cards from functions, bars and dining rooms on nostalgic display. Even the addition of American-style eateries in the late '60s could not stop it from being demolished in the era that ensued, unfortunately, unable to compete with the demand for commercial American-style hotels. In 1971 it was demolished to make way for the MLC centre and the area which was known for its theatre life, eateries and bohemian vibe ironically slowly evolved into a business region.

The official souvenir booklet program of the tour was released during the Sydney season. With a stunning cover in Venetian red, black and grey, it was edited by Australian art critic, journalist and bookseller, Tatlock Miller and designed by his partner Loudon Sainthill, who was a stage designer and artist. The *Sydney Sun* wrote that the old playbills and prints used as inspiration for the book were found by Tatlock in an astounding discovery at the Public Library. Tatlock and Sainthill were part of the avant-garde group of artists who boarded at the famous bohemian 'Merioola' at Edgecliff along with others like Donald Friend and Alec Murray. There were many creative collaborations including this souvenir program. The Oliviers were pictured browsing through what may have been their personal copy and were particularly impressed, promising to help Tatlock and Sainthill out if they came to London. They did just that and moved permanently in 1949, being engaged almost immediately by Robert Helpmann. The Tatlock and Sainthill partnership was not only a romantic lifelong one but also successful career-wise. Tatlock would go on to be a Director and later Chairman of the Redfern Gallery and was responsible for gaining much-needed international exposure for other Australian artists like Sidney Nolan and Russell Drysdale. Sainthill would continue to write more books and become one of the most prolific theatre designers of the twentieth century. In 1973, the Loudon Sainthill Memorial Scholarship Trust was established to help young Australians study abroad.

The opening night at the Tivoli Theatre was as much a glorious success if not more so than all the other openings with its more luxurious atmosphere. It was described as the most stimulating first night since the visit of the Russian ballet before the war. The female audience was dressed to the nines in furs and glamorous, floor-length formal gowns, while the gentlemen were in tuxedos and some even in top hats. Leaders of Sydney's diplomatic circle, the Lord Mayor, Lady Mayoress, the Governor-General, and social and theatrical figures all attended. Police were called to allow the first-night audience to get through the crowd of onlookers with all the 1900 seats occupied as the curtain rose. Amongst that first-night audience was also a young prominent up-and-coming Australian actor by the name of Peter Finch; a name that would become synonymous with the Oliviers' eventual marriage breakdown.

The Tivoli was just slightly smaller than the Capitol in Perth but had better acoustics. It was the theatre that was renamed from the Adelphi in 1911 and sat on the corner of Hay and Campbell Streets. Its use declined when TV arrived in the

Left:
Reading their copy of the official tour booklet. Credit: Private Collection

Right:
At Greta Army Camp, NSW. Credit: State Library of NSW, PXE 1692/vol.43, photo c/o Alicia Powell

late '50s and was badly damaged by a fire in 1967, eventually preempting its demolition in 1969.

On the 31st of June, Vivien and Olivier along with thirty members of the company were invited to the Mayor's civic reception at the Town Hall. Two hundred and fifty people greeted them inside waiting eagerly to be introduced. The social scene in Sydney had not seen anything like it since they said the Mountbattens had come to visit. To spare the Oliviers from being totally overwhelmed, the ceremony was kept low-key. It was informal enough for Olivier to check karma lines on his hands with the Minister for Housing, Mr Evatt, and Vivien commented that her favourite Aussie meal so far had been barbeque chops cooked over lemon gum.

The opening night of *Richard III*, on July 3rd, was again generally well received with obvious attention given to Olivier's acting. The lighting was duller than it had been for *The School for Scandal* to create the right atmosphere for medievalism.

> *Shakespeare in his hands ceases to be subject to flamboyant operatic flourishes – instead is made to live. On the shoulders of Sir Laurence falls the mantle of the great Shakespearean actors who have gone before him. His acting is a privilege of our time. Lady Olivier revealed herself as an actress who is not only aware of Shakespeare's soul but is capable of expressing it. Hers is a dignity that is the violin's when it is at its unaccompanied greatness.*[3]

Richard III was the hot ticket in Sydney and teenage Michael Blakemore gives an insight into young set Australian one-liner culture at the time; 'Have you got a ticket to "Richard d'Turd or Dick the Shit?"' You didn't buy tickets – you had to apply for a seat by posting a cheque in the mail and keeping your fingers crossed, like buying shares. From a first-hand account, Blakemore gives another fabulous description of the impact of the production and of course Olivier himself.

> *My first sight of him was the long hobble to the footlights at the beginning of Richard III, and after Hamlet he seemed a very long way away. We were a restless house and took a while to subdue. But what amazing sounds the actor sometimes made! 'A horse! A horse! My kingdom for a horse!' – the fabric of the theatre seemed to be vibrating with it, one of those pitched sounds that can crack a tray of glass tumblers. By the curtain, like the marvelous George Relph's, Duke of Buckingham, we had all sunk to one knee.*[4]

A rather contradictory review appeared in *Bulletin of Sunday Shows*, with the writer observing that Olivier's *Richard III* was not at all on the same par as *School for Scandal*. That it in fact had a crack right across it, with Olivier having performed in detached amusement, as if making fun of the role instead of assuming it. He further writes, confusingly, that the two roles of Sir Peter Teazle and Richard were not connected – but were they meant to be? At the same time, he writes that it's impossible not to admire Olivier's superb acting even while criticising it. Olivier seems to have taken particular offence at the mention that Sydney had seen better Shakespeare because this was something he made a point to write home about begrudgingly.

Left:
The Oliviers after a performance of *The School for Scandal* at the Tivoli.

Right:
Vivien in her Tivoli Theatre dressing room.

Credit: NAA:SP1011/1, 3605 (ABC publicity photos)

Blakemore felt the other two productions were more enjoyable and seemed to enlighten him more than *Richard III* but that the three plays were a perfect contrast to each other. On *School for Scandal,* he wrote that the most celebrated moment was when Lady Teazle is discovered behind the screen by Olivier, in his usual flamboyance, and the audience is momentarily stunned – realising the pain in his frozen outline.[5] He noted that the choice of *The Skin of Our Teeth* was perfect for those who were vying to see their Scarlett O'Hara in a fast-paced American play, and of course that had been Olivier's intention all along – to give Vivien her play. In any case, having watched all three plays and being mesmerised by Olivier, Blakemore was convinced to give up his medical career and pursue acting.

In Sydney, something shifted in not only their personal relationship but also professionally. As if to foretell the turn of fortune that was to come to Olivier, during one of the battle scenes in the matinee on the 4th of July, he turned and fell, twisting his ankle and spraining his right knee badly. Doctors were called and after being examined he managed to finish the performance in pain. He returned for the night's show still in considerable pain but with no intention of not continuing with the performance. Olivier, from then onwards, played the parts with a crutch but he never considered stopping and he never complained. The term 'the show must go on' took on its literal meaning.

Professionally, a big blow also came during the Sydney season when Olivier received a letter from The Old Vic's Chairman Lord Esher, informing him that the triumvirate's (Olivier, Richardson and Burrell) contracts would not be renewed after the next London summer season in 1949. Burrell took great offence to such a big decision being made while Olivier and Richardson were overseas and not confiding in him. He saw it as an attempt to wedge a divide between them when they were separated. Olivier was so shocked with disbelief that his initial reaction was hysterical laughter. In his response back to Esher, which he took a while to pen, he wrote that he felt like a pioneer disowned by his country in the middle of a very distant campaign. Peter Hiley told Olivier biographer Terry Coleman in 2003 that Olivier was angry, offended and deeply hurt by Esher's letter.[6]

The reason behind this decision has never been discovered but there seems to have been some very serious plotting and gameplay. Olivier's friend George Devine wrote from London to express his disdain '… clandestine methods which have been borrowed from international politics and are inexcusable.'[7] Some felt there were those who were envious and disapproved of The Old Vic becoming Olivier's and Richardson's theatre, considering their spectacular rise in fame meant it could no longer be classified as the 'people's' theatre. With the tour's feverish publicity, the Australian press had started referring to The Old Vic as Olivier's company, which was all fed back to the British press. Strachan provides an alternative theory – that most at the time believed it to be the underhand work of Tyrone Guthrie, who had harboured ill feelings towards Olivier after he had removed him from directing *Oedipus*.[8] O'Connor writes that Bronson Albery was also ardently opposed to Olivier and Richardson being absent for long periods of time for filming and tours, and Lord Esher had become an ally of Guthrie's.[9] Whoever and whatever the cause, this news deeply wounded Olivier, who now had to complete the tour knowing he had been fired from his job with his dream of creating a National Theatre aligned to The Old Vic ruined.

On August 1st, they were invited to lunch with Leo Buring and his wife Ida at their home in Emu Plains. Chips Rafferty drove them there. Buring, a trained oenologist, was a prominent figure and major shaper of the Australian wine industry, acting as its ambassador. Although Australia was a cultural backwater in 1948, those who had travelled overseas were educated and in the upper crust of society enjoyed more than the meat and three-veg staple diet with a bottle of Resch's Dinner Ale.

The ranch-like home was built in 1920 with the Nepean River at its front and the foot of the beautiful Blue Mountains to its back. Buring planted a vineyard too. Emus and wallabies roamed freely and the sound of bellbirds filled the air. He also built a nineteen-hole golf course on it called the Leonay Country Club (Buring's wife's name was Ida but was nicknamed Nay) which became the Penrith Golf Club.

The seven-course meal Vivien and Olivier were served that day was included in the 'Memorable Meals' chapter in Andre Simon's book *Gourmet's Weekend Book*. Starter was oysters 'a la leonay', followed by baked snapper soaked in champagne, lamb cutlets grilled on the barbeque, potatoes roasted on ashes and green peas. The dessert was strawberries flambé with ice cream. All of it washed down with seven accompanying wines including a 1940 Leonay Liqueur Brandy, an 1893 Great Western Hermitage and a 1920 White Hermitage from Dame Nellie Melba's own vineyard.

The Buring vineyard was sold after Leo Buring's death in 1961, the surrounding land was subdivided as residential property and the area eventually became the suburb of Leonay. Today the house still exists, insignificant and unnoticeable unless you know which it is, a little piece of history lost in the mundaneness of suburbia with not even a sign to respect its former story.

After lunch, the couple decided to stop at Centennial Park to watch the cricket match between The Old Vic side and the Tivoli Theatre team in what was a whitewash by The Old Vic. The journalist covering the game used Shakespearean wit in recording the match in the next day's paper:

Barrackers barracked in the language of Shakespeare. Instead of 'Take him off the park rang with cries of 'Off with his head!' ... Actor James Bailey, who took six for two in Tivoli's first innings, acted the role of Grimmett, with every delivery, 'like to bowl upon a subtle ground' (Coriolanus). He got his wickets so efficiently that his opponents felt they had been 'bowled to death with turnips' [Merry Wives]. But as an opening batsman, Mr Bailey failed. A rueful glance at the scoreboard showed him that he was out 'For O! for O!' [Hamlet]. And his shamefaced smile cried out, 'Eyes do you see? How

Left:
Thomas Heathcote, Mercia, Vivien and possibly Peggy Marshall at Blue Mountains look out.

Right:
At Blue Mountains look out.

Photos credit: Author's collection

Bottom:
Leonay in the 1930s. Credit: Nepean District Historical Society

can it be? O dainty duck! O dear!' [Midsummer Night's Dream].[10]

They were running late for a marathon four-hour show at the Independent Theatre, *Mourning Becomes Electra* by Doris Fitton's group and the speeding car got pulled over by the police. The show was postponed by over an hour. Doris Fitton founded and ran the experimental Independent Theatre. In an oral history recorded by Hazel de Berg, she said, 'When I started the Independent Theatre in May 1930, I had two objects. The first one was to present the world's best plays as we possibly could, and the other object was the development of Australian talent.'[11] Fitton connected well with the company manager, Elsie Beyer, as she had shown great interest in the potential of Australian theatre. Beyer would return to Australia in 1949. Surprisingly, when the car was stopped by police, the crowd that had gathered rushed to get Rafferty's autograph – having not recognised the Oliviers were in the car, too.[12] The photo taken on that day graces the theatre entrance today.

It was also while in Sydney that Olivier received the first transcript of his biography written by his sister Sybille, which he had authorised before leaving England, with the working title *He That Plays the King*. Its 229 pages still exist in the Olivier Archive at the British Library. It's obvious that he took particular care in proofreading and editing, going by the quality of his pencilled markings and notations. For example, when Sybille wrote of Vivien in 1937 that no portrait showed her delicious vitality and happiness, he commented, 'At this stage … Sounds as if she was hatched-faced now.' He also corrected that the reason they ended up giving the ticket money back in the New York run of *Romeo and Juliet* was gangsters had scared him into it. But for whatever reason, he suddenly became quite distressed and anxious and decided he didn't want it published, quickly backtracking. He sent Tennant a telegram on 5th August, advising him that it had distressed him much and to reimburse all costs incurred to Sybille and even suggested buying the publisher out. Terry Coleman, in his authorised biography on Olivier, suggests that Sybille might've been too candid in her writing style and too open in her descriptions of their childhood and her first marriage, causing him angst.[13] In any case the book was not published, much to his relief, but again this occurred while in Sydney – adding to the bad vibes the city gave them.

In correspondence and from observations made by those in the company, Olivier began to withdraw from this point onwards, and some noticed a sullenness – maybe even a midlife depression – at only forty-one. In retrospect, this was completely understandable. How was he to complete the rest of the tour with its never-ending demands, representing the very organisation that had fired him mid-tour, having to plan also the coming season in London knowing that his tenure was not going to be extended? He did not confide this to anyone else on the tour, apart from Vivien, who had started to suffer from mental and physical exhaustion; possibly an offshoot to the stress they were both under, and another cycle of bipolar.

Left:
L to R Olivier, Mollie Brown, Doris Fitton, Vivien, Haydee Seldon at Independent Theatre after watching *Mourning Becomes Electra*. Credit: Presented to Wenona School, owners of the Independent Theatre, by the Seaborn, Broughton and Walford Foundation. Kind permission to reproduce by Dr Caroline Lowry OAM

Left:
On a picnic. Photos credit: Author's collection

In a testament to both of their professionalism, no matter what was transpiring in their personal and professional lives, they didn't stop fulfilling their roles as the leaders of the tour and keeping the group's spirits up. Peter Cushing remembered how the group was very close-knit and harmonious and this was mainly due to their leaders Vivien and Olivier, who went to great lengths to make sure everyone was happy, never putting on airs or demanding the best. On most free Sundays, the Oliviers organised sight-seeing trips, picnics or games days. He fondly recalled how in Melbourne they even organised a cricket game at the great MCG. In Sydney, they picnicked in the Blue Mountains with the whole company on Sunday, to see the majestic Three Sisters rock formation and dared to walk across to Lady Darley lookout. It's interesting to note the change in geography in the photos to today with obvious wear away in the mountain landscape and rocks.

Everyone's birthdays were also celebrated. For the May-June-July birthday team members, Vivien and Olivier organised a drive to Whale Beach via two Australian National Airways coaches. Here they lunched at Jonah's and spent the day on the beach. Whale Beach residents observed how the English were much hardier than they were, jumping into the winter cold waters without any fuss. As far as they were concerned, when the sun shone it was summer.

Jonah's is still operating today and is an exclusive retreat on the spectacular spot. Back in 1928, an English lady called Constance Vidal was widowed and subsequently followed her daughters to Sydney when one married Geoffrey Hughes; the son of Sir Thomas Hughes. Constance bought land overlooking Whale Beach in Sydney's Northern Beaches for 750 pounds and built a roadhouse diner on the clifftop, calling it 'Jonah's', with her private quarters at one end. Her daughter Mary would help her run it. A description of it by a visitor in 1930 writes:

The interior is designed after the fashion of the famous old roadhouses in Britain. The guest rooms include one of the most picturesque dining rooms in the neighbourhood of Sydney. Painted white and green, the kitchen, with its built-in cupboards and array of old Worcester china in the great dresser, is one of the show corners of the house. And in this lovely Old World English atmosphere, the most mundane but all-important matter of food is carefully considered and cooked and served in a manner, both for quality and for service, that is memorable. French doors lead onto the spacious loggia, where on fine warm days, meals are served on little green tables with an incomparable ocean view as an appetizer.[14]

In the '50s, the Vidals sold the property, and it became solely a restaurant. It went through many facelifts and changes of hands, including once being a nightclub in the '60s and an Italian restaurant in the '70s. A clifftop pool was built and an accommodation wing added on. It went from strength to strength and received a Mark of Excellence Award in 2008. Today it's one of Sydney's most exclusive retreats, managing to retain a small part of its long history – the lounge and bar areas are the original dining room, and the fireplace is also the same one that welcomed

Left:
Those celebrating their birthdays in May, June, July cut their cake at Jonahs.

Right:
The group at Jonahs to celebrate May, June, July birthdays.

Photos credit: Athol Shmith, 1948 – Australian Tour 1948, Laurence Olivier and Vivien Leigh and The Old Vic Company, Bib ID 3044576. Credit: National Library of Australia

The Old Vic guests back in 1948. In that area near the bar, two black and white photos hang on the wall of Olivier and Vivien, unfocused but special enough to be given a priority location.

After getting back in the evening that day, Vivien had further arranged for the birthday celebrants to have a private showing of the film, *Blanche Fury*. Elsie Beyer wrote to Tennant in her reports that everyone had had the most wonderful day thanks to Vivien and Larry.

Sydney boasted the best restaurants in Australia in 1948. Melbourne's superb café culture and the world's best coffee accolade were still many decades away. The Oliviers, always accustomed to good food and fine wine, made it a point to take advantage of the better restaurants in Sydney. One was *Romano's*, Sydney's best and smartest. A marble bust of Napoleon stood at the entrance of its Martin Place building with a full orchestra and at one time an astounding 370 dishes. Out of its Oyster Bar, the Manager at the time Tony Clerici created a dish specifically for the Oliviers called 'Oysters Olivier', which Vivien later said was her favourite. The oysters still in a shell would get a few drops of vinegar, topped with chopped garlic, parsley, celery, salt and pepper, be placed on a bed of sea salt, and grilled till brown in the oven.

On Wednesday, July 7th, a cold and blustery Sydney winter's morning, Vivien opened the Killara Camellia Flower Show on her own without the shadow of Olivier over her, at what was then the Soldiers Memorial Hall. It was again to raise funds for the Food for Britain Appeal, and an invitation extended to her by the Ku-ring-gai Horticultural Society. There is a fifty-five-second film footage existing today of this opening where it's obvious how radiant Vivien looked on the day (contradicting O'Connor's account of her looking weary, worn and strained during this time) and gives a visual confirmation of how big the crowd was that winter's morning. The crowd was described in sexist terms as unruly, hysterical females who broke through a cordon of police, one even fainting. A display of rare and prized blooms was ruined but Vivien managed to be escorted inside safely.

She delivered what was to be a prophetic speech:

> *Thank you very much, for your kindness. There is no show I would rather open than a flower show, and no flower show I would rather open than a camellia show ... Let me take this opportunity too, to encourage and implore you to use the funds at your disposal for preserving and fostering the theatre in Australia. I advise the reclamation, wherever possible, of existing theatres, since theatres are not easy to build. They should be carefully arranged to produce an intimate atmosphere. This hall, for example, would be ideal for a theatre. Perhaps, in time, you might consider the use of such halls as creative spaces for the expression of theatre.*[15]

Long-time Sydneysider, Alicia Powell – a lifelong Vivien Leigh fan, who is passionate about the preservation of theatre history – wrote in her monograph for the Marian Street Theatre, that resulted seventeen years later from the hall, 'Officiating at the ceremony was Ku-ring-gai Mayor, Alderman HJ Brown and Mrs Brown, Professor EG Waterhouse and Mrs Waterhouse, and Judge HF Markell and Mrs Markell.' During the show, Vivien was presented with prized camellias in a cellophane box, and an illustrated book by Professor Waterhouse. This book was one of the signed limited editions of 550 copies and is considered 'the most beautiful garden book published in Australia.' In 1966 the hall was transformed into a community theatre and evolved into Marian Street Theatre for Young People. Unfortunately, it is currently closed due to ongoing issues and is in the midst of a complete remodel and revamp, hampered by Covid-19 lockdowns during 2020 and 2021. The building is even deemed too hazardous to enter. It stands as it did back in 1948, even the surrounding area still evoking a 1940s vibe with house blocks unchanged, but the theatre is in an abandoned, sad state.

The book that was presented to Vivien that day was part of the Australia Lot auctioned from *The Vivien Leigh Collection* in 2017 and was written by Waterhouse, who was the founder of the Australian and New Zealand Camellia Research Society – a garden designer and scholar. It's widely said he influenced the gardens of Sydney's North Shore – an influence that's still visible today.

Powell's mother, Marie Thomas, was a seventeen-year-old Law student at Sydney University in 1948 and belonged to its dramatic society. Along with her date and some friends from the group, dressed to the nines, they attended the lunch given by the British Drama League in the Olivier's honour at the Trocadero on July 21st. The Trocadero was Sydney's most glamourous dance palace hall and one of its major attractions. In

Left:
Vivien opening the Killara Flower Show at the Soldiers Memorial Hall, now Marion St Theatre. Eight-year-old Julie Sinclair at the end. Credit: Alicia Powell Collection

Right:
At Killara Flower Show. Credit: Australian Performing Arts Collection, Arts Centre Melbourne

art deco style, it was stunning with granite walls and polished marble floors, and able to seat 2000. Although it hosted many classy events, it was also a favourite for the University balls which at times became rather rowdy. The Trocadero closed its doors for the last time in February 1971 when it was sold and eventually demolished as the young set found other places to dance with the change in music styles. The Event Cinema now stands in its place.

Marie Thomas recalled to her daughter Alicia Powell how exquisite and beautiful Vivien was, but her only memory of Olivier was his 'rambling' long speech that day – a trait he would often be guilty of, even in his writing style. Her date from the lunch, to impress her, discreetly took a plate from the Trocadero under his dinner jacket to give to her as a memory of the lunch.

That afternoon, the couple were invited to visit the State Library of New South Wales by its Principal Librarian John Metcalfe to view the Shakespeare Tercentenary Memorial Library first and second Shakespeare's Folios. As a token and to give authenticity to their visit, a binding of the programs of the plays they were performing in Australia were autographed and photographs were taken – albeit unfocused photographs, probably by what someone noted as an over-excited staff member. Metcalfe felt it would be valuable for posterity and for students of Shakespearean productions in Australia in the future.

If you are to visit the library today, the photographs, correspondence from Metcalfe to Olivier, the autographed title page, and the theatre programs can be viewed in a specially made-bound volume. The Shakespeare Memorial Library is also exquisitely maintained exactly as it was in 1948.

That Friday, *Hamlet* premiered at the Embassy Theatre, where the crowds again were into the thousands. Remaining footage shows the celebrities that attended and Vivien and Olivier beaming. The newspapers that week had front-page headlines and photos about the film. The reviews were all glowing for Olivier and his production. Michael Blakemore had been charting the film's progress for months, equating its premiere in Sydney to a long-expected meteorological event; 'Hurricane Harry'.[16] When he saw its first screening at the Embassy in Pitt Street, it was the rhetoric of the speeches and the outline of who had spoken them that lingered in his mind. 'Not for the last time would the tattoo of Olivier's extraordinary delivery go on beating in my head for days after I had heard it.'[17] It was that performance which placed Olivier as his hero along with Orson Wells and James Cagney, igniting a teenage show business imagination. Blakemore even wrote a review on it for his University newspaper titled 'The Film's The Thing!' with an opening line, 'A magnificent new film is verifying a current furfy that we have with us now in Sydney the theatre's most brilliant personality' and, when it was published, sent Olivier a cutting to which he surprisingly responded graciously. Blakemore was seduced even further.

A wonderful insight into Olivier's dressing room and the unseen value of a dresser was given when Joan Powe interviewed Pat Legh for *The Australian Woman's Weekly* in August. Pat Legh had been Olivier's dresser for the past four years

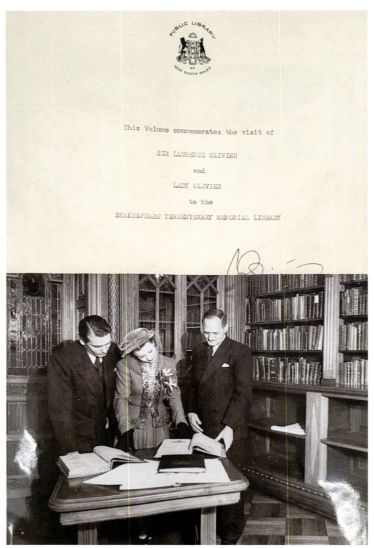

Left:
Marie Thomas and her date attend the British Drama League lunch at The Trocadero. Credit: Alicia Powell

Right:
At the Shakespeare Room, State Library of NSW with principal librarian John Metcalfe. Credit: State Library of NSW c/o Alicia Powell

and travelled with The Old Vic to Paris and New York and now Australasia. She did not have any experience in the theatre when she had applied for the job, having been a script writer for an American broadcasting unit, and had only a love for it. Having lost her husband and son, she felt in need for a desperate change in life and was lucky to get an interview with Olivier upon applying. She expressed nothing but gratitude and admiration for the Oliviers and, like all the touring group, showed devotion and loyalty to them.

> *They are both wonderful and Sir Laurence is the kindest, best person anyone could ever work for. He is never temperamental, never gets moods or becomes hard to please. He insists on doing most of the making-up himself, but there are lots of little things I can do for him. It's wonderful to feel that someone like Sir Laurence is even a little dependent on you.*[18]

Mrs Legh's role as a dresser was to keep all his costumes and wigs in order, neat, clean, and undamaged and ensure the right one was set up for each costume change. She also had set up the dressing room, ensuring it was always kept tidy and homelike. For this, she would decorate it with personal cushions, photographs (five out of six of them of Vivien), and flowers. She also told Powe that Olivier didn't believe in any superstitions nor did he have any lucky charms that other theatre people did. He was a very easy person to look after, with his only insistence being a cup of tea between scenes. Powe noticed a brown grass strip hanging from one of the walls that looked like a skirt. It was apparently a native grass skirt a fan had sent him from Darwin. Olivier did have the sweet habit of displaying fan gifts in his dressing room wherever possible.

Through the Sydney run, still knowing he had another season left with The Old Vic upon returning to London, his most pressing dilemma seemed to be finding another suitable play for Vivien. He wrote to Tennant to express his frustration, having read approximately seven unsuitable plays and still obvious was his concern for her health. 'Darling Puss is not v well, I cannot find a drug to waft away her cough …'[19] Vivien wrote on the bottom of the same letter that they were missing Tennant terribly, inserting some photos they had taken together of kookaburras.

Sydney delivered another fateful meeting of souls. It was here that they met and befriended the man Olivier would take under his wing and Vivien would go on to have a life-shattering affair with – Peter Finch. If there are specific words to describe Finch from those who knew him in life, they'd be; mercurial, tormented, complex, talented, orphan, non-committed, restless, childlike, unlikely, irresponsible, poetic, happy-go-lucky, hellraiser, sensual and – contradicting all those words – spiritual. His story is one worthy of a chapter on its own if his impact on the Oliviers' lives, and to an underrated acting legacy, is to be seen as a whole.

Vivien and Finch shared quite a few things in common, specifically what she saw as an abandoned childhood, a short Eastern upbringing and influence, love of life, hard-drinking, sensuality, philosophy and even the mystical – which would explain part of the mutual fascination they developed for each other. O'Connor, without going into specifics, mentions that upon their meeting, there would've been the unconscious acknowledgement of 'like meeting like' even between Olivier and Finch where Olivier might've seen a younger version of himself in him.[20] Finch wrote a telling description of himself which eerily echoes an aspect of Vivien's personality. 'Always, too, some strange inner compulsion has driven me to cram as many experiences of life and love and living into as few years as possible.'[21]

Who was Peter Finch and how could he have secured himself such a close and personal gateway into the exclusive world of the Oliviers? And why would he have such an impact on their lives that Olivier unkindly said in old age that he had been glad to hear of Finch's passing?

Peter Finch was born in London in 1916 to an Australian-born father, George Finch (although much later in life, Finch was to learn he was not the biological father), and an English mother. His childhood was unconventional, bohemian, confusing and extremely unsettled. He was virtually kidnapped by his supposed father at the age of two, from – in his opinion – a wayward and unfaithful wife, looked after by an aunt short term, then left with his eccentric grandmother, Laura, in France. His mother did not put up a fight to get him back – something he would question and would affect him emotionally and mentally later in life. Finch wrote:

> *I was forced into the harsh reality of life when I was two years old. My father had come home from France at the end of the First World War and he and my mother decided to end their marriage, so as a child I never knew what it was to have my parents' love.*[22]

Finch only saw his father once after that, when he arrived in London as a man with a wife and child and questioned his parentage. The meeting lasted but a few minutes when his father confirmed that he was not Finch's biological parent.

His grandmother Laura would have a profound influence on Finch as a child, with her adopted mystical and cultish existence in Paris. 'She taught me to explore the frontiers of experience; she encouraged me to explore new places, to meet new people.'[23] Laura took him to India when he was nine on a pilgrimage to study Buddhism and attend the Theosophical Society's golden jubilee. What happened to him in India remains somewhat a mystery with Finch himself retelling in later years different versions to different people, depending on his mood, but it is certain that at one stage he had shaved his head, became a child monk and disappeared, threatening to upstage their religious leader. The Society, finding out this out-of-control child had relatives in Sydney, decided to take control over Finch's life from the grandmother who they deemed as an unfit guardian. They sent him to Sydney to their headquarters in Mosman. Laura left them to it and went to Darjeeling, where she died in her old age. Another mother figure who didn't seem to care what happened to him and didn't put up a fight to keep him.

Nine-year old Peter was packed off on a ship alone and sent to Sydney where he was taught by The Manor; the Theosophical Society's headquarters, until his grandfather caught wind of his whereabouts and, disapproving of the Society's teachings, took Finch out. Being too old to care for a young child, Finch's grandfather handed him over to his spinster niece, who took him unwillingly.

The years that followed were cruel and left lifelong scars on the boy; he played up, got into trouble, wasn't interested in school apart from participating in the school plays, and as a result was reprimanded badly by his great aunt. They were traumatic years that resulted in addictions and demons when he became a man. His childhood abandonment by his parents and supposed other relatives made to feel unwanted and created a confused character that craved women's attention but also ran from responsibility and conflict. Elaine Dundy, in her comprehensive Finch biography, wrote, 'Peter Finch was a fine actor, touching genius I believe in certain performances. But that he was able to leave any mark on the world at all after a childhood and adolescence composed mainly of abandonment, chaos and cruelty is, perhaps, an even more impressive achievement.'[24] Dundy does not go into specific details about the childhood abuse bar a few mentions and dedicating the book to Finch's English teacher, whom she wrote as encouraging him in his 'darkest' days. We do not have to do so in this book either, but providing a brief backstory to Finch's childhood helps shed light on a character who is often painted as ungrateful and cowardly, and is credited with causing the breakdown of the Olivier marriage.

Below:
Peter Finch, 1948. Credit: Alicia Powell Collection

It's speculated that the Vivien-Finch affair began in Australia during the tour, which it did not. Olivier, by writing in his autobiography that he somewhere, somehow 'lorst' Vivien in Australia straight before he introduces Finch as the possible cause, further gives credit to this wrong narrative.[25] In retrospect, it's not surprising that Olivier came to look at Australia as being the place where he lost Vivien: he must've associated his sombre change in mood as having started during the Sydney run, due mainly to his sacking by The Old Vic board, his troubling knee injury and also the meeting place of the person who would eventually have an affair with his wife.

By 1948, at the time of the tour, Finch was certainly not an unknown discovery as it has been said. He had left the clutches of a cruel and controlling family environment when he turned sixteen to work as a copy boy for a newspaper. He had also served in the army, developed an unusual kinship and respectful understanding of Australia's Indigenous culture, and become very successful in radio acting work (winning the Macquarie Award – radio awards in 1946 and 1947). He had also travelled Australia with an acting troupe and had a few films under his belt, after which point, he had decided his life belonged to acting. His acting talent had always been there. During his war service, his good friend poet John Quinn remembered, 'I've seen Peter, jump on a table awash with a stale beer in a mess tent full of howling AIF, and, waving a schooner, start spouting yards of speeches from *Henry V*. It got 'em too. They really listened.'[26] In 1943, at twenty-six, he married raven-haired Russian ballerina, Tamara Tchinarova, and set up the travelling Mercury Theatre with John Kay, a composer musician and theatre fanatic. The Mercury Theatre started out as an acting school and one of its first students was Trader Faulkner, another Australian personality who would touch the Oliviers' lives after the tour. Finch had convinced Faulkner to take up acting as a career and eventually became his lifelong mentor and a sort of older brother figure.

The Mercury Theatre initiative, after a tepid start and a pause to allow Finch to film *The Eureka Stockade*, reignited with a brilliant and innovative concept – that of taking the theatre to the masses with a fold-out stage that could be set up in fifteen minutes. They could take their plays to schools, factories, and surf clubs during lunchtime with ease. It was during one such performance that Vivien and Olivier first met Finch.

Olivier had taken it upon himself to talent scout during the tour and initially felt his duty to find someone to take under his wing to mentor; to ensure a local boy made good under his guidance. If Olivier had started out encouraging talent to stay in Australia, by the time he knew he was sacked, he started to think of his own interests. In 1947, on the advice of his agent Cecil Tennant, he formed Laurence Olivier Productions (LOP), a £100-limited liability company. Talent scouting became a way to secure actors for himself and his company, which he eventually did with Finch.

Olivier also met Peter Hiley in Sydney. In 1948, Hiley was employed by the British Council to look after the social side of the tour. He was born in Kensington, London, educated at Eton, and served in intelligence during the war, after which he went to work for the British Council. He was twenty-six in 1948 and became completely mesmerised by Vivien and Olivier. Hiley was poached by Olivier and offered a job back in London as his company secretary. His attitude towards The Old Vic and thereby his purpose on the tour had completely changed.

A lot of the time, when Olivier had enquired who were Australia's good actors, most said Peter Finch. Ironically Olivier did not go looking for Finch himself. It was Kay who wrote to him, rather brashly, to invite them to a performance of their current production of Moliere's *Imaginary Invalid* with Finch starring. Olivier reluctantly accepted, finding a gap in his hectic schedule to attend one performance at O'Brien's Glass Factory on August 19th, much to the surprise of Finch himself. They were impressed beyond measure and soon enough Olivier had offered him his help if he decided to relocate to England, meaning he would sign him under Laurence Olivier Productions and hire him. Olivier wrote in his autobiography:

He had developed a way of boiling down the classics to one hour in order to give them to factory workers during their lunch breaks. To one such performance, we went, and did not notice the hardness of the wooden planks on which we sat. We were watching as brilliant a performance of Tartuffe in as expert a production as could be imagined.[27] *[He got the role wrong.]*

It's commonly quoted that Olivier said after that performance, 'If you ever come to London, look me up.'[28]

During the remaining weeks in Sydney, they developed a good rapport with the tawny-haired, lean Australian, who showed them around town to clubs and other nightlife. It might've been during such an outing that Vivien and Finch felt an attraction and some flirting may have started but that is only an assumption. Floy Bell, Vivien's Australian secretary, told Hugo Vickers that she had remembered the meeting with Finch and was certain nothing had started between them in Australia.[29] In the last week he helped prepare an interstate radio broadcast by them and in the photo that exists of that engagement, Finch looks in awe.

Trader Faulkner, Australian and UK actor, raconteur and one-time flamenco dancer, was a boy who had grown up in the beachside town of Sydney's Manly and in 1948 was being mentored and employed by Finch. He was taken as a supernumerary for the Sydney run for *The School for Scandal* – for the crowd scene. Trader was his childhood nickname that he formally adopted after John Gielgud said his official name, *Ronald*, was too boring.

A few months before he was to pass away, Trader Faulkner reminisced fondly. Sydney had an electric vibe in 1948 with the tour and young Trader was mesmerised, even though he was just an insignificant extra. He had asked Olivier if he could watch all the performances from backstage and recalled how attractive Olivier was to both men and women with a charm he had never encountered. Before the first rehearsal, the chief technician took offence to working for 'stuffy poms' as he called them. He decided to be spitefully problematic and not help with the curtains that

Left:
Watching the *Imaginary Invalid* at O'Brien's Glass Factory. Credit: State Library of NSW, Sydney John Kay Scrapbooks, ML MSS 7164/Boxes 1X-SX

Right:
Olivier as *Richard III*.
Credit: News Ltd/Newspix, Newscorp Australia

had to go up and down fast between scenes. In an act of defiance, he went up the flies and refused to come down. Olivier arrived and worked his charm in a near-perfect Australian accent. He asked him to call him Larry instead of Sir Laurence and told him how at the New Theatre in London, they had never got the timing right and could the chief technician help him here, being the expert. Hook, line and sinker, Mario fell, replying, 'Larry, leave it to me. I've got it.'[30]

Olivier's performance in *Richard* was menacing, his movements lethal, as if a scorpion ready to sting was lying beneath his character. Vivien was exquisite, and her performance in *The Skin of Our Teeth* was unique and eclectic, most certainly her standout and 'her' play. It was endearing to see how Olivier had picked the play to allow her to shine alone, even if it was an odd pick which baffled most Australians.

But what stood out to Trader was both of them had a common touch that endeared them to Australians. Their love for each other was still very visible and extremely physical. He noticed no signs of trouble; in fact, quite the opposite. He remembered how they would steal kisses behind the curtain between scenes and, tellingly, he reminisced on a very specific memory – that of Olivier's dressing room being locked just before curtain call for *Richard* and everyone becoming frantic. They were then told by David Kentish, the Stage Manager, that Olivier was most likely making love to Vivien before his performance, as he normally did, and not to worry. Faulkner thought it a very human aspect to this man, hailed as the greatest Shakespearean actor at the time.[31]

Dundy notes an interesting Australian trait that seems to exist even today – one sprouting no doubt from the *cultural cringe* and Australia's geographical isolation: once someone becomes successful in the Australian arts field, they had to leave Australia, as real success and recognition only came from overseas. This was also taken advantage of by Britain. Peter Finch and his wife Tamara left for England within three months of that fateful meeting. His success was immediate. Olivier had been right.

Interviewed by Tess van Sommers in 1949, after his terrific impression on London audiences, Finch started by saying, 'A lot of the time I'm homesick for Australia – really homesick.'[32] He had intended to stay six months of the year in England, getting new ideas, recruiting new people, learning and bringing them back to Australia, where for the next six months he would produce and act. Tess sensed behind the nostalgia there was a deep connection and appreciation for the country that had adopted him, giving Finch his first taste of success as an actor and even a writer. But those intentions never materialised. Tess ended the interview by predicting that, after Finch flowered as an artist in England, Australia would harvest the fruit. Peter Finch only returned again in 1957 to film *The Shiralee* and *Robbery Under the Arms*, but to an indifferent reception. A classic Australian habit was to cut the tall poppy at its head. Australia never reaped the harvest or, better put, never appreciated it when it came back. Finch never returned.

But he never forgot his adoptive home. In 1962, Vincent Firth asked Finch if he considered himself an Australian in an interview, to which Finch replied, 'I suppose I do really. Although I have been back in England for fourteen years, I grew up "down under" and I served in the Australian Army – these are the factors which I feel decide a man's nationality.'[33] Finch is classified as an English/Australian actor, the first to be awarded a posthumous Academy Award for Best Actor for his role in *Network*. Ironically the second posthumous academy award in history would be another Australian, Heath Ledger, in 2008.

Trader Faulkner would leave Australia in 1950 and be part of the 1955 Stratford-upon-Avon season with the Oliviers, becoming especially close to Vivien. Long after Vivien's death, he became an Honorary Member of the *Vivien Leigh Circle* – a fan and member-based society created in 1968, reignited in the last twelve years and very active today. He attended Vivien's 50th Death Anniversary Memorial, organised by the Circle, on the 7th of July 2018, along with an intimate gathering of her fans and select family. In his last few years, he toured with the *Letter to Larry* production, recounting his witty memories to the audience, specifically those of the Oliviers. Trader Faulkner passed away in April 2021. During the interview with the author in October 2020, six months before his passing, his effervescent personality, wit, love for life and charisma had not dimmed. In fact, he told the author he was planning a trip back to Australia to partake in a swim at Geelong pier.

In 1959, after Finch had had an on-and-off affair with Vivien which everyone seemed to have known about (except the press), and having attempted to elope once, Vivien decided to stay with Olivier. Finch could not compete with the great Olivier, and never would. He acknowledged this willingly and separated from his wife Tamara permanently. He told Tamara that he could not go back to his old life and that his affair with Vivien had changed him irrevocably. (Incidentally, the 1963 film *The VIPS* starring Elizabeth Taylor and Richard Burton was based on that attempted elopement.)

It's more than likely that the mutual attraction between Vivien and Finch sparked at the time of the meeting in Sydney, and only possibly reached an affair status in Sri Lanka (what was then Ceylon) in 1953, when they filmed the ill-fated *Elephant Walk* together. In a heady sub-tropical

Below:
Preparing for their farewell broadcast. Credit: News Ltd/Newspix, Newscorp Australia

climate, where both she and Finch must've felt a sense of a homecoming – having shared an Indian childhood – alone without their partners, in the onset of a 'high' phase of her bipolar condition, it was probably inevitable.

Do we ever get to pick the people we are attracted to regardless of its possible destructive nature? To Vivien, it was always going to be Olivier, for even in that phase she was following Finch around calling him 'Larry'. The insistence that Finch leave his wife for her also seemed like an attempt to relive and replay her chase for Olivier when he had been married to Jill Esmond. Just as Olivier may have seen a younger version of himself in his selected protégé, so too may Vivien; a younger version of the man she had fallen in love with in 1936. Olivier would remain the love of her life. It's a tragic twist, that when it was obvious the marriage had broken down irrevocably, Vivien sought Finch and told him she was ready to give him his chance. By then Finch had moved on and turned her down.

The affair was devastating enough to ruin his own marriage to Tamara and drive him close to suicide on a number of occasions. A voice better to make a judgement call was Yolande Finch, his second wife, who wrote, 'He had met the greatest actor in the world and he had met the woman who was to be his greatest passion, his mistress and very nearly the death of him.'[34] Vivien was the only flawed masterpiece he had ever met and quite possibly the love of his life. When she passed in 1967, his enduring image of her was one of her walking briskly like a young boy amongst the ruins of an ancient Ceylonese civilisation.

Faulkner, in his biography on his good mate, wrote that in later life, Finch had said that no film award he received ever compared to the fulfilment he had felt seeing one of his poems published in an anthology of Australian poetry in 1945.[35] There is a verse written in Dundy's book that is a poem written by Finch, which can easily be said to have been inspired by Vivien.

Bound and entwined by our mutual love of Chopin waltzes,
    the surge of feeling at an encounter with some historic spot,
    the vital words of a poet, the wisdom of philosophies … till time withers us gently as old autumn leaves and blows us gaily into the dark pathways of afterlife.[36]

Chapter 12

BRISBANE

FAREWELL AUSTRALIA

*And as Wigi Wigi sleeps he dreams of to-morrow and the long trek to Arnhem Bay and the sugar bag honey and the dream time legends, of his people in a country that is theirs by right of wisdom and time.**

* Peter Finch, *Wigi Wigi of Arnhem Land*, published in *Talk* magazine, October 1947, Papers of Peter Finch N_A MS 7003.

The Brisbane stint came close to not happening at all when it was not guaranteed they could be flown directly to Auckland by chartered Skymasters. The allocation of petrol was based on the flight's national value and the Director-General of Civil Aviation, Air Marshal R. Williams, could not understand why there was a need for private charters when there was a regular service to New Zealand. For the company, though, it was imperative to stick to their schedule as they also had to have their London opening date confirmed when they got back. Eventually, the sets and costumes were approved to be flown by charter while everyone else had to go by the normal service.

The Oliviers arrived at Archerfield Airport at 6:30pm, three hours later than expected. By that time the crowd that had waited for them had dissipated to only forty-odd. They had completed the last two performances in Sydney the day before, utterly exhausted. Vivien had been seen trembling after the matinee and rushed to take a rest between shows.

They stayed at Lennons – Brisbane's best hotel. In 1948 it was still located on George Street, having been rebuilt into a simpler but bigger building in 1941 with bricks in light salmon. The rooms were all air-conditioned, so it boasted being the most modern hotel in Australia at the time, where the most notable guests stayed and dined. In 1972 the Council bought it to be demolished while the new Lennons was built on Queen Street.

Brisbane was a two-week, more subdued stint with only *The School for Scandal* being performed, much to the disappointment of Queenslanders. There had developed jealousy between the States

Preceding spread, on left:
Farewell Australia.

Left:
Arriving in Brisbane's Archerfield Airport.

Right:
Signing into Lennons Hotel.

Photos credit: Author's collection

and they felt snubbed with only a two-week program and only one play out of the three. Olivier was questioned about this relentlessly and at one point appeared to onlookers irritated. It had been nearly a no go and he felt it should be appreciated Brisbane was ever considered at the expense of a shorter period in Australia's biggest city, Sydney.

Brisbane is the capital of the Sunshine State, Queensland, and was originally inhabited by the Turrbal people who called the area Mianjin. Sir Thomas Brisbane gave instructions for a further penal colony to be established in 1823, around the Moreton Bay area. Non-convict settlement started in 1838 with a boom. Most of the immigrants were of German and Scottish descent in the early days and were given land, good wages and free passage through the day's immigration programs. Later in the early 1900s, the Russian migration started.

The land surrounding the meandering river was named Brisbane like the river itself. Brisbane was much like Rome, which has the Tiber running through it, with its surrounding hills; so much so it is often referred to as 'Later Rome'. During the Second World War, Brisbane actually held an important role as the South-West Pacific headquarters for General MacArthur at its AMP Building (later MacArthur Central). In 1948, post-wartime Brisbane – although known as the 'big country town' – was still the third biggest city in Australia.

Cicely Courtneidge, touring Australia at the same time, thought Brisbane the most primitive of the cities she played in, being cut off from the modern world altogether: 'A sort of Mrs Wiggs of the cabbage patch world in which hard work is only just catching up with good living.'[1]

Ticket sales for the two-week Brisbane stint did not generate the anticipated big rush. Police arrived outside Palings the night before tickets went on sale, to keep the crowd calm. People only arrived early in the morning and even then, less than a dozen formed a queue by 6am. Laurence West was the first to buy a ticket. He had woken at 3:30am, arriving at 4am to get his tickets at 6am when the shop opened.

The opening night of *The School for Scandal* was another grand success. All the who's who of Brisbane arrived brilliantly dressed in fur coats and top hats. Reviews were glowing with headlines 'Old Vic Superb', and 'Theatre Brilliant as Before War'. Warwick Lawrence wrote for *The Courier*:

To the music of Handel, to the backdrops of Beaton, last night's opening performance of Sheridan's 'The School for Scandal' by The Old Vic Company was a ballet with words. As beautiful and delicate as the birth of a leaf, the great traditions of British Theatre and its heritage unfolded to a single instrument – the simple playing of a five-act play.[2]

Cecil Beaton's backdrops were again called works of art. The Oliviers' acting was compared to the giants of the past like Kean, Kemble and Sara Siddons. George Relph, Eileen Beldon, Terence Morgan and also Peter Cushing were applauded too.

The Oliviers' social duties continued at a more relaxed pace to match Brisbane's warmer, tropical balmy climate. There was a cricket match against

Left:
The Oliviers watching the cricket match between the Brisbane Wanderers and The Old Vic team. Credit: Author's collection

Right:
Vivien possibly in Moreton Bay. Credit: Athol Shmith, 1948 – Australian Tour 1948, Laurence Olivier and Vivien Leigh and The Old Vic Company, Bib ID 3044576. Credit: National Library of Australia

Bottom:
Taking a bow after a performance. Credit: Author's collection

the Brisbane Wanderers with the Tivoli staff and this time it was a draw, with the Oliviers watching on. The Royal Queensland Yacht Club took the whole crew in nine vessels to Moreton Bay where they picnicked on the beach and swam. Their most memorable excursion was to the Great Dividing Range at 5am to enjoy a bush breakfast of steak. Most felt the landscape was the real Australia that they had envisioned before starting the tour. Eileen Beldon, writing to Sir Barry Jackson in England from Brisbane, wished she could send back all the rare, peculiar tropical Australian flora as well as the more traditional roses, daffodils, freesias, and sweet peas that were in profusion. She wrote:

> *… this I shall remember – this and the cleanness of the atmosphere so that in the country it is possible to see for eighty miles and think you could walk it in a few hours; the very sunlight is reflected from the glossy leaves of the gum trees and the red baked hills.*[3]

It's interesting to note that Beldon wrote in this letter that Olivier was disappointed in the reception he had received in Australia for *Richard III*, compared to London, New York and Paris. Beldon felt he was overreacting, as they were dealing with an audience unaccustomed to live theatre and performing in what she described as 'barns' for theatres. At this stage of the tour, she was also very ready to come home, although not regretting she had been a part of a memorable and unique experience. It goes without saying that most of them were probably at that same stage but Australia definitely had not had enough of them and New Zealand had not even started. It is certainly the first correspondence to surface where a principal member of the tour had also expressed irritation with Vivien and Olivier as spoilt, immature and over-reactionary to bad criticism and ready to come home.[4]

Another memorable social event the Oliviers took part in was the St George's Society Ball at Cloudland Ballroom, the night before their eighth anniversary, after the day's performance. Looking regal as their roles required, Olivier in white tie and tails and Vivien in a long silk embossed dress, a fur stole over her slim shoulders, shook hands with twenty-nine debutants. After that, they enjoyed a private four course meal and slept for most of their anniversary the next day.

The Cloudland was an icon of Brisbane city culture for a long time. Originally built as a fantasy land – Luna Park, on top of Bowen Hills in 1940, its ballroom, Cloudland, was its centrepiece, with its domed skylights, luxurious seating, opulent chandeliers, private alcoves and dreamy feel. In 1940 it was renamed Cloudland Ballroom and quickly became Brisbane's premier entertainment centre. Its parabolic roof arch, eighteen metres high, was visible from all over Brisbane. When it was bought by developers in 1982, even with a National Trust listing, it was demolished in the middle of the night with no warning in an act that can only be called barbaric. The security guard on duty that night was shocked to be told close to 11pm to go take whatever he wanted as the building was about to be taken down within an hour. The only thing he managed to get at was the clock that was above the dance floor – to be forever stopped at the exact time he took it

Left:
The Oliviers attend the St George's Society Ball.

Right:
At St George's Society Ball.

Photos credit: Author's collection

down. Brisbane woke in shock to the devastation the next morning, too late to do anything. The dreamy ballroom in the sky, with over thirty years of memories – including the night theatre royalty-bewitched Brisbane – disappeared in under an hour. Today, the only reminder that there once existed such a place is the discreet memorial arch erected close by with pictures and stories of the ballroom engraved into it – a shrine to a time and place long gone.

At the University of Queensland's speech in George Street (Old Parliament House), where close to a thousand students sat on the lawn, Olivier spoke about drama and was again questioned why he had not brought all three plays for Brisbane. O'Connor was told by the then-Student's Union Vice-President that he looked drained and irritated answering the same question yet again.[5] The weariness and frustration with the endless tiresome schedules, the 'same old same old' was beginning to irritate visibly now.

The Food for Britain Appeal rally held at the Exhibition Grounds was disappointing. They expected a crowd of 10,000 but only 2000 attended. Only four of the sixteen trucks hired to take the expected number of food parcels were needed in the end. Despite that, Vivien still managed to say thanks in the speech: 'If your ears are burning today, it is because the British people are sending thanks with all their hearts.'[6]

At the end of the Oliviers' time in Australia, they did a goodbye broadcast in the form of a reminiscent chat between themselves. They spoke of the things, people and incidents that they would never forget. Olivier asked, 'Do you remember the scent of the gum miles out to sea before we reached Western Australia?' Vivien responded, 'Do you remember our first day in Perth -and how we went to the beach the next day and a swan flew overhead?' A barbecue while driving from Adelaide to Melbourne, a cheque pressed into Vivien's hand by a well-wisher for Food for Britain, and the unforgettable Theatre Royal in Hobart were among the other memories.

Brisbane delivered a cruel blow this time to Vivien, marking their final days in Australia with sad overtones. Her love and bond for cats were one that formed very early. As a six-year-old, having been left at the Convent of the Sacred Heart, Roehampton, then their youngest student, the nuns felt sorry for her and allowed a small kitten to be taken to bed – a big concession considering how strict convent life was back then. In later life, she told Trader Faulkner that the dormitory hall where they slept was big, dark and lonely – scary at night. During holidays she'd often be the only child left at school with her family still in India. The kitten would've been her only comfort and company all those nights she was alone – a daunting experience for a young child. Further, she also told Trader that in her first scene in *Streetcar Named Desire,* where she arrives in New Orleans and searches for her sister's house, she drew on the feelings of being lost and abandoned by her parents at Roehampton. It's understandable where her connection and comfort with cats came from.

Although she had cats from then onwards, her most loved and first Siamese was gifted by Olivier for her birthday in 1946 and aptly named New Boy, after the New Theatre in St Martin's Lane,

Below:
Olivier giving his speech (far left) at University of Queensland, Old Government House. Credit: Author's collection

Left:
Vivien helped up the steps at the University of Queensland. Credit: Author's collection

Right:
Speaking at the Food for Britain rally at the Exhibition Grounds. Credit: News Ltd/Newspix, News Corp Australia

Left:
With Deputy Lord Mayor at the Food for Britain Rally.

Right:
Preparing for their final broadcast.

Photos credit: Author's collection

CHAPTER 12

Left:
With the black cat that came to Vivien at Brisbane airport.
Credit: Author's collection

later the Noël Coward Theatre. New Boy became quite a celebrity in his own right. He accompanied her everywhere, to lunches at The Ivy, to the set of *Anna Karenina* at Shepperton Studios, to the theatre as a good luck charm. He was even featured in magazines and was adored by both his owners. Olivier had bought an elegant collar with charms from Paris for him which he wore handsomely. Vivien said in an interview, 'Once you have kept a Siamese cat you would never have any other kind. They make wonderful pets and are so intelligent they follow you around like little dogs.'[7]

Initially, they had wanted to bring New Boy with them on the tour, but quarantine laws prevented it. To compensate, Vivien had got into the childlike habit of writing letters to him and one of her secretaries would write back to her telling her of his daily activities with a paw print as his sign-off. During the final week in Brisbane, New was taken to Notley for a break and sadly ran out the front gate to be run over by a passing motorist. Vivien was devastated when she was advised.

A small black cat had made an appearance when they had arrived at Archerfield Airport, gravitating immediately to Vivien like a magnet. Ominously the same cat again came to her as they left Brisbane to bid her farewell.

As the Skymaster plane flew them away from Australia towards an awaiting New Zealand, the extent of Vivien's underlying health issue was revealed – her fragility since birth. The crew noted her pale complexion and sombre mood. A weak and grieving Vivien startled everyone when she started gasping for air mid-flight. O'Connor wrote that the pilot had to immediately bring the plane down to 4000 feet while the hostess put an oxygen mask on her.[8] On top of her mental illness, which would only be diagnosed years later and become worldwide news as a 'nervous breakdown' in 1953, Vivien had caught TB during the North Africa tour. These two conditions would exacerbate her medical decline and eventual premature death in 1967. Living during a time when lithium had still not been discovered, Vivien would be treated with primitive procedures like prolonged ice baths to induce sleep, fed egg whites only, and undergo numerous electric shocks to the temples. Olivier observed after the first shock treatment, Vivien – his life force and inspiration – had changed irrevocably. Eventually, these personality changes and health deterioration, coupled with their excessive lifestyles – smoking, drinking, and overworking – along with their numerous infidelities, meant the Oliviers' legendary marriage would crumble.

Vivien would go on living life preciously on the edge, defying the warnings given at birth and then later by doctors. The fight for air mid-flight provided the prelude to what was to come as they bid Australia of Wigi Wigi farewell.

— *Chapter 13* —

NEW ZEALAND

THE LAND OF THE LONG WHITE CLOUD

You may not know it, but you are talking to two walking corpses.*

* Laurence Olivier, *Old Vic Celebrities*, Otago Daily Times, Issue 26890, 30 September 1948, pg. 6

AUCKLAND

New Zealand, *Aotearoa* in Māori, has an almost unearthly quietness to it and a surreal mythical beauty. A two-island country (North and South), it is the south-westernmost part of Polynesia. Its landscape brought *The Lord of The Rings*' Middle-earth to life, many decades later, with its active volcanos, dazzling fjords, deep glazier lakes and snow-caped mountains. Vivien was disappointed to have not had enough time to see its legendary beauty more thoroughly but had been able to get its feel almost instantly. Writing to her first husband, Leigh Holman, she observed the nation's unearthly, subdued quality.[1]

If they started in Perth, the most isolated city in the world, they ended up in New Zealand, the most isolated country in the world. It was the last main large liveable country to be inhabited by humans and although, ignorantly, people often class it as another state of Australia, it is distinctly different in every way; geographically, landscape-wise, culturally and historically. Very young in terms of human history, it was only inhabited by Polynesians (thought to be from Hawaii, Cook Islands and Tahiti) between 1200 and 1300 AD. These were the ancestors of the Māori people – the term 'Māori' only being introduced by Europeans.

Although it was Abel Tasman who 'discovered' New Zealand, it was the British who colonised it, signing the Treaty of Waitangi in 1840 – a formal agreement between the Māori leaders and Britain, giving Britain the right to rule. It is a treaty that, even today, is controversial and a cause for disharmony. However, it is still regarded as New Zealand's founding papers.

NEW ZEALAND

Preceding spread, on left: Farewell Aotearoa – Vivien, Olivier in wheelchair and presumably George Relph and Mercia Swinburne.
Credit: Athol Shmith, 1948 – Australian Tour 1948, Laurence Olivier and Vivien Leigh and The Old Vic Company, Bib ID 3044576.
Credit: National Library of Australia

Top:
In front of the Australian National Airlines aircraft, Auckland.

Bottom:
Walking to arrival gate as baggage gets taken off from their Australian National Airlines aircraft.

Photos credit: Alexander Turnball Library, Wellington, New Zealand, Whites Aviation Collection

Top:
Heading into the arrival area besieged by admirers.

Bottom:
Signing autograph for Michalle Kennedy.

Photos credit: Alexander Turnball Library, Wellington, New Zealand, Whites Aviation Collection

Unlike Britain, New Zealand recovered well after the war and was also involved in the Food for Britain Appeal. In 1948, it was starved of real theatre and attention from Mother England, so the Oliviers served as replacement royalty even in New Zealand, perhaps more so than in Australia, with its greater isolation and smaller land space. Still, New Zealanders were cinema-loving people and the Oliviers were household names and suitable royal surrogates.

The announcement of the tour was received with great appreciation in New Zealand and was called *A Notable Visit*. Many recognised the cultural and historic significance. A piece by *The Northern Advocate* mentioned that it would greatly help the future sponsorship of cultural movements after the previous two years had seen a marked revival of interest in music and dramatic art.[2]

Upon arriving in Auckland, Vivien agreed to have an x-ray of her lungs and treatment at Greenlane Hospital. With the benefit of hindsight, and also medical advances, maybe subconsciously she knew from the start, as she preferred to live life on the edge – never sleeping, always on-the-go, trying to squeeze every minute with activity, living. In the end, Vivien lived her fifty-three years enough for at least three lifetimes; more than one who lived well into their eighties could've hoped for.

New Zealand definitely got the short end of the straw in terms of getting the best out of the company in those last five weeks of the tour. At this point, it was certainly an anticlimax. The overtired, disheartened and unwell Oliviers were really just desperate to finish off the tour and get back home. For a husband-and-wife team working twenty-four/seven, non-stop, it was no wonder that the only known and recorded 'fight' between them occurred in New Zealand, Christchurch, nearing the end of the tour. They declined many social events and did the bare minimum, which seems a pity considering New Zealand is a stunning country, landscape-wise, and the people friendly and laid-back. The company noted it looked a lot like England, cooler in climate and pretty. During one interview both Olivier and Vivien specifically commented that New Zealand audiences were remarkably enthusiastic, appreciative and well-mannered.[3] Vivien also wrote to Leigh about New Zealanders being a better-mannered audience.[4]

They had five weeks left in New Zealand, starting in Auckland, then Dunedin, Christchurch and Wellington. They flew into Whenuapai Airport, Auckland and were obliged to sign a few autographs. The press noted how beautiful Vivien was even with no sleep on the six-hour flight, but Olivier was obviously tired from his looks and admitted to being unable to sleep on flights. Waiting patiently and nervously was a young Michalle Kennedy with her autograph book and pen in hand. Upon a bewitching smile from Vivien, she mustered the courage to approach her. Vivien signed it graciously and ran after Olivier who had gone ahead of her and stopped him. She then beckoned Michalle and got Olivier to also sign her book. Michalle scurried back into the crowd holding tight to the book like the crown jewels, as the watching press noted.

The tenderness they still had for each other was evident in inconsequential acts; Vivien noting a smear on Olivier's face, took out her handkerchief to wipe it away before they both faced photographers.

Auckland, known as 'Tamaki-makau-rau' (maiden with a hundred lovers) to its original Māori settlers, who created terraced villages in its volcanic peaks in and around 1350, is based around two harbours; one falling into the Pacific and the other to the Tasman seas. Prominent are the islands spotted around them, especially the iconic extinct volcano, Rangitoto. Their island beaches were fringed with the stunning Pohutukawa trees, and their hills with a scatter of magnificent grand old houses – all the beauty of which seemed to have been a blur and lost on most of the team. Georgina Jumel couldn't remember it at all.

Upon arriving, Vivien and Olivier were driven straight to the Grand Hotel where almost immediately local millionaire Sir Ernest Davis, an ardent admirer of Vivien, started sending daily bouquets of flowers and gave to their disposal a chauffeur-driven car. Sir Ernest was Mayor of Auckland from 1935 to 1941. He was the imminent businessman of the country, a skilled political manipulator, generous philanthropist and was invested in an astounding array of social, business and sporting ventures. For over fifty years he was at the centre of Auckland's civic arena, a city he adored. Sir Davis was to entertain Vivien in 1961 too, taking her on a cruise of the Hauraki Gulf on board his yacht *Alert*. Vivien wrote to her sister-in-law, 'We all loved Auckland. I particularly because a spritely nonagenarian took a shine to me & spoilt me greatly which I thoroughly enjoyed.'[5] A young Clifford Gascoigne was taken in by the

Left:
Waitemata Harbour, with Waiheke Island in the background, most likely from their hotel. Credit: Athol Shmith, 1948 – Australian Tour 1948, Laurence Olivier and Vivien Leigh and The Old Vic Company, Bib ID 3044576. Credit: National Library of Australia

Davis family in 1947 and met Vivien on many occasions. Davis's daughter, Mollie Carr, after her father passed away, handed down to him a ring that Vivien had given Davis as a token of their friendship.

Sir Ernest also purchased a small house on Wynyard Street, Auckland which was refurbished to become the Vivien Leigh Theatre, which she opened during her solo tour, on 19th February 1962. The theatre never had a play performed in it, but more so acted as a rehearsal centre, which today is the James Henare Māori Research Centre.

The Grand Hotel was in fact owned by Sir Ernest and his brother Eliot Davis. It opened in 1889 and survived a major fire in 1901, to be refurbished and become a part of Auckland's social scene and its finest hotel. But like so many

Left:
Reading letters in their dressing room at St James Theatre. Credit: Alexander Turnball Library, Wellington, New Zealand

buildings from yesteryear, it became old-fashioned and unmaintained. In 1966 it began to wind up, starting with the guest rooms and then the bars. At the end of the year, its furnishings, fittings, paintings and even mirrors were auctioned off. The nineteenth-century painting collection was Sir Ernest's who had passed away in 1962. His daughter managed to keep the most important piece in the collection in the family, one by Sir Edwin Landseer, which Sir Davis had bought in 1913 for an undisclosed amount. The hotel was replaced by an office but its front façade was protected and remains.

In Auckland, the Oliviers played at St James Theatre, which they both approved of, likening it to the Lyceum and although the same size as the Capitol in Perth, this theatre had a back wall that made it appear smaller. Built in 1928, it was designed by Henry Eli White, who designed many of New Zealand's theatres and was originally meant for vaudeville acts. Its Spanish Renaissance-style interior was well conserved through decades of renovations and additions, like a cinema complex. For the best part of a century, it was the centre of Auckland's social life, until a fire greatly damaged it in 2007. Unfortunately, although classified as a Category 1 historic place by the New Zealand Historic Places Trust, it still remains closed to the public and has not been restored. A notable contingent of the public continues to fight for its rescue.

At the end of the eleven-day run, Auckland broke the record in attendance and gross receipts. The Manager of St James Theatre, Mr Ian Donald, told the press that the most comparative figures over a same time period for The Old Vic was when Katherine Cornell presented *The Barretts of Wimpole Street* in Chicago ten years previously. The season saw more than 33,000 people attend a performance to see the great Oliviers.

It was foggy and drizzling on the 19th of September causing their flights to Christchurch to be delayed. Olivier found himself entertaining those that had come to see them off. He burst into an impromptu comedy act, the drama was mimicked and famous lines from Shakespeare were replayed in a great show of his acting ability and sense of humour. For the twenty-odd fans that had waited up to six hours to catch a glimpse of the Oliviers, it was a reward that left a lifelong memory.

CHRISTCHURCH

Christchurch is the biggest city of the South Island, known for its English heritage having been a sponsored settlement by the Church of England. With its abundant beautiful parklands, the River Avon wandering through its centre and Gothic-revival architecture, it is known as it was then, as the most English city in New Zealand.

That 1948 day had started off bright and sunny but by twilight when the Oliviers landed at Harewood Airport, it had turned grey and cold. Christchurch had just come out of a long and harsh winter. Only about fifty out of the approximate 250 that had waited all day to catch a glimpse of them had survived but close to the plane arriving late, the crowd had swelled again to around 150. Vivien obliged to photographs and reluctantly moved to what the photographers thought was better lighting. They went to the United Services Hotel, on the corner of Colombo Street and Hereford Street in Christchurch's famous Cathedral Square. Crowds had gathered there, too, and one passer-by was lucky to have had Vivien give her a dazzling smile which she felt unable to return, having had two front teeth removed.[6] The hotel seemed especially significant with a carving of Shakespeare on the right way at the Cathedral Square entrance. (In 1988 a demolition order was on the building and it was eventually demolished in 1990.)

When they arrived, much to their bewilderment, they had been given a room with two single beds on the second floor. Olivier and Vivien were not used to sleeping apart and insisted on a double bed. Matters didn't get any better when it came to food. The dining rooms closed at nine and they had to find someone to make a small supper for them in their bedroom. One of the complaints the group had about New Zealand was that hotels were over-priced, and their services were not suitable for the theatre timetable.

From this hotel, Olivier started a letter to Thornton Wilder in his usual rambling and long-winded style – a letter that he would only finish a few days into their journey home on the high seas. He started by saying how deeply impressed both of them had been reading Wilder's latest book *The Ides of March* and that Vivien had actually started it, but he had pulled it off her on the plane down and now she was beyond annoyed at him writing to Wilder to say so first. It was the only book he managed to finish during the tour.

I have finished it – Vivien is under the drier and I look up occasionally to stare at a huge Mobil Oil sign across the street, there are dusky green, rather interesting hills beyond the town – V ancient geological structures I have no doubt. It is 5.20 and we open 'School' here tonight.[7]

He goes on to write, coming to the end of the tour, they are only holding onto a tither before getting on the ship home and how it has imposed too much of their time and energy.

The St James Theatre was also a cinema theatre that had been a skating rink and a venue for opera performances. After being closed for eight years, it reopened after renovations but in 1960 – coming under the management of Kerridge-Odeon – it was renamed Odeon Theatre with extensive renovations. In 1983 it closed to become a church for the Sydenham Assembly of God but was severely damaged in the 2010/2011 Canterbury earthquakes resulting in a demolition order in 2012. As of 2017, it was hoped the grey stoned façade would be saved, but all work has come to a standstill.

They found the theatre had no heating and unpacking the costumes took unusually longer, with an industrial dispute having delayed their arrival from the wharf to the theatre. Before opening night, as recounted in O'Connor's *Darlings of the Gods* the only public fight recorded between the God and the Angel supposedly occurred, in front of three temporary theatre staff. Lady Teazle's red shoes could not be found and Vivien had stormed at the three girls. Vivien's temper could make a grown man cower at the best

Left:
Daffodils on the banks of the River Avon.

Right:
Christchurch, most likely from their hotel room.

Bottom:
Vivien with two unidentified ladies, possibly at the Botanic Gardens looking at the rock gardens.

Photos credit: Athol Shmith, 1948 – Australian Tour 1948, Laurence Olivier and Vivien Leigh and The Old Vic Company, Bib ID 3044576. Credit: National Library of Australia

of times and the young girls were terrified. When Olivier appeared to get Vivien on stage she angrily refused as the girls pulled back into shadows to hide but lay witness to what ensued.

If we assess the supposed exchange, a present-day marriage counsellor might conclude that it was a normal, if not aggressive, fight between a husband and wife suffering from underlying, *unresolved* issues between them, as triggered by a long, tiring and stressful tour. Olivier slapped her, calling her a bitch, and she hit him back, calling him a bastard. He then reminded her who the real bastard was – alluding to her desertion of her child and first husband (sexist and hypocritical to say the least, as he had done the same to his son and first wife). Vivien succumbed to tears, saying that he always threw that at her. Olivier then took her into his arms, calming her, saying he'd find some shoes for her, and cajoled her onto the stage.

The opening night was extra special, however; the fight having created some kind of stimulus to their performance. The lines between Sir Peter and Lady Teazle took on an extra dimension and they gave a stunning act.

Knowing what we know now about how the Olivier marriage eventually broke down, this altercation highlighted how tumultuous the relationship could become, especially how it was characterised by a destructive communication pattern, which escalated into physical aggression, which in the present day would be considered an unhealthy or toxic relationship.

The willows on the riverbank in the botanic gardens had yet to come to full foliage. Avid gardeners Vivien and Olivier took time out during their week in Christchurch to visit. Olivier photographed the daffodils in the woodland area across the River Avon and Vivien eagerly examined the rock garden and the spring flowers. They had also made the habit of taking cuttings from all over Australia and now New Zealand to plant back home at Notley.

Olivier's knee pain flared up again during a *Richard* show and he made enquiries about getting it operated on either before leaving New Zealand or as soon as they returned to England, although that would leave him only three weeks to heal before he was due back on the stage. After a surgeon in Christchurch confirmed it was cartilage damage and then a second opinion from one from Wellington, a decision was made to have it operated on before they left, allowing him a month on the seas to rest.

Despite health issues, underlying tensions between the God and the Angel, and a few social obligations, the birthday celebrations continued. They kept the united front in front of the crew. Vivien wore what O'Connor mentions was a daring and overtly sexy split-to-the-waist black dress to a performance of *Six Characters in Search of an Author* by Canterbury University Club's Dramatic Society on September 27th to get attention, and in defiance of Olivier.[8] We can't assume what her motivations were but it seems strange why no press photos exist that we can find in newspaper archives of the event if the dress was that sensationalist.

The Oliviers were welcomed by the Māori clans of the South Island at the St James Theatre after their matinee performance on September 28th, at which traditional dances and chants were performed much to their delight. Two special carved figures, one male and another female, were presented to them. They were the last of the works by the Rotorua tohungas and the clan suggested they be kept in the archives at The Old Vic but Olivier interjected saying he would be keeping them himself, obviously by now feeling he owed nothing further to the company that had fired him mid-tour.[9]

The planned picnic day out for the birthdays of those who fell in August and September had to be cancelled due to bad weather. They were called instead to have lunch in the Oliviers' hotel flat. Olivier stayed in bed in his silk pyjamas, carving two large hams and chatting. They were given a big lunch and plenty of drinks. The rain eventually subsided and the group decided to risk a drive to the countryside as originally planned in the hired buses.

It was a beautiful, but wistful setting. They wandered through the pastoral plains with hills covered in daffodils with the peak of an ancient volcano in the background. It was the gardens of noble Otahuna Lodge, built in 1895 as the residence of politician, philanthropist and sportsman, Sir Heaton Rhodes. Back then it was especially famous for these fields of daffodils, the largest in New Zealand, whose surplus bulbs were donated to the city. 'Otahuna' in Māori means 'little hill among hills'. The lodge, built in Queen Anne style, sits on a hill overlooking its vast gardens and ponds and then onto the Southern Alps. It was lovingly restored into a luxury retreat by an American couple, still surviving today through the

Left:
Olivier in bed cuttung two hams. Credit: Athol Shmith, 1948 – Australian Tour 1948, Laurence Olivier and Vivien Leigh and The Old Vic Company, Bib ID 3044576. Credit: National Library of Australia

Canterbury earthquakes and each September, like in 1948, the hills still bloom in a vista of yellow bulbs to charm its guests. Thankfully, unlike other buildings of that time, it's protected as a Category 1 listing by the New Zealand Historic Places Trust, dedicated to preserving local heritage and the environment.

As the sun made its appearance for the first time that day, melancholy shadows started to dance on the daffodil-covered hillsides making overtures to the impending curtain fall on their tour. Olivier had chosen to stay back alone in his hotel room in bed, ironically also an overture to the voyage home – a voyage he would spend mostly alone in his room.

Left:
Otahuna Lodge.

Right:
The group in the daffodil fields Otahuna Lodge.

Bottom:
Daffodil fields at Otahuna Lodge.

Photos credit: Athol Shmith, 1948 – Australian Tour 1948, Laurence Olivier and Vivien Leigh and The Old Vic Company, Bib ID 3044576. Credit: National Library of Australia

DUNEDIN

The Oliviers drove with their secretary Floy Bell and the Relphs to Dunedin from Christchurch, appreciating the chance to see at least a little of the countryside which they had not had much of a chance to do. Uniquely, Dunedin was known as the Edinburgh of the South with its Scottish history. Although initially inhabited by the pioneering Polynesians at the same time as the rest of the country (exact date is still contested) it was formally settled by the Europeans of the Lay Association of the Free Church of Scotland in 1848. In this picturesque setting at the foot of a canopy of mountains and a pretty harbour, the surveyor of the city was given the brief to reproduce the characteristics of Edinburgh.

They were to perform at His Majesty's Theatre, originally the city's agricultural hall that eventually became a theatre. In the '70s, much of its exterior was remodelled to become Dunedin's iconic music venue Sammy's. In 2017, it was bought by the Council and currently awaits feedback from the public as to its preferred future, standing neglected with no progress.

The box office had opened on September 27th to limited seats and as usual the line-up had started the day before to hundreds of people. Dunedin had never seen such an unbroken queue before. They stayed at The City Hotel and all of Dunedin's three cinemas were showing *Caesar and Cleopatra*, *Waterloo Bridge* and Olivier's *Pride and Prejudice*.

Olivier said to the interviewer of the *Otago Daily Times*, when he visited them backstage, 'You may not know it but you are talking to two walking corpses.'[10] It is an often-quoted line. He noted that it was a big ask of anyone to perform nine shows a week but they were insistent on completing the tour so as not to deprive anyone from seeing them.

They were welcomed to the city by Dunedin's Mayor Sir Donald Cameron at a function held in the Council Chambers. Various theatrical associations of the country had been present.

Otago in New Zealand's South Island is renowned for its brown trout and Olivier's observation that trout season had started and how he would love to taste the New Zealand fish was taken to heart by a group of trout farmers. The journey to get a decent trout to them was filled with angst and mishandling. First, they couldn't find one suitable and when they did, it got lost in transit. Eventually, once the Oliviers had left the South for Wellington, the lovely 'five-pounder in the pink of condition' found its way to their plates, much to Olivier's delight! He commented it was 'delicious' and cooked exactly as New Zealand trout should be.[11]

When he addressed students at Otago University in the still-existing Allen Hall, the topic of a National Theatre was brought up as it had been all the way through the Australian cities. Olivier's respected opinion was sought by all. He admitted he didn't know but made suggestions:

> *I think you should, first of all, get a few people like your chancellor, and your best painter, best poet, and other learned gentlemen to get together and form a trust, perhaps bring out a*

Left:
Picnic on the way to Dunedin. Credit: Athol Shmith, 1948 – Australian Tour 1948, Laurence Olivier and Vivien Leigh and The Old Vic Company, Bib ID 3044576. Credit: National Library of Australia

line producer from England and then go to the Government for money. I think they would give it to you provided your proposals had some sort of canopy of respectability.[12]

He made sure to emphasise the possibility of pomp and ceremony to take over enthusiasm and enterprise if it's on a national scale and to also point out that acting was not a 'sissy' career but one that needed considerable talent, strength, energy and toughness.[13]

It rained throughout their time in Dunedin, coating the week in a depressing cloud. Georgina Jumel did remember Dunedin, though; not because it was impressive but because it was a personally miserable time. She wrote that it was here that Olivier observed she had talent, but her voice was not good enough for theatre. When she asked if she'd be more suitable for film, he seemed to have compared her to Vivien and shook his head, crushing her confidence and making her cry for days.[14] As expected, a sigh of relief came after their final performance on Saturday, 2nd October.

They bid farewell to the South after entertaining nearly a 7000-person audience, leaving many disappointed in not having secured a seat. As in every airport, this time at Taieri, a crowd had gathered to see them off. Five flights were engaged to take them and the sets to Wellington. This time the God and the Angel only managed a quick wave of their hands before bidding farewell to the South of New Zealand.

Below:
Georgina Jumel feeding a Canterbury lamb. Credit: Athol, Shmith. 1948, Australian tour 1948, Laurence Olivier and Vivien Leigh and the Old Vic Company Bib ID 3044576. National Library of Australia

WELLINGTON

Windy Wellington, as it's referred to, sits at the southern end of the North Island and was chosen as the capital over Auckland in 1865 because of its ideal central location to both the island masses and the fine hook-shaped harbour. Over the years earthquakes altered the landscape and the area of flat land lessened, causing early Māori tribes to move to enclaves in hills and build shelters. Only around 1840 with the arrival of British settlers did the area – originally named Britannia – begin to take urban form with the building of churches, pubs and houses. Soon it was renamed Wellington after the Duke of Wellington. Two unfavourable aspects seem to define New Zealand's capital: its frequent tremors and, as some would say, its umbrella-shredding winds – but today, its vibrant café and bar culture, award-winning coffee and restaurants combined with a quirkiness sets it apart from other New Zealand cities.

Wellington, their last city on the tour, followed suit to every other city and a whole day before tickets were to be released, people started queuing to secure tickets. They were coated, carried lamps, and set themselves up on rubber mattresses with thick blankets on Panama Street. They withstood the cold and biting wind, cramming into available doorways for a little warmth. Within a few hours, the line had extended a further forty yards and continued to grow until the morning.

The team were billeted out to host families in Wellington, too. Michael Redington stayed in Oriental Bay with a lovely view of the harbour and the added incentive of being able to see the *Corinthic* docked on the bay awaiting its return home. He wrote:

> *... and there, right across the harbour on the other side of the Bay, is the Corinthic. So, if I see it creeping out one morning I shall swim after it, no matter how cold the water is, or what state I am in! I've waited for eight months for the boat home and I am not going to miss it now!*[15]

He thought Wellington resembled Hull, the port city in Yorkshire, but probably like the rest of the crew was too preoccupied with going home to appreciate it fully during that last week. The impatience to get back home contributed to these last five weeks being a blur to most. Georgina Jumel admitted to not remembering much about New Zealand, apart from a few incidents that stood out because of their impact emotionally.

The Oliviers would stay at the Hotel St George, one of Wellington's beautiful art deco buildings and at the time Wellington's best. The hotel went through many refurbishments and upgrades over the years with it becoming Victoria University's student hostel from 1994 to 2009. It remains a Category 1 listing with Heritage New Zealand.

With Olivier limping about in excruciating pain, they only committed to the bare minimum civic engagements. On the 4th of October they attended the State Reception in the Wellington Parliament buildings. Some 500-odd guests were invited and it seemed the biggest social event they agreed to attend in New Zealand. Mr Nash, the Acting Prime Minister, continued with the

British push by thanking the British Council and The Old Vic for their efforts to preserve and disseminate British culture. He further cheekily said that when one looked at Vivien Leigh, they forgot her famous husband Laurence Olivier, to which Olivier agreed on his return speech:

> *When I appear alone, people's faces fall about three yards. I take this as a compliment to myself because she is my wife and as a tribute to the English cameraman. But I know how they feel – when I think of Vivien Leigh, I find it impossible to think of anything else.*[16]

This sort of public preference for the wife of the celebrity couple bore uncanny similarities to another couple who would also tour decades later – a real royal couple – Prince Charles and Lady Diana. Eerily, Prince Charles also said something around the same lines as Olivier: that when he appeared alone, people's faces would drop. Georgina Jumel remembered that Olivier would look at Vivien with a proud smile whenever this happened in contrast.

That night they performed *Richard* and marked a new era in Wellington theatre history with a full capacity theatre – something that had not happened in years. The audience sat transfixed by Olivier's opening soliloquy and thereafter as he took them into his sardonic world with a performance never to be forgotten. With only one interval, the tension was not broken, enabling the audience to be continually enthralled.

The Wellington week impressed everyone and they continued to charm interviewers. One lucky person who managed to get a ticket to all three plays was dazzled by the versatility of the company. They observed the lustiness and thrill of *Richard*, the charming romantic comedy of *School* and the truth underlying the fantastic impressionistic *Skin*.

New Zealand's famed painter, Peter McIntyre, managed to fit in an enchanting portrait of Vivien as Lady Teazle while in Wellington. McIntyre is a ghost in the international art world today but was once renowned. His painting of Vivien is also one that even the most ardent and dedicated Vivien Leigh collector and fan is unaware of.

McIntyre was New Zealand's official war artist during World War Two and those paintings became icons of her war effort. He started a Journalism Degree in Dunedin which he abandoned to travel to London to study at the Slade School of Fine Art instead. Afterwards, he

Left:
Otago Daily Times, Issue 26916, 30 October 1948, Page 8.

worked as a commercial artist and when the war started, enlisted with the Second New Zealand Division, where his art caught the attention of the Major. He was then appointed as the official war artist, travelling to Egypt, Italy, Tunisia and Libya. Returning to New Zealand after the war, he continued to be a professional painter, although he admitted to finding it hard to adjust to peacetime painting after the war. McIntyre also wrote several art books that covered not only his own war art, but other New Zealand and other Pacific Islands art, which were important in bringing his work to the attention of a wider audience. He was awarded an OBE and remains one of New Zealand's most noteworthy artists. With his portrait of Vivien in 1948, instead of having her sit for him, he stood as far back as possible backstage in between acts of *The School for Scandal* and disturbed no one. [17]

The city also screened just about all their movies during that week to a somewhat bewildered and embarrassed Olivier. Asked if he approved of the re-releases, he shuddered. 'We would like to forget some of them. After all, they were made a long time ago; let me see – 1948, 1938 ... Ugh!'[18] He must've alluded to *Twenty-One Days Together* which both continued to be embarrassed about all their lives.

After the 10th of October performance, Olivier entered Lewisham Private Hospital to finally have his knee operated on, to remove a cartilage in that nagging right leg. This would allow him time to recuperate on the way home as he was not to put any weight on it for the following two weeks. During the four days he was there, the team visited him and, in typical Olivier fashion, he was cheery enough to make crude jokes about being cared for by nurses. He told Thornton Wilder that he spent his time in hospital doing absolutely nothing, as tired as he had been, and that he was extremely concerned about Baba having to play with an understudy and handling all the farewell speeches and tributes on her own – but was reassured that she had done so brilliantly.[19] He wasn't doing 'nothing', as he had written. He was making plans for the following season back in London. He sent a detailed and long letter to Cecil Beaton, instructing him of the costume and set redesigns that he wanted for *The School for Scandal* upon their return. The costumes and sets from the tour were donated to a Wellington theatre school. In order to not upset Beaton with the number of the redesigns he insisted on, Olivier seems to sweeten it with compliments: 'This letter has been written in great haste, and does not convey to you one thousandth part of the brilliant success that your work has been and how gloriously happy a little show the whole thing is. ... You, Sheridan, Handel and me – quell combination – particularly with little Puss [Vivien] to crown our cake.'[20] Olivier never stopped working, even with an operated knee and in hospital.

It seemed New Zealand was reluctant to admit that the tour was as influential as it had been to Australia based on the length of it. Five weeks did not seem enough to make a profound impact and some people felt a sense of disappointment.

Despite the success of the tour and the joy the productions gave playgoers who were able to get into the theatres, it is doubtful if it was an

CHAPTER 13

Below:
Olivier's last performance in Wellington before admitting himself into hospital for knee surgery. Credit: Greta Ritchie Collection

unqualified success in its effect on the theatre in New Zealand. A lot of ill feelings and disappointment were created by the manner in which the seats were allotted, and there is a general feeling that a company that could play a longer season, with everyone able to see the performances and at less than a guinea a seat, would do more to create permanent interest in the theatre in New Zealand.[21]

However for those that were lucky enough to have seen a performance by the fine performers, they did leave an unforgettable memory. Vivien's instinctive sense of comedy was remembered in *Skin,* as it was still her stand-out role, and the Oliviers were beyond any criticism from the vast majority of New Zealanders.

They did a farewell broadcast on Sunday night from Olivier's hospital room, involving various scenes from their stage and screen triumphs – which was also a success – closing with a toast to England from Noël Coward's *Cavalcade*. Olivier said that the warmth and appreciation of his 'dear New Zealand listeners and audiences' meant something that could not easily be conveyed.[22] The intimate nature of its length and number of shows meant the New Zealand season was much more subdued and, as one newspaper wrote, it was more like a family reunion and leave-taking. The broadcast was, according to one local resident, a memorable classic; with the trademark Wellington banshees in the background making it even more special.

Wellington's skies wept and the banshees whimpered on their departing October morning. Olivier's last glance of Wellington was from a canvas sling hoisted thirty feet above the ground as he was carried on board only half an hour before departure. The rest of the troupe, along with Vivien, had boarded the night before. Although he chatted happily with the ambulance crew and laughed as he was lifted, the scene was shadowed by a melancholy ambience. A young girl ran forward to hold an umbrella over his head as he waited to be lifted. Vivien's figure was seen waving to the small group that had gathered to bid them farewell from the *Corinthic* as it set sail. The Oliviers had arrived in Australasia to a burst of sun, the scent of eucalyptus, flashbulbs, bouquets and their enthusiasm intact, in stark contrast to the tone of their departure.

As man disappears from sight, the land remains.
— Māori Proverb

— *Chapter 14* —

THE CURTAIN FALL

Shouldst thou some others suit prefer
I might return thy scorn to thee,
And learn Apostasie of her
Who taught me first Idolatry*

* Thomas Stanley Esquire, Third verse, *The Divorce*.

An interesting analogy to the break-up of Australasia's 1948 surrogate royal couple is that of Prince Charles and Lady Diana, who were put under more media and public scrutiny decades later. They, too, faced similar media hounding at a much more intense pace with the emergence of the 'paparazzi' which did not help their already-present tensions while touring. These tensions were exacerbated by Diana's eating disorders, and both hers and Charles' infidelities – paralled by Vivien's bipolar and TB. Not to mention, both Vivien and Olivier had their share of infidelities to contend with. Certainly, the 1948 tour was not just theatrical but a replacement royal tour, including all the civic duties that came with it. The two tours, decades apart, further demonstrate Britain's enduring patriotic hold over Australia and New Zealand through monarchical structures and traditions. Two referendums have failed to cut the ties that bind Australia to Britain and the Commonwealth still.

The amount of pressure was never more intense than it was on the 1948 tour for Vivien and Olivier. Olivier took on the tour after having become public property, following his knighthood, and felt obligated to accept, although in the back of his head he had the personal aim of forging his own National Theatre in due course. They were both also very patriotic and not likely to have said no to begin with. The added incentive was incorrectly assuming that the tour would help Vivien's health and their relationship. Olivier thought the sea air would help her weak lungs. Interestingly, a palm reading done on 23rd September 1947, now in the Victoria and Albert Vivien Leigh Archive, recommended sea air to help her health.

We warn you here, that you are using up too much vital force and energy in pushing on your fate line, as small lines across this fate line, show nervous vitality is being used over-rapidly and without correct placement. On comparing this with your health line, we would advise a complete change of surroundings and a restful sea voyage.[1]

This seemed to have been taken very seriously as, without doubt, the main reason Olivier had decided to travel by ship to and fro was to give Vivien that exact chance to recuperate.

The month's journey back was an anticlimax for most. Georgina Jumel recalled a sombre mood compared to the excitement of the outgoing one. In the Atlantic Ocean section, they hit a storm and were forced to stay in their cabins. Vivien celebrated her birthday onboard on November 5th. The company gave her a book signed by everyone, *Sweet Thames Run Softly*. They inscribed it 'To Our Aunt in Law'. They cut the customary cake and drank black velvets.

Olivier – stuck in his room trying his hardest to not disturb Vivien with a bed pan – tried to gallantly manoeuvre himself into the bathroom instead and ended up extending his knee too much. He had to be pumped with as much codeine, aspirin and morphine as the ship doctor had to numb the pain in order to drain the plaster of the profusion of blood that resulted. He felt it had been the same sort of vanity that had killed du Maurier and felt bad for having to give Baba more to worry about.[2]

Three of the company had decided they didn't want to return to England, opting to go back to Sydney. John Barnard, James Bailey, and Hugh Stewart had asked for permission to do so and Olivier agreed.

Barnard (Pip to his good friend Redington) was the son of successful British character actor Ivor Barnard, who joined the New Theatre and used the pseudonym of Phillip Humphrey or Phillip Humphries, performing in many of its productions and also directing. By 1962 he went back to using his real name, after it's said, McCarthyism wore off. In 1962 he acted in The Elizabethan Theatre Trust's production of *The Ham Funeral*. He revisited England again in 1969 when he took a year's leave – twenty-one years after he came with the tour. His copy of the official tour program was signed affectionately by Vivien: 'Joy & good wishes dear Pip – a truer wish was never wished.' Olivier signed, 'Unmannered Dog … Now bind up thy wounds & take affectionate wishes for a full and fine life … Sir R' – in reference to his small part. By the end of the tour, he had a permanent scar on his elbow from being hit down by Olivier during the performance. He remembered, 'There was a special warmth woven in that 1948 tour which I doubt has ever quite been equalled for any member of the company since. We enjoyed the times we were together as a company, and especially those moments when we were close to Larry and Vivien.'[3]

When Vivien toured again with The Old Vic in 1961, this time without Olivier, Barnard and Stewart came to see her in Sydney. She was as warm and welcoming as she had been in 1948. Barnard noted, 'I had not seen her on stage since 1948. She moved one utterly. She was the Lady of

Preceding spread, on left:: Fans waving goodbye, possibly Essendon Airport, Melbourne. Credit: Athol Shmith, 1948 – Australian Tour 1948, Laurence Olivier and Vivien Leigh and The Old Vic Company, Bib ID 3044576. Credit: National Library of Australia

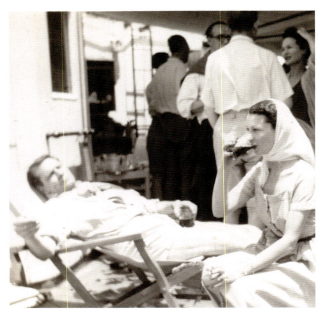

Left:
Vivien cutting her birthday cake on the journey home. November 5th, 1948.

Right:
Drinking Black Velvets.

Bottom:
Olivier in his wheelchair on the trip back.

Photos credit: Athol Shmith, 1948 – Australian Tour 1948, Laurence Olivier and Vivien Leigh and The Old Vic Company, Bib ID 3044576. Credit: National Library of Australia

the Camellias. It was her *tragedy* … Yet even as I rejoiced that she had joined the ranks of the great ones, I also felt a sense of foreboding.'[4]

In 1982, when Michael Redington sat down with Australian broadcaster and interviewer Margaret Throsby in Sydney, a surprise reunion occurred. His great friend Pip – John Barnard – came on the air. They had met at the side of the stage on the first day of rehearsal and had been the best of friends since staying at each other's places whenever one came to visit. They recalled their 'giggling' reprimand by Olivier in peels of laughter. Pip and Redington had the habit of giggling under the canopy in a scene in *Richard III* when the Little Princes would ask Richard to show them his weapon. The canopy would shake uncontrollably. Olivier had called them into his dressing room after one such performance and cautioned them in no uncertain terms.

Barnard was forever grateful for being a part of the tour and a staunch admirer and defender of Vivien after she passed away. When Hugo Vickers' definitive Vivien biography was published in 1988 and a bad review was given by Joel Greenberg, headlining Vivien's small talent and outdated performance in *A Streetcar Named Desire* – not understanding her mystique – Barnard wrote to *The Sydney Morning Herald* in her and the book's defence. He said that he had been enthralled by Vivien's performance during the 1948 tour and this admiration had not diminished after forty years. An excerpt of the letter which follows shows quite clearly the inspiration Vivien had, to draw thousands of fans, a star that has ascended after death and continues today to rise.

Captivated by her 'Dresden China' Lady Teazle (The School for Scandal), *and excited by her witty Sabina* (The Skin of Our Teeth), *it was in her 1961 tour that I was privileged to be profoundly moved by her Lady of the Camelias. She had blossomed into a tragedienne of power, the image of which I carry forever, perhaps strengthened by her personal tragedy. Last year I discovered her film version of Streetcar Named Desire. Having missed the initial showing, I expected to find it dated. Far from feeling it 'creaks rather noisily' (Joel Greenberg) it held me spellbound as a cinematic masterpiece; through it all, quivering and shimmering, the pathetic, sad and final tragic madness of Vivien Leigh can be found. Greenberg may not be impressed by her mystique but to let this influence his assessment of Hugo Vickers' fascinating account is to ignore the emotions of those still drawn to the Leigh legend.*[5]

Barnard continues in trying to understand Greenberg's review and assumes that he may've been offended by colonist references to Australia of 1948 and instead of being culturally cringed was having a cultural whinge.

Barnard was a prominent participant in the Australian amateur theatre scene, marrying two times and loving the country he had adopted after the tour. He died on 8th August 2016; twelve days shy of a masterful innings of ninety-three.

James Ibsen Bailey (Jimmy) was born to theatrical parents in Manchester, England in 1909. Following in their footsteps, he gained experience in classic and modern theatre and even travelled through England as part of the family touring company. Jimmy would say that his father warned him never to get into theatre but failed to tell him what to do otherwise. Nevertheless, both he and his elder brother Eddie decided the theatre was for them. After a minor role in Olivier's *Hamlet*, which didn't even make the credits, Olivier had no qualms in picking him to join the tour.

During the heatwave in their two weeks in Perth, their first port of call, Jimmy fell in love with Peggy, a girl who ran The Tavern on London Court. Peggy (Margaret Laidlaw Paterson) was of strong Scottish heritage. Her nephew Graeme Gillespie, who would become one of their guardians and administrators, recalls her having been a stunner with a gregarious personality which would certainly account for Jimmy falling in love with her within the two-week run in Perth.[6] Peggy followed the tour and Jimmy to Sydney and they married there that year. After the tour ended, Jimmy went back to Perth with Peggy to settle.

The Baileys didn't have any children and lived next door to Peggy's mother in Doubleview in a small cosy house. Not having children didn't mean they were short on memorable family catch-ups and support. Jimmy never ended up getting his driver's licence, preferring to be driven around by his wife, and the extended family always enjoyed their convenient location next door to their grandmother's.

His love of acting and entertaining extended outside of the theatre. In the backyard, he would fill the tank with water and film model planes with cotton wool for clouds and he'd always have a camera on hand to film the play-acting at family gatherings and entertain them all. A regular visitor when he was in Australia was Jimmy's good friend Peter Cushing. Of course, there was a lot of reminiscing about the tour that had helped forge their friendship.

During the years in Perth, Jimmy became a prominent participant in the local theatre scene even honouring Olivier in his role as *Richard III* in 1953, which launched the first Festival of Perth in UWA's Somerville Auditorium. His wig and hump had been flown in specially from England. The wig is on display today at His Majesty's Museum of Performing Arts.

Although he gave many stage performances, it was in radio and broadcasting that he made his mark in Perth. He was the star performer is Alexander Turner's radio plays, acted in the ABC's school broadcasts and was outstanding on 6WF's Variety Show. He even worked alongside a newsreader and interviewer Peter Holland at the ABC for many years. In 1982 he was given a life membership to Australia's Actors' Equity.

The Baileys moved into the Kimberley Nursing home in West Leederville in their older years, where Jimmy continued to entertain the residents with recitations and Christmas lunch performances in the recreation area. After Peggy passed away in 2001, Jimmy slowed down considerably, but his love for the films stayed with him until the end, going to a movie once a week before he passed away. Little did James Bailey know that when Olivier picked him to join his *tour de force*, it would be a journey that steered him towards the love of his life and to the country where he would make a considerable contribution.

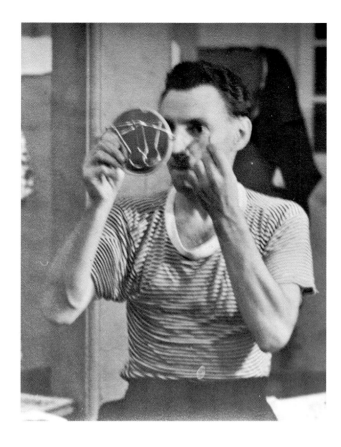

Left:
John Barnard applying makeup. Credit: Author's collection

Right:
James Bailey broadcasting for ABC. Credit: State Library of Western Australia

In return, Australia honoured him by including his name in a memorial at St George's Anglican Cathedral, Actor's Corner. James Ibsen Bailey passed away on 5th March 2003, buried in true theatrical style with two of his favourite hats.

Unfortunately, little is known about Hugh Stewart due to various discrepancies. Hugo Vickers lists his birth year as 1910 but incoming and outgoing passenger lists for the *Corinthic* record an 'HRS Murray' an actor, as being born in 1907. We know he returned to England with The Old Vic as he was part of the cast for the 1949 Old Vic season in *Antigone, Richard III* and *The School for Scandal*. He was listed still acting in England up until 1957 and an 'HRS Stewart-Murray' is recorded as returning to Australia with a wife in 1958. We also know Stewart was in Sydney in 1961 to meet Vivien with John Barnard and was still acting in 1963 in Australia. The confusion and inability to find much information on him may be because he seems to go by various names. Although acting as Hugh Stewart, sometimes we see his surname spelt incorrectly as Stuart. Incoming and outgoing records show different variations of his name: there is a Hugh Stewart born in 1910 in England, who was also a film editor, adding to the confusion.

Another member of the tour who had a considerable impact on Australian theatre thereafter was Elsie Beyer. She had left her job with HM Tennent, and actor Hugh Beaumont to join the tour. It's said starting around the Melbourne season, the Oliviers started to tire of her, especially Vivien. Initially endearing as a mother figure to the company, the Oliviers kept her well within their intimate inner circle, often letting her join private dinners and engagements. However, her need to control everything and be a killjoy so to say, eventually made them resent her. Vivien had wanted to send her home but Olivier resisted, employing others to do the jobs she was doing and leaving her with not much to do. Beyer must've realised she had been cast aside as her lengthy reports to Cecil Tennant changed in their tone and length after Melbourne. The reports start out enthusiastic, detailed, and personal but wane out to short, sparse and more direct towards the end of the tour. On the journey home she was mostly alone in her room and depressed. Olivier, in his long letter to Thornton Wilder on the return journey home, makes a reference to this when he writes that he should've had a nervous breakdown on the tour, but that Elsie Beyer is now suffering one instead.[7] Although in public she continued to praise the Oliviers and was always grateful for the opportunity, the relationship didn't end well.

When she returned to England, Beyer worked for a short time as the General Manager to the Shakespeare Memorial Theatre in Stratford-upon-Avon as the first woman in that role but requested release in 1950 to return to Australia. She saw Australia as an opportunity and a challenge. She aimed one day to build a National Theatre to keep Australian talent in Australia and wanted to do a tour to England with Australian actors – the 1948 tour in reverse. In 1954 the foundation of The Australian Elizabethan Theatre Trust was laid, and she became one of its three female directors. In 1962 she resigned as Assistant Executive Director, feeling a younger person should take over and offered herself special assignments only, the first of which were visits to Jakarta, Singapore, Hong Kong, Tokyo, Bangkok and Manila to inspect theatres, investigate costs and examine audience potential. Beyer passed away in Bromley, England in 1975.

Today The Australian Elizabethan Theatre Trust still exists as a not-for-profit, relying on private donations to operate and with the same purpose it was established for back in 1954: to support the arts in Australia, for Australia and by Australians. Before its inception, there were homemade productions like Finch's Mercury Theatre, but these were not consistent in all the States and towns. The Australian Elizabethan Theatre Trust has helped establish many independent companies like NIDA (National Institute of Dramatic Art), Bell Shakespeare Company and The Australian Ballet Foundation, and today is known for its International Music Scholarship Program.

Terence Morgan's film debut was in Olivier's *Hamlet* as Laertes which earned him many fan letters from swooning teenage girls. Olivier had spotted him in his first West End performance in 1946 and is credited as being his discoverer. Morgan felt a great deal of obligation towards Olivier because of this and had agreed on joining the tour at the expense of the lead in the film *The Blue Lagoon*, opposite Jean Simmons. It was a decision both Morgan and Georgina later regretted, realising how much they missed out on their baby's development and, had Morgan chosen to star in the film, it would've had more of an impact on his career. Even with the release of *Hamlet* during the tour, he was forbidden to talk to the press and missed out on the attention it might've generated. Upon returning to England after the tour, he continued acting in films mostly in loutish roles and although relatively successful, Hollywood never beckoned. In 1961 he got the title role in ATV's *The Adventures of Francis Drake*, which earned him an American following but again no offers came. He remained married to Georgina Jumel, who retired from acting to become a full-time mother to their only daughter, Lyvia Lee – named after Olivier and Vivien. In 1958, they moved to Hove where he retired to run a small hotel and dabbled in property development. He was also a Director of the Brighton Festival. In 2000 he suffered a heart attack and his health deteriorated over the next five years. Georgina said, 'We were very happily married for fifty-eight years. He was a very kind man with a sense of humour which he had right up to the end.'[8] Morgan died on August 25th in 2005 in Nuffield Hospital with Georgina and Lyvia at his side. Georgina died in 2021, sixteen desolate years without the love of her life Morgan, and as she wrote in a poem at the end of her autobiography – waiting only to join him:

Come back my love, come back to me,
Or shall I come to thee?[9]

Mercia Swinburne was the only Australian member of the troupe but could hardly be called such, having only been born in Sydney – she left for London when she was a baby. When questioned by the press on the tour, she referred to having been born in Australia as a bit of an accident. It appears

Left:
A scene from *The School for Scandal*. Credit: Alicia Powell Collection

Right:
Getting ready for a performance at the Tivoli Theatre. Credit: Author's collection

Left:
Walking down Spring Street, Melbourne with Mercia Swinburne. Credit: Kendra Bean Collection

Right:
Vivien photographed in a chauffer-driven limousine. The car passed between lines of cheering people as it left the Archerfield Aerodrome. Credit: John Oxley Library, State Library of Queensland

Mercia was the result of an affair her mother Leah was having with Charles Swinburne and by the time she was born, her mother was in the midst of a nasty divorce. After the divorce, her mother took the children with Charles to London. There was a short period back to Sydney in 1912 but they returned to London within two years. Mercia was acting from the age of fifteen and became quite the socialite, modelling and furthering her acting. In 1925 she married the actor George Relph, appearing together in many shows.

Mercia and Relph were Vivien and Olivier's closest friends during the tour. Upon returning they continued to act together until 1950 when it appears Mercia retired while George continued. Relph died in 1960, and Mercia in 1993.

Eileen Beldon recalled the tour many years later with fondness, aware of the strain it had on the leaders, especially on Vivien's already precarious health.

> *They worked tremendously hard, Larry and Viv. They had to go out every single day, to cocktail parties and to visit this and that, and they never went to bed until about two in the morning. I don't think they could have enjoyed it very much, and what it must have taken out on Vivien one can only imagine. She had very little stamina, was such a tiny thing, and of course she had tuberculosis.*[10]

It was a tour that must've been a strain on her too, having had to leave a twelve-year-old son, David Jon, back home in the care of a nanny. Beldon was a seasoned actress, with what others thought a 'husky voice' and a wicked sense of humour. She had toured America twice, and her career ranged from Shakespeare to Shaw. Beldon continued to act after she returned to England. She was with the Birmingham Repertory Theatre through the early '60s. She died in Aylesbury on 3rd August 1985.

Michael Redington went on to become a successful producer and director. After returning from the tour, he married Ann Connell and gave up acting to take on the role in ATV as a live TV producer. In the mid-'80s he went back to the theatre but as a producer. He worked with many notables such as Judi Dench, John Gielgud, and Derek Jacobi in West End shows during that time. He always held the Oliviers in the highest esteem and believed Olivier's performance as *Richard III* a theatrical epiphany. He was always grateful for having been a part of the tour, saying it was the highlight of his life, and credited it as having created him. Redington appears to have been Garry O'Connor's main point of reference for *Darlings of Gods*. He died on December 15th, 2016 in Westminster, London.

There were people apart from those who were part of the touring group for whom the tour was life changing. Australian Michael Blakemore, for instance, was born in Sydney and a medical student at Sydney University at the time of the tour. He was influenced so much by seeing Olivier's performance as Richard that he changed his career to training as an actor instead. Leaving Australia in 1950 to study at RADA, he made his stage debut in 1952 as a doctor in *The Barretts of Wimpole Street*. He would go onto become an accomplished Tony Award-winning director and ironically ended up being an Associate Director of

The National Theatre. In an experience he found intimidating, he directed Olivier in *A Long Day's Journey into Night* in 1971 (Olivier was also his boss at the time).

Peter Hiley, who was in Sydney working for the British Council, went to work for the Oliviers as the Company Manager and eventually became indispensable, earning the name 'fixer of fixers'. There he ended up managing not only the company but also anything else they threw at him, including Notley Abbey, which included negotiating with the Ministry of Agriculture for sugar for the bees at Notley, arranging for the willow trees to be made into cricket bats and even Olivier's brother's funeral at sea with the Navy. After Olivier and Vivien divorced, he returned to Australia for a year, where he still had family. He kept doing the odd paperwork for both, becoming a go-between confidant, albeit unpaid, for the rest of his life. Hiley was the first person Jack Merivale (Vivien's end-of-life partner) called upon Vivien's passing in July 1967, and it was he who notified Olivier. Likewise, Hiley arranged Olivier's funeral in 1989 and executed his estate as he had done for Vivien in 1967. Vivien, characteristically generous and thoughtful, left Hiley a prized Sickert oil painting in her will, which moved him deeply.

After both their deaths he continued to be helpful to their estates and extended families until he died in June 2008. Close to sixty years he devoted to the pair he had met and been enchanted by in 1948, Sydney.

In terms of the success of Great Britain's use of the tour for political and commercial interest – cultural diplomacy – the results were contradictory, according to one thesis conclusion by James Lee Taylor in 2018. Tyrone Guthrie himself followed up the tour with a lecture tour on British Drama of his own, aiming to meet theatre representatives to discuss the setting up of a National Theatre, the inadequacies of the Australian theatre scene and how it could be remedied by the British via an import-export scheme funded by the Australian Government. His report was handed to the British Council which noted that the proposal had been discussed in Canberra with the Prime Minister pledging £30,000 if the States contributed likewise.[11] James Taylor asserts that this was a continuation of the cultural exploitation and dismissive attitude by the British Council to Australia's own post-war theatre scene that had begun with the tour. However, this proposal was also scrapped when Ben Chifley was defeated by Robert Menzies in December 1949.

Between 1951 and 1954, the British Council had many cuts made, and in 1954 its operations in Australia, New Zealand and Ceylon (now Sri Lanka) were shut down following a recommendation to reduce Government expenditure on Information Services. Regardless of the impact that the coronation of Elizabeth II in 1953 had on showing 'historical continuity' and stability, British imperial culture was slowly becoming old-fashioned and stale. Britain was still struggling to figure out its post-war identity and global role with decolonisation, the rise and influence of America and the threat of communism. However, there were plenty of Australians who were dismayed at the withdrawal of the British Council and what looked like an abandonment of her Dominions, those that still felt an enormous affinity and inspiration in British ideals, culture, and history.

A boom in Shakespearean culture did result, though, with John Alden's Australian Shakespeare Company doing a national tour between 1951 and 1952. Alden was an Australian radio and theatre actor who, in 1937, had gone to England and spent time with David Woltif and The Old Vic, gaining invaluable experience before returning to Australia. His productions of *Measure for Measure* in 1948 and *King Lear* in 1950 at the Independent Theatre were critically acclaimed and commercially successful. His company's Shakespearean tour in 1951/1952 was partially sponsored by the Government, leading certain circles to speculate that it was the beginning of a true National Theatre. Challenging indoctrinated ideals and allowing and embracing Australian accents was a refreshing change, which was followed suit by radio and screen.

The tour was a great success, covering Sydney, Melbourne, Brisbane, Perth, Launceston, Hobart and even Canberra much to the unease of the British Council as this did not in any way benefit Britain culturally, politically or commercially. One British Council representative criticised Alden, comparing him to actor-manager tours from the UK a few years prior and their faults and also putting him down as an actor.[12] However successful the enterprise was, Alden got very uncomfortable when a yearly Commonwealth grant was proposed as it would entail him giving up control of his company. With that, he suddenly disbanded the company and the idea of an Australian National Theatre with it. Alden, however, continued to be an integral part of the Australian classical theatre scene until his death in 1962, acting and directing at the Independent Theatre, producing *Titus Andronicus* in 1958, relaunching another company, and organising the 1961 Sydney Shakespeare Festival.

Although an Australian National Theatre did not materialise, The Australian Elizabethan Theatre Trust Fund (AETTF) did in 1954, aiming to sponsor artists mainly from the UK. It secured a lease on Majestic Theatre in an attempt to emulate The Old Vic and Hugh Hunt from the British Council arrived in Australia in 1955. But by 1956, as James Taylor in his thesis concludes, '… pro-British ardour of the immediate post-war years had cooled considerably, the opposition was raised further by the realization that, like Hunt himself, the Trust's four leading associates (Elsie Beyer, John Sumner, James Mills, and Robert Quentin) were all British and previous Old Vic employees.'[13] He does, however, concede that Shakespearean tours used for cultural diplomacy had more success in Australia than in fascist Europe, especially the 1948 one with the Oliviers' star power pull, and its imperialistic character, with them being seen and treated like Royal surrogates. It appealed to the masses in a time of unique historical duress, with the Dominions craving attention from the Motherland after the war. But in the 1950s, although there was a change in cultural diplomacy from advertising the British way of life – for altruistic and non-specific goals to more obvious political practices – it did so having achieved certain goals by the time of the British Council's withdrawal.

Left:
Arriving back in England.
Credit: Greta Ritchie Collection

The tour was undoubtedly a financial success. Gross takings were an enormous £226,318, of which the British Council received £42,000 after tax. The Oliviers, on top of the £100 a week pay, received a percentage and were given a £5000 share. Most other members of the company were given £60, which was not even enough to cover their personal expenses while on the tour. The Old Vic, on the other hand, received enough to wipe out the London losses and make a surplus for 1948 and the 1949 season.[14]

There was an irony to The Old Vic's decision to let go of Olivier and Richardson with the reason being they needed an independent person with no prejudice and a non-actor. For when, finally, a body resembling the National Theatre emerged in 1963, it was Olivier who they turned to. The money that was promised with the passing of *The National Theatre Bill* took fifteen years to be produced and an actual building was only opened in 1976.

The Australia and New Zealand tour left an undeniable lasting impression on the Oliviers, no matter how stressful and overworked they were. The tour won their hearts in different ways. Because of the power of film before television, they had a worldwide celebrity presence in the collective minds of the population even if it was Down Under and isolated New Zealand. After they returned, Olivier said this to Australian press: 'Let's say how we like Australians. They gave us a wonderful time. We had never dreamed of such a warm reception. They are very, very nice people. Give them our love.'[15]

All indications point to it being true what Olivier wrote in his autobiography about having lost Vivien somewhere, somehow in Australia. Strachan used an apt analogy of tectonic plates that kept their passionate love together having shifted during the tour, even though it may not have been obvious. Terence Morgan, in the documentary *Larry and Vivien: The Oliviers in Love,* said he remembered on the trip to Australia that the Oliviers' lust for each other, a big part of their relationship, was still evident, recalling how embarrassing it had been to witness Olivier getting aroused just watching Vivien rehearse. Georgina Jumel pointed out in the same documentary that at the end of the tour, something had definitely changed which they kept from the group: 'At that time, they were very tired, very exhausted … We did sense something was wrong towards the end. Something was cooling between them.'[16] Further, in her autobiography in 2011, Georgina confirmed that there had been flirting between Vivien and Dan Cunningham on the tour that was more pronounced on the journey home. Olivier noted in 1951, when they took the two Cleopatras to New York, he had noticed a peculiar change in Vivien's behaviour towards him. She started to behave like a frightened child, leaning close to him and wanting him to put his arms around her. Although it was not passionate in nature and somewhat mystifying, he still welcomed it, as it had been the first time in three years she had given him some sort of happiness by making him feel important and reliable.[17] If that is to be believed, the time frame to when a change had occurred correlates to somewhere during or straight after the tour.

Vivien and Olivier's love, veiled in a fairy-tale aura not of their own creation – having to justify it even to themselves, deserting young children and good-hearted partners to be together – forced them to maintain the façade of the perfect theatrical couple at any cost. Journalist and author Elaine Dundy likened Vivien to having been blessed by the gods, but also being abandoned by them. Garry O'Connor referred to them as 'darlings of the gods' in his book on the tour, and the crew called them God and Angel. Noël Coward wrote this to a friend a few days after Vivien passed, 'To have seen her and Larry together in their prime was to have glimpsed a kind of divinity.'[18] Divinity seemed to surround their personas. Trader Falkner said it best:

> *They reached the pinnacle, they had money, they had everything. I've never seen a couple so adored, so admired. But there was a terrible price to pay. In the end you saw all the beauty, all the riches, all the success was worth little. The only thing that was priceless were the moments where people went 'ahhh'. These moments will live forever. And in these moments are a glimpse of God. It is a glimpse of God.*[19]

God and his Angel.

Below:
In their Surfers Paradise apartment with Olivier's camera. Credit: John Oxley Library, State Library of Queensland

— *Postscript* —

*Then you go on living and there you are, with it, knowing what has happened, remembering its details. Yet what else is there to do?**

* Curtis Bill Pepper, 'Talking With New York Times', March 25th 1979. Laurence Olivier remembering about his marriage to Vivien Leigh.

In 1977, when Olivier was in Newport filming *The Betsy*, strolling through the gardens of Rosecliff mansion, being interviewed by Australian television personality and journalist Ray Martin without his prompting, he remembered Vivien and their tour in 1948. He recalled with fondness the short holiday in Broadbeach and how beautiful Vivien had been. "'Australia was where I lost Vivien," he said. "But I don't hold it against you darn Aussies." Then he laughed, still very handsome in old age, and gave that enigmatic smile of his.'[1]

Vivien maintained a special connection to Australia in the way of a unique fan, Joyce Attwood, from Fitzroy, Melbourne. Joyce was an unassuming and humble girl from a working-class family, brought up by her grandmother and father, marrying late in life, living in one house all her life until she had to go to a nursing home.

She had seen all the shows while the tour was in Melbourne in 1948 and, during what we presume to be the 1961 Old Vic Tour that Vivien did on her own with Robert Helpmann and Jack Merivale, she befriended Vivien's assistant Trudi Flockhart at the stage door. Like most ardent fans she maintained and kept detailed scrapbooks, wrote to all the newspapers for their press photos and devotedly to Vivien over the ensuing years. Some of her letters are now part of the Vivien Leigh Archive at the Victoria and Albert Museum and some in the Laurence Olivier Archive at the British Library.

Vivien was generous and thoughtful, treating her fans better than most stars. Although there are those that say she was not sentimental, her habits, tendencies and items she cherished most beg to differ. Cast members' birthdays were remembered, cards, telegrams and letters cherished, and phone calls came without a care for time differences. For example, she kept Noël Coward's 'get well note' that he sent while she recuperated at Netherne Hospital in Surrey after her worst breakdown in 1953 in her handbag, re-reading over and over, whenever she needed comfort. When Notley Abbey was robbed one year, while she was recuperating from her 1953 breakdown, it was not the mink or jewels they took that saddened her. The one item she missed most was a simple ring, of no major value, that Olivier had given to mark a particular incident in both their lives.

The custodian of Joyce's Vivien Leigh Collection, her niece Judith Koop, puzzles over the dedication and commitment Joyce had to a star, considering the geographical distance between them.[2]

But relationships, especially those formed through fandom, are complex, and connections happen between people without reason or motive. Possibly Joyce's admiration for Vivien provided an avenue for cathartic release that need not be understood but simply accepted and appreciated.

After Vivien's death, a number of personal effects were sent to special fans from around the world, including Joyce. Having no children of her own, Joyce's niece Judith Koop inherited these mementos and her collection after Joyce herself passed away.

In 1965, for Vivien's birthday, Joyce had sent her a book, *The Lore of the Lyrebird*, inscribed, 'To Dear Miss Leigh, along with the recording I hope this brings back pleasant memories of your visit to Sherbrooke Forest. Sincerely Joyce.' A few years prior, she had sent Vivien a recording of a lyrebird that she found wonderful and listened to often at Tickerage, her country home. In 1961, when Vivien had been in Melbourne, she – with her usual curiosity and the need to experience a place fully – had dragged Jack (her end-of-life partner), Robert Helpmann and Trudi out of bed before the crack of dawn to drive up to Sherbrooke Forest to try and catch one. The lyrebird's most notable talent is the ability to mimic any sound, either natural or artificial. They are rare to see and many people go time and time with no luck. She wrote to Peter Wyngarde, actor and her friend, about how lucky she had been to have seen not one but four birds during close to a forty-five-minute display – a truly remarkable experience was how she described it.[3]

The Lore of the Lyrebird made its way back to Melbourne in 2017. Vivien had kept it all her life. It came to belong to another lifelong Vivien Leigh fan – the author of this book. Fandom and love for Vivien Leigh had come full circle, serendipitously.

Do not seek the because – in love there is no because, no reason, no explanation, no solutions.
— Anais Nin

Preceding spread, on left: The Olivers walking on a beach in Australia. Credit: Author's Collection

Following spread: Credit: Angus McBean Photograph. © Harvard Theatre Collection, Houghton Library, Harvard University

Endnotes

INTRODUCTION

1. OLIVIER Laurence, *Confessions of An Actor*, Weidenfeld & Nicolson, 1982, pg. 168
2. BLACKMORE Michael. *Arguments with England, A Memoir*. Faber and Faber Ltd, London 2004 pg. 5

CHAPTER 1

1. POUND Reginald, *Knight Errant*, newspaper clipping, paper unknown, Kendra Bean Collection
2. GALLOWAY Stephen *Truly Madly: Vivien Leigh and Laurence Olivier: The Romance of the Century,* Grand Central Publishing, pg. 179
3. COLEMAN Terry, *Olivier,* Vivien Leigh Archive, V & A Museum, LO to VL 1945 June, pg. 169
4. Ibid pg. 169
5. STRACHAN Alan, *Dark Star; A Biography of Vivien Leigh*, I.B Tauris & Co. Ltd London, New York 2019, pg. 127
6. GALLOWAY Stephen, *Truly Madly: Vivien Leigh and Laurence Olivier: The Romance of the Century*, Grand Central Publishing, pg. 90
7. Picturegoer, August 1947
8. BARKER Felix, *The Oliviers,* Cornwall Press, 1953, pg. 308
9. BEAN Kendra, *Vivien Leigh An Intimate Portrait,* Running Press, Philadelphia, 2013, pg. 105
10. STRACHAN Alan, *Dark Star; A Biography of Vivien Leigh*, I.B Tauris & Co. Ltd, London, New York 2019 pg. 129
11. VICKERS Hugo, *Vivien Leigh, A Biography,* Little Brown and Company, London 1988 pg. 2

CHAPTER 2

1. BARKER Felix, *The Oliviers,* Hamish Hamilton, 1953, pg. 314
2. LAWSON Valerie *Dancing Under the Southern Skies; A history of Australian ballet*, Australian Scholarly Publishing Pty Ltd, 2019, pg. 177
3. TAYLOR James Lee (2018), *Shakespeare, Decolonisation, and the Cold War.* Ph.D. Thesis. The Open University, pg. 84
4. LAWSON Valerie *Dancing Under the Southern Skies; A history of Australian ballet*, Australian Scholarly Publishing Pty Ltd, 2019, pg. 177
5. Ibid pg. 178
6. THORNDIKE Dame Sybil *'Of Pioneering'* Best Available Plays and Operas For The People, noted date 7.9.48. Newspaper clipping. *Kendra Bean Collection*
7. WILMOT Charles, *The Old Vic Theatre Company. A Tour of Australia and New Zealand.* Official Theatre Program, foreword, pg.4
8. THORNDIKE Dame Sybil *'Of Pioneering' Best Available Plays and Operas For The People*, noted date 7.9.48. Newspaper clipping. Kendra Bean Collection
9. TAYLOR James Lee (2018*), Shakespeare, Decolonisation, and the Cold War*. Ph.D. thesis. The Open University, pg. 78
10. COLEMAN Terry, *Olivier, The Authorised Biography*, Bloomsbury, London 2005, pg. 204
11. OLIVIER Laurence, *Confessions of An Actor*, Weidenfeld & Nicolson, 1982 pg. 166
12. COLEMAN Terry, *Olivier, The Authorised Biography*, Bloomsbury, London 2005, pg. 191
13. BLAKEMORE Michael. *Arguments with England. A Memoir*, Faber and Faber Ltd, 2004 pg. 148-149

14. CUSHING Peter. *An Autobiography* Weidenfeld and Nicolson, London. 1986 pg. 102
15. COLEMAN Terry, *Olivier, The Authorised Biography,* Bloomsbury 2005, pg. 164
16. WALKER Alexander, *Vivien, The Life of Vivien Leigh*, George Weidenfeld and Nicolson Ltd 1987, pg. 241
17. STRACHAN Alan, *Dark Star, A Biography of Vivien Leigh,* I.B. Tauris & Co. Ltd, 2019 pg. 121
18. Ibid
19. COLEMAN Terry, *Olivier,* Bloomsbury 2005, pg. 191
20. O'CONNOR Garry, *Darlings of the Gods*, Hodder and Stoughton, 1984, pg. 17
21. Unknown title, author, newspaper clipping. *Kendra Bean Collection*
22. Ibid
23. BARKER Felix, *The Oliviers,* Hamish Hamilton, 1953, pg. 134
24. TAYLOR James Lee (2018). *Shakespeare, Decolonisation, and the Cold War.* PhD thesis, The Open University
25. Ibid

CHAPTER 3

1. QUICK Harriet. 2017 'Vivien Leigh: Icon of Style.' Sothebys.com, *https://www.sothebys.com/en/articles/vivien-leigh-icon-of-style. Accessed 10 August 2021*
2. *Vivien Leigh Actress and Icon*, Chapter by Keith Lodwick; Dressing the part: costume and character, edited by Kate Dorney and Maggie B. Gale, Manchester University Press, 2018
3. THE MAIL '"Vivvy" – Dresses by Britain' author unknown, March 13, 1948
4. VIZARD Steve. The curly encounter of Larry and Mo. In Beyond the Stage: Creative Australian Stories from the Great War, edited by Anna Goldsworthy and Mark Carroll Wakefield Press, 2020. p.110
5. STRUTTON Bill. *World Famous Old Vic Company on its way to Australia.* In The Australian Women's Weekly, February 1948. p.20
6. D'ORTHEZ Vicomtes. *Their Business is Fashion,* British Vogue, Fashion Edition, July 1948
7. BRITISH VOGUE, May 1948, untitled article, author unknown. p.55
8. Untitled Newspaper Clipping, 1948, author unknown, Kendra Bean Collection.
9. JAN Tomes. 2017 '*The New Look: How Christian Dior revolutionized fashion 70 years ago*' dw.com https://www.dw.com/en/the-new-look-how-christian-dior-revolutionized-fashion-70-years-ago/a-37491236 Accessed 2 September 2021
10. SYDNEY MORNING HERALD '*Vivien Leigh Plans an Australian Wardrobe',* 28 January 1948
11. AUSTRALIAN WOMEN'S WEEKLY '*World Famous Old Vic Company on Its Way to Australia.'* 21 February 1948
12. THE SYDNEY SUN, '*Perth Crowds Welcome to Olivier, Leigh.'* 15 March 1948
13. THE WEST AUSTRALIAN '*In a Star's Wardrobe'* 23 March 1948
14. THE AGE, '*Lady Olivier is her husband's favourite actress.'* 20 April 1948
15. HAMILTON Madeleine. 2009 *Glamour returns to post-war Australia.* https://www.eurekastreet.com.au/article/glamour-returns-to-post-war-australia Accessed 13 July 2021
16. THE WEEKLY NEWS, *Royalty of English Theatre Sir Laurence Olivier and Vivien Leigh Enchant Auckland,* 15 September 1948
17. LAMBERT Joyce. *Australian Clothes Wonderful Says Vivien Leigh*, The Sun, 30 November 1948

CHAPTER 4

1. OLIVIER Laurence, *My Trip Abroad,* Journal, February 14th 1948, Add MS 79980 – Vol. CCXV, British Library, Laurence Olivier Archive
2. BEYER Elsie, British Library Add MS 89150/3/5
3. OLIVIER Laurence, *My Trip Abroad,* Journal, Add MS 79980 – Vol. CCXV, British Library, Laurence Olivier Archive
4. Ibid

CHAPTER 5

1. National Archives of Australia, series A1265, Report by the Public Relations Officer on the postponed Royal Visit 1949 Original Typescript
2. TAYLOR James Lee (2018). *Shakespeare, Decolonisation, and the Cold War*. PhD thesis The Open University
3. LAWRENCE James, *Churchill and Empire: Portrait of an Imperialist*, Phoenix, 2013, pg. 287
4. https://www.nma.gov.au/defining-moments/resources/postwar-immigration-drive National Museum of Australia *Post War Immigration Drive* date accessed 20 April 2022
5. https://www.dailytelegraph.com.au/news/today-in-history/shakespeare-had-an-impact-on-early-colonial-australia-centuries-after-his-death/news-story/2c843c9e6febca8e5bc9ea03bf196e85. Date accessed 21 April 2022
6. BOWDEN Bradley *The Rise and Decline of Australian Unionism: A history of industrial labour from the 1820s to 2010* Griffith University, 2011
7. Adelaide Mail, Saturday 7th February 1948
8. OLIVIER Laurence, *My Trip Abroad,* Journal, 1948, Add MS 79980 – Vol.CCXV, British Library, Laurence Olivier Archive

CHAPTER 6

1. THE WEST AUSTRALIAN *'Perth in Wartime: This delightful City.'* 13th March 1942
2. Ibid
3. CUSHING Peter. An Autobiography. Weidenfeld and Nicolson, London, 1984. p. 105
4. THE WEST AUSTRALIAN *Old Vic Company Lands at Fremantle,* Tuesday 16th March, 1948
5. The Sun (Sydney), *Perth crowds welcome to Olivier,* Leigh, Monday 15th March, 1948
6. Ibid
7. O'CONNOR Garry, *Darlings of the Gods,* Hodder & Stoughton, London, 1984 pg.18
8. Barbara to author June 18, 2019. Contact details for Barbara have been lost during Covid lockdowns and the phone number given has been disconnected
9. 1982 Radio Segment, Michael Redington, City Extra with Margaret Throsby date listened 19 June 2019
10. CUSHING Peter. *An Autobiography*, Weidenfeld and Nicolson, London, 1986, pg. 105
11. O'CONNOR Garry, *Darlings of the Gods,* Hodder & Stoughton, London, 1984, pg.43
12. THORNE Ross, *Picture Palace Architecture*, Sun Books Pty Ltd, 1976, pg.2
13. https://www.news.uwa.edu.au/feb-2008/uwas-sunken-garden-theatre-celebrates-60-years. Accessed 8 July 2019
14. O'CONNOR Garry, *Darlings of the Gods,* Hodder & Stoughton, London, 1984, pgs. 47, 48
15. *Glamourous Occasion is Old Vic Premier*, Sunday Times, Sunday 21st March, 1948, pg.9
16. Ibid pg.51
17. By Fidelio Old Vic Opens, The West Australian, Monday 22nd March, 1948, pg.4
18. SUNDAY TIMES *'Old Vic Premier, Acting is Perfect – Acoustics Bad'* Sunday 21 March 1948
19. Brent Bellon to author 15 May 2019
20. THE WEST AUSTRALIAN *'Old Vic Season',* 23 March 1948 1948
21. THE COURIER-MAIL BRISBANE *'Adelaide Q For Oliviers'* Monday 22 March 1948
22. OLIVIER Laurence, *My Trip Abroad,* Journal, 23 March 1948, Add MS 79980 – Vol.CCXV, British Library, Laurence Olivier Archive
23. Ibid
24. BEYER Elsie, British Library, Add MS 89150/3/5 Laurence Olivier Archive
25. OLIVIER Laurence, *My Trip Abroad,* Journal, 27th March 1948, Add MS 79980 – Vol.CCXV, British Library, Laurence Olivier Archive
26. THE WEST AUSTRALIAN *'Tumultuous Farewell To The Oliviers',* Wednesday 31st March 1948

CHAPTER 7

1. O'CONNOR Garry, *Darlings of the Gods* Hodder & Stoughton, London, 1984, pg. 60
2. LAMBERT Joyce, *'Australian Clothes Wonderful Says Vivien Leigh'* THE SUN, Sydney November 30th, 1948

3. STEAD Lisa. *Reframing Vivien Leigh, Stardom, Gender, and the Archive,* Oxford University Press, 2021 pg. 107
4. Peter Goers to author 3 May 2021
5. Ray Oberman to author 15 May 2019
6. THE WEST AUSTRALIAN *First Night Triumph,* 5th April 1948, pg. 9
7. Lyn Sharp to author 6th February 2023
8. THE ADVERTISER *'Old Vic Company Welcomed'* April 6th, 1948
9. *The Skin of Our Teeth,* Letter to the Editor, The Advertiser, 16th April, 1948
10. ARMITAGE Mary, News, *Play That Dazzles and Bedevils,* 13th April, 1948
11. OLIVIER Laurence, *My Trip Abroad,* Journal, Add MS 79980 – Vol.CCXV, British Library, Laurence Olivier Archive
12. Adelaidean *Alumni News* Vol 5 No 21, November 18th 1996
13. THE HERALD *The Oliviers Liked Us,* 18th November 1948
14. *www.escape.com.au Take a look inside famous Aussies artist's home.* Elizabeth Fortescue, May 11th 2019. Date accessed February 16th 2022
15. BARKER Felix, *The Oliviers,* Cornwall Press 1953 pg.326
16. DENTON Meg, 'Sir Robert Helpmann, CBE', SA History Hub, History Trust of South Australia, *https://sahistoryhub.history.sa.gov.au/people/sir-robert-helpmann-cbe,* 17th September 2014, Date accessed 28th June 2021
17. OLIVIER Laurence, *My Trip Abroad,* Journal, April 19th 1948 Entry Add MS 79980 – Vol.CCXV, British Library, Laurence Olivier Archive

CHAPTER 8

1. O'CONNOR Garry, *Darlings of the God,* Hodder & Stoughton, London, 1984, pg. 76
2. OLIVIER Laurence, *My Trip Abroad,* Journal, Add MS 79980 – Vol. CCXV, British Library Laurence Olivier Archive, April 19th 1948 entry
3. HOLDEN Anthony, Laurence Olivier; A Biography, Random House 1991 pg. 233
4. THE ARGUS *Famous Stage Couple in Melbourne,* F. Keith Manzie, 20th April 1948
5. THE AGE Women's Section *Lady Olivier Is Her Husband's Favourite Actress,* 20th April 1948
6. SPICER J Chrystopher, *Duchess: The Story of the Windsor Hotel,* Loch Haven Books, 1993, pg. 35
7. Ibid
8. THE AGE *'Free rent and $8000 back pay for 101-year-old Melbourne tenant'* July 22nd, 2014
9. THE ARGUS, *Police Break Up Ticket Ques,* May 1st 1948
10. *https://www.historyvictoria.org.au/collections-lounge/princess-theatre/ Princess Theatre – Royal Historical Society of Victoria* Date assessed 28th September 2021
11. SYDNEY MORNING HERALD *Olivier Pleased at Success of First Night,* 21stApril 1948
12. THE AGE Melbourne, *The School for Scandal Old Vic's First Night Triumph,* 21st April 1948
13. Mass Museum, *Textile Designs by Prestige Ltd https:/ma.as/*319417, date accessed 3rd October 2021
14. O'CONNOR Garry, *Darlings of the Gods,* Hodder & Stoughton, London, 1984, pg. 82
15. OLIVIER Laurence, *My Trip Abroad,* Journal, Add MS 79980 – Vol. CCXV, British Library, Laurence Olivier Archive, April 24th 1948 entry
16. THE HERALD *Theatre* 27th April 1948
17. THE AGE *Olivier Excels in Richard III,* 27th April 1948
18. Listener In (sp) 1-7 May 1948, Newspaper clipping, *Joyce Attwood Collection*
19. THE SUN *Olivier's Richard III,* April 27th, 1948
20. O'CONNOR Garry, *Darlings of the Gods* Hodder & Stoughton, London, 1984, pg. 84
21. THE ARGUS *Had Bonzer Time You Beauts said Olivier,* 13th May 1948
22. Truth, 8th May 1948
23. ABC media abc.net.au Old Vic Theatre Company Australian Tour 1948: Michael Redington, 1982, date listened/accessed 4 October 2021
24. CROMBIE, Isobel. *Athol Shmith Photographer,* Schwartz Publishing (Victoria) Pty Ltd, pg. 120
25. Ibid
26. O'CONNOR Garry, *Darlings of the Gods,* Hodder & Stoughton, London, 1984, pg. 83

CHAPTER 9

1. O'CONNOR Garry, *Darlings of the Gods* Hodder & Stoughton, London, 1984, pg.91
2. THE MERCURY, *Spontaneous Acclaim for Old Vic Show at Hobart*, 15th June 1948
3. Fortysouth.com.au *Voices from the Theatre*, Date accessed 7th October 2021
4. The Mercury, *Plea for Retention of Theatre* 15th June 1948
5. Ibid
6. British Library, Olivier Archive, Elsie Beyer reports Add MS 89150/3/5
7. THE MERCURY *Old Vic Season*, 17th June 1948
8. Carole Freeman to author 17th April 2023

CHAPTER 10

1. MARTIN Ray, *Stories of My Life* William Heinemann Australia, 2010, pg. 142

CHAPTER 11

1. DAILY TELEGRAPH *Oliviers Like Their Mementos Lively*, 29th June 1948
2. SYDNEY MORNING HERALD *The Australia Hotel*, June 20th 1891
3. THE HERALD *Shakespeare in his Splendour* July 3rd 1948
4. BLACKMORE Michael, *Arguments with England, A Memoir* Faber and Faber Limited, 2005 pg. 6
5. Ibid
6. COLEMAN Terry, *Olivier*, Henry Holt and Company, New York, 2004, pg. 196
7. Ibid
8. STRACHAN, *Alan Dark Star*, I. B Tauris & Co. Ltd, 2019 pg. 139
9. O'CONNOR, Garry. *Darling of the Gods,* Hodder & Stoughton, London, 1984, pg. 114
10. SYDNEY MORNING HERALD *'Batsmen Cry "O Dainty Duck! O Dear!"'* August 2nd 1948
11. Doris Fitton interviewed by Hazel de Berg in the Hazel de Berg Collection, Oral History and Folklore Collection, National Library of Australia
12. FITTON Doris, *Not Without Dust & Heat; my life in the theatre.* Harper & Row, 1981 pg. 71
13. COLEMAN Terry, *Olivier,* Henry Holt and Company, New York, pg. 198
14. *https://www.pittwateronlinenews.com* Issue 209 April 5-18, 2015, accessed 14th October 2021
15. Footage lip reading and parts of newspaper articles deciphered by Alicia Powell
16. BLAKMORE Michael *Arguments with England. A Memoir.* Faber and Faber Ltd, London 2004, pg.3
17. Ibid
18. POWE Joan. *'Olivier's dresser is a shy English widow'* The Australian Women's Weekly. pg.17
19. OLIVIER Laurence letter to Cecil Tennant 14th July, 1948. British Library Add MS 89150/3/5 Laurence Olivier Archive
20. O'CONNOR, Garry. *Darlings of the Gods,* Hodder & Stoughton, London, 1984, pg. 126
21. FINCH Peter, *I Lived as I Liked,* Woman's Own, September 1961, Papers of Peter Finch, 1937-1954, NLA MS 7003
22. Ibid
23. Ibid
24. DUNDY, Elaine. *Finch, Bloody Finch. A life of Peter Finch.* Holt, Rinehart and Winston, New York. 1980. pg.13
25. OLIVIER, Laurence. *Confessions of An Actor* George Weidenfeld & Nicolson Ltd 1983 pg.168
26. SOMMERS van Tess Interview for People October 24 1949, Peter Finch Papers, 1937-1954 NL MS 7003
27. Ibid (Olivier incorrectly writes it was as Tartuffe that Finch acted. It was in Imaginary Invalid.)
28. DUNDY, Elaine. *Finch, Bloody Finch. A life of Peter Finch by Elaine Dundy.* Holt, Rinehart and Winston, New York. 1980. pg.129
29. VICKERS Hugo, Vivien Leigh, Little Brown and Company, 1988, pg.188
30. Faulkner, Trader. Phone interview with author 25th October 2020

31. Ibid
32. SOMMERS van Tess, Interview for People, October 24 1949, Peter Finch Papers, NLA MS 700
33. FIRTH Vincent. *Down Under to The Top*, Film Star Interview, publication unknown, 1962
34. FINCH Yolande, *Finchy*, Wyndham Books, New York, 1981, pg. 28
35. FAULKNER Trader, *Peter Finch, A Biography* Angus & Robertson, UK, 1979 pg. 110
36. DUNDY, Elaine. *Finch, Bloody Finch. A life of Peter Finch*. Hclt, Rinehart and Winston, New York. 1980. pg. 339

CHAPTER 12

1. COURTNEIDGE Cicely, *Cicely*, Hutchinson & Co Ltd, 1953, London pg. 160
2. LAWRENCE Warwick, Old Vic superb, The Courier-Mail, Brisbane, Wednesday 25th August, 1948, pg.3
3. LEWIS Roger, *The Real Life of Laurence Olivier*, Century Books Ltd 1996. pg. 182
4. Ibid pg.132
5. O'CONNOR, Garry. *Darlings of the Gods,* Hodder & Stoughton, London, 1984, pg. 132
6. TRUTH Brisbane, *Food Rally Was Dismal Flop*, 29th August 1948
7. Illustrated London News 1948
8. O'CONNOR, Garry. *Darlings of the Gods,* Hodder & Stoughton, London, 1984 pg.133

CHAPTER 13

1. VICKERS Hugo, *Vivien Leigh,* Hamish Hamilton, London, 1988 pg. 186
2. *A Notable Visit*, Northern Advocate, 7 September 1948
3. *The Oliviers; Old Vic Company Principals* Press, Volume LXXXIV, Issue 25604, 20 September 1948, Page 6. Paperspast.natlib.govt.nz
4. VICKERS Hugo, *Vivien Leigh,* Hamish Hamilton, London pg. 186
5. MONIN Paul, *Matiatia: Gateway to Waiheke*, Bridget Williams Books, 2012 pg.52
6. O'CONNOR Garry, *Darlings of The Gods,* Hodder & Stoughton, London, 1984, pg. 13
7. OLIVIER Laurence, September 20, 1948, Letter to Thornton Wilder, Thornton Wilder Papers, Yale Beinecke Library
8. O'CONNOR Garry, *Darlings of The Gods,* Hodder & Stoughton, London, 1984 pg. 144
9. *Presentation to the Oliviers* Press Volume LXXXIV, Issue 25612, 29 September 1948. Paperspast.natlib.gov.nz
10. OTAGO DAILY TIMES *Old Vic Celebrities*, 30 September 1948
11. OTAGO DAILY TIMES *True Fish Story*, Issue 26894, 5 October 1948
12. OTAGO DAILY TIMES *Professional Theatre*, Issue 26892, 2 October 1948
13. Ibid
14. MORGAN Georgina, *Laughter in the Air*, The Book Guild Ltd, 2011, pg. 95
15. O'CONNOR Garry, *Darlings of The Gods,* Hodder & Stoughton, London, 1984 pg. 147
16. WANGANUI CHRONICLE *Compliments Fly at Reception to The Oliviers,* 5 October 1948
17. OTAGO DAILY TIMES Issue 26916, 30 October, pg. 8
18. HUTT NEWS *Old Vic Tour Ending*, 13 October, 1948
19. OLIVIER Laurence, September 20, 1948, Letter to Thornton Wilder, Thornton Wilder Papers, Yale Beinecke Library
20. OLIVIER Laurence, October 15th, 1948, Letter to Cecil Beaton, Victoria & Albert Museum, Vivien Leigh Archive, THM 433/2/1-2
21. HUTT NEWS *Good-Bye to Old Vic. Impressions of Tour,* Volume X11, Issue 19, 20 October 1948, pg. 11
22. NORTHERN ADVOCATE *Oliviers' Farewell To 'Dear Audiences'* 18 October 1948

CHAPTER 14

1. Kindly provided by Keith Lodwick – V&A, palm reading, Vivien Leigh Archive
2. OLIVIER Laurence, September 20, 1948, Letter to Thornton Wilder, Thornton Wilder Papers, Yale Beinecke Library
3. VICKERS Hugo, *Vivien Leigh*, Hamish Hamilton, London,1988, pg.197
4. STRACHAN Alan, *Dark Star* I.B Tauris & Co. Ltd, London, New York, 2019. pg. 278
5. BARNARD John, *Leigh and a Cultural Whinge*, Sydney Morning Herald, May 7 1990
6. Graeme Gillespie to author 25 February 2022
7. OIVLIER Laurence, Letter to Thornton Wilder, Thornton Wilder Papers, Yale Beinecke Library, 20 September 1948
8. THE ARGUS *Funeral of Drake TV actor,* 2 September 2005
9. MORGAN Georgina. *Laughter in the air. A Tale of Love, Stage and Screen,* The Book Guild Ltd, 2011 pg. 159
10. COTTRELL John, *Laurence Olivier*, Weidenfeld and Nicolson, London, 1975 pg. 237
11. Taylor, James Lee (2018). *Shakespeare, Decolonisation, and the Cold War*. PhD thesis, The Open University, pg. 97
12. Ibid
13. Ibid pg. 123
14. Ibid
15. THE HERALD *The Oliviers Liked Us.* 18 November 1948
16. *Larry and Vivien: The Oliviers in Love*, BBC documentary, 2001
17. OLIVIER Laurence, *Confessions of an Actor,* George Weidenfeld & Nicolson, 1982, pg. 140
18. COWARD Noel letter to 'Marya' 13 July 1967 from Les Avants, Sur Montreux image Heritage Auctions, HA.com
19. FAULKNER Trader, *Larry and Vivien; The Oliviers in Love*, BBC documentary 2001

POSTSCRIPT

1. MARTIN Ray, *Ray: Stories of My Life*, William Heinemann, Australia, 2010, pg. 142
2. Judith Koop, personal communication with author, 23 November 2020
3. LEIGH Vivien, letter to Peter Wyngarde, September 6th 1961, on Bellevue letterhead, Brisbane. *Greta Ritchie Collection*

Bibliography

BOOKS

ARAYA Margarida. *Laurence Olivier Stage Work,* Amazon Digital Services, 2019

BARKER Felix. *The Oliviers*. London: Hamish Hamilton, 1953

BEAN Kendra. *Vivien Leigh, An Intimate Portrait:* Running Press, Philadelphia, 2013

Beyond the Stage, Creative Australian Stories from the Great War, edited by Anna Goldsworthy and Mark Carroll, Wakefield Press, 2020

BLAKEMORE Michael. *Arguments with England A Memoir,* Faber and Faber Limited, London, 2004

COLLIS Rose. *Coral Browne: 'This Effing Lady',* Oberon Books Ltd, 2007

COTTRELL John. *Laurence Olivier,* Weidenfeld & Nicolson, London, 1975

COLEMAN Terry. *Olivier,* Henry Hold and Company, New York, 2005

CROMBIE Isobel. *Athol Shmith: Photographer,* Schwartz Publishing Pty Ltd, Melbourne, 1989

COURTNEIDGE Cicely. *Cicely,* Hutchinson & Co. Ltd, London, 1953

CUSHING Peter. *An Autobiography* Weidenfeld and Nicolson, London, 1986

DUNDY Elaine. *Finch, Bloody Finch. A life of Peter Finch by Elain Dundy,* Holt, Rinehart and Winston, New York, 1980

FAIRWEATHER Virginia. *Cry God for Larry,* Calder & Boyars, London, 1969

FAULKNER Trader. *Peter Finch, A Biography* Angus & Robertson, UK, 1979

FITTON Doris. *Not Without Dust and Heat; My Life in Theatre,* Harper & Row, Sydney, 1981

GALLOWAY Stephen. *Truly Madly: Vivien Leigh, Laurence Olivier and the Romance of the Century,* Grand Central Publishing, 2022

HOLDEN Anthony. *Laurence Olivier: A Biography,* Macmillan Publishing Company, New York, 1988

Historic Houses of Australia, Australian Council of National Trusts, Wilke and Company Ltd, 1974

LASKY Jesse & Pat Silver. *Love Scene,* Berkeley Books, New York, 1978

LAWRENCE James. *Churchill and Empire: A Portrait of an Imperialist* Weidenfeld & Nicolson, London, 2013

LAWSON Valerie. *Dancing under the southern skies: a history of ballet in Australia,* Australian Scholarly Publishing Pty Ltd, 2019

LEWIS Roger. *The Real Life of Laurence Olivier* Century Books Ltd, 1996

MARTIN Ray. *Ray: Stories of My Life,* William Heinemann, Australia, 2010

MONIN Paul. *Matiatia; Gateway to Waiheke,* Bridget Williams Books, 2012

MORGAN Georgina. *Laughter in the Air,* Book Guild Publishing, 2011

O'CONNOR Garry. *Darlings of the Gods. One Year in the lives of Laurence Olivier and Vivien Leigh:* Hodder and Stoughton, London, 1984

OLIVIER Laurence. *Confessions of An Actor,* Weidenfeld & Nicolson, London, 1982

Vivien Leigh Actress and Icon, edited by Kate Dorney and Maggie B. Gale, Manchester University Press, 2018

SPICER J Chrystopher. *Duchess The Story of the Windsor Hotel,* Lord Haven Books, 1993

STACKER Lorraine. *Pictorial History Penrith and St Marys,* Kingsclear Books, 2002

STEAD Lisa. *Reframing Vivien Leigh, Stardom, Gender, and the Archive* Oxford University Press, 2021

STRACHAN Alan. *Dark Star, A Biography of Vivien Leigh,* I.B Tauris & Co. Ltd, London, New York, 2019

VICKERS Hugo. *Vivien Leigh A Biography,* Little Brown and Company, London, 1988

THORNE Ross. *Picture Palace Architecture* Sun Books Pty Ltd, 1976

WALKER Alexander. *Vivien, The Life of Vivien Leigh,* George Weidenfeld and Nicolson Ltd, 1987

Index

Italic numbers refer to images and captions.

A

Actors Equity, Australian 66–7, 78, 122, 218
Adelaide (SA), and 1948 tour: city's character/ attractions 88, 90, *91*, 92, 97, *98*, 99, 101; company's performances *86* (*89*), 92, 94, 96; relaxing/ sightseeing (incl. road trip eastwards) 92, 97, *98*, 99, *100*, 101, 109, 184 (see also Mount Gambier); ticket sales 81–2, 92, 94, 96, 112; Oliviers' arrival/ departure *89*, 90; ambassadorial workload *44*, 46, 92, *93*, 94, *95*, 96–7, 109
Agate, James 35
Albery, Bronson 156
Alden, John 226
Amies, Hardy 42, 43, *44*, 46, 49
Andrews, Robert (Bobbie) *59*, 61
Anna Karenina (film) 22, 23–4, 189
ANZAC Day, and Oliviers 114
Archerfield Airport, Brisbane *176* (*179*), 178, *179*, *188*, 189, *223*
Armitage, Mary 96
Atheneum Theatre, Melbourne 133
Atherton, Barbara 75
Attwood, Joyce 14, 125, 232, 233
Attwood, Mary Ann 125
Auckland (NZ), and 1948 tour: city's character/ attractions 196, *196*, 198; company's performances 198; ticket sales 198; Oliviers' arrival 178, *193*, *194*, 195; ambassadorial workload 49, *194*, 195, 196, *197*, 198
Australia Hotel, Sydney 149
Australia/ Australians post-WWII, and Britain 10, 28, 31, 49, 65, 88, 90, 94, 108, 118, 119, 214, 225–6
Australian Elizabethan Theatre Trust, The 215, 220–1, 226
Australian flora/ fauna/ landscape: and Oliviers 14, 36, *62* (*65*), 66, 73, 76, 82, 96, 101, *102*, 103, 122, 167, 184, 233; and other tour members 182
Australian Government, and post-war theatre policy 36, 225, 226
Australian High Commissioner (in London) *29*, 36
Australian theatre architecture/ heritage, and Oliviers 75, 76, 78, 92, 112, 130–1, 133, 136, 163, 184
Australian theatre talent/ scene: Oliviers' encouragement of/ impact on 12, 36, 78, 97, 112, 158, 163, 171, 174 (see also National Theatre); other 1948 cast/ crew members' impact on 158, 215, 217, 218, 220–1

B

Baddeley, Angela 35
Bailey, James (Jimmy) 35, 156, 215, 217–18, *219*, 220
Bailey, Margaret (Peggy) 218
Ballet Rambert 28, 31, 67
Banks, Norm 109
Barker, Felix 23, 28, 37
Barnard, John (Pip) 35, 215, 217, *219*, 220
Barr Smith, Ursula 96
Bayliss, Lilian 31, 32
Beasley, Mr 36
Beaton, Cecil 22, 23, 36, 81, 114, 180, 209
Beaumont, Hugh 101, 220
Beaumont, Robert 35
Beck, Helen (also Helen Cushing) 33, 75
Beldon, Eileen 35, 180, 182, 224
Bellon, Brent 81
Beyer, Elsie 53, *53*, 58, 61, 82, 85, 119, 133, *134*, 149, 158, 162, 220–1, 226
Blakemore, Michael 15, 33, 153, 155, 165, 224–5
Blue Mountains (NSW), and Oliviers 156, *157*, 161
Bonython, Sir Lavington 94
Bowers, Raymond 81
Boyd Neel Orchestra 28, 31
Brereton, Austin 112
Brisbane (Qld), and 1948 tour: city's character/ attractions 178, 180, 182, 184; company's performances 178, 180, *181*; relaxing/ sightseeing *181*, 182; ticket sales 180; Oliviers' ambassadorial workload *44*, 180, 182, *183*, 184, *186*, *187*, *223*; arrival/ departure *176* (*179*), 178, *179*, *188*, 189, *223*

British Council, and politico-cultural diplomacy generally 28, 31, 42; and Old Vic's 1948 tour specifically 32, 33, 35–6, 37, 42, 49, 67, 73, 75, 94, 114, *115*, 133, 170–1, 208, 225, 226, 228; in 1950s and beyond 225–6

British cultural ambassadors, Oliviers as: overview 10, *29*, 31, *32*, 33, 36, 37, 40, 42, 43, 46, 48, 49, 61, 73, 92, 94, 114, 118, 148, 214, 224, 228 (see also Food for Britain Appeal); specifically: attending civic/ cultural/ society engagements 10, 33, 37, *44*, 45–6, 48, *74*, 76, *77*, 78, *79*, 82, 85, 92, *93*, 94, *95*, 96–7, 114, *115*, *116*, *117*, 118, 119, 122, *132*, 133, 148, *150*, *152*, 153, *159*, 162–3, *164*, 165, *166*, *182*, *183*, 184, *186*, *187*, 195, 201, 204, 206, 207–8, 224; demonstrating local knowledge/ interest 64, 73, 80–1, 85, 99, 109, 119, 153, 173, 204; encouraging worthy local endeavour 12, *77*, 78, 158, 163, 201; engaging with media 12, 18, 33, 36, 45–6, 49, 61, *68* (*71*), *72*, 73, 76, 80, 81, 85, 92, *93*, 94, 106, 108, 109, *110*, 119, *130*, *146* (*149*), 149, 180, 184, 204; interacting with fans/ public 36, 61, 75, 76, 78, 80, 82, 85, 92, 94, 96, *110*, 111, 125, 129, *183*, *194*, 195, 196, 198, 199, *223*, 232; making speeches/ broadcasts 10, 12, 33, 61, 76, 80–1, 82, 85, 96, 112, 118, 119, 131, 163, 165, 171, *174*, 184, *185*, *187*, 204, 206, 209, 211; maintaining connections/ return visits 78, 111, 125, 133, 165, 196, 232, 233; manifesting charm/ grace 36, 73, 81, 82, 85, 106, *113*, 125, 165, 171, 173, 195, 198, 204, 208, 211; promoting best of British: see celebrity couple; royalty of British screen/ stage; royalty surrogates; Vivien as fashion/ style icon; Olivier as finest Shakespearean actor of era; receiving gifts/ tributes *68* (*71*), 81, 82, 94, 109, *110*, *113*, 114, 122, *154*, 163, 165, 167, 196, 202, 204, 209

British Drama League, Sydney 163, *166*

British High Commissions: in Canberra 31; in Cape Town 59, 61

British patriots/ nationalists, Oliviers as 33, 108, 114, 118, 214

Broadbeach (Qld) see Surfers Paradise

Brown, Mollie *159*

Browne, Coral *115*

Buckingham Palace, London, Oliviers at *25*

Buring, Leo and Ida 156 (see also Leonay)

Burrell, John 12, 20, 119, 155

Bushell, Anthony 23

C

Caesar and Cleopatra (film) 204

Calwell, Arthur 65

Cameron, Sir Donald 204

Canary Islands see Las Palmas

Canberra (ACT), and 1948 tour: city's character/ attractions 114, *117*; Oliviers' arrival *116*; ambassadorial workload *8* (*11*), 67, 114, 118

Canterbury University, Christchurch 201

Cape Town (South Africa), and 1948 tour 43, *59*, 61

Capitol Theatre, Canberra 118

Capitol Theatre, Perth 75–6, 80, 81, 151, 198

Carrick Hill estate (Adelaide) 96, 97, *97*

Carr, Mollie (née Davis) 196

Carroll, Garnet H. 112, 122

Cedars estate, The (Adelaide Hills) 99, 101

celebrity couple, Oliviers as 10, 12, 15, 33, 36, 48, 228–9 (see also British cultural ambassadors; royalty surrogates); embodied style and glamour *8* (*11*), 10, *11*, *13*, 15, *16* (*19*), *21*, *25*, *29*, 33, *37*, 48, *68* (*71*), *74*, *84*, *89*, *93*, *110*, *116*, *132*, *154*, *174*, *176* (*179*), *179*, *183*, *186*, *187*, *193*, *227*, 228, *229*, *230* (*233*), (*233*) 234–5 (see also Vivien, as fashion/ style icon); professional partnership 10, 22, 24, *29*, *32*, 33, 35, 36, *37*, 58, 61, 118, *137*, 155, 158, 161, 167, 173, *181*, 195, 199, 201, 202, *202*, 204, 208, 209, 215, *222*, 228, 229 (see also Old Vic's 1948 tour, and individual cities); romantic partnership 10, 12, 14, 20, 22, 23, 24, 46, 144, 155, 173, 174, 175, 184, 189, 195–6, 199, 208, 215, 228–9, 232, 233; stress points for 10, 12, 22, 23, 24, 35, 37, 61, 119, 140, 148, 155, 167, 168, 169, 170, 189, 195, 201, 214, 228, 232

Centennial Park, Sydney 156

Chifley, Ben 64, 67, 114, 225

Christchurch (NZ): city's character/ attractions 198, 199, *200*, 201, 202, *203*; welcome to traditional Maori land 201–2; company's performances 201; relaxing/ sightseeing 201, 202, *202*, 204; Oliviers' arrival/ departure 198–9, 204; ambassadorial workload 199, 201

City Hotel, The, Dunedin 204

Claremont Yacht Club, Perth 82 (see also *Sabina*)

Clarke, James 96

Clerici, Tony 162

Cloudland Ballroom, Brisbane 182–3

Coffin, Clifford *41*, *47*

Coleman, Terry 22, 155, 158

Coleman and Sons (UK company) 45

Cooper, George 35

SS *Corinthic* (ship) *50* (*53*), 52–3, *53*, 54–6, 58, *60*, 61, *72*, 73, *190* (*193*), 207, 211, 215, 220

Cotton, Louis (Lewy) 90

coughing theatregoers, and Olivier 119
Courtneidge, Cicely 180
Coward, Noël 11, 23, 90, 223, 229, 233
cricket matches, Old Vic team vs others: in Brisbane *181*, 182; in Melbourne 161; in Sydney 156, 158
'cultural cringe', Australian 49, 88, 90, 108, 119, 120, 173
Cunningham, Dan 35, *55*, *56*, *121*, 122, 136, 140, 144, 228
Curtin, John 65
Cushing, Helen see Beck, Helen
Cushing, Peter 33, 73, 75, 81, 119, 161, 180, 218

D
Daneman, Meredith see Kinmont, Meredith
Daneman, Paul 94
Dare, Zena *59*
Davis, Eliot 196
Davis, Sir Ernest 196, 198
Davis, Mollie see Carr, Mollie
de Valois, Ninette 103
Delanghe, Angele 45
Denham Film Studios (UK) 18
Devine, George 155
Dior, Christian 43, 45, 48
Donald, Ian 198
Donaldson, Marie 75
Dundy, Elaine 169, 173, 175, 229
Dunedin (NZ): city's character/ attractions 204; company's performances 204, 206; relaxing/ sightseeing *205, 206*; ticket sales 204, 206; Oliviers' ambassadorial workload 204, 206; departure 206
Durham Cottage (Oliviers' London home) 36

E
Eager, Sir Clifden 117
Eager, Muriel 117
Elephant Walk (film) 174–5
Embassy Theatre, Sydney 165
Empire Youth Rally (Melbourne), and Olivier 120
Esher, Lord 32, 155, 156
Esmond, Jill (Olivier's wife #1) 22, 175, 201, 229
Essendon Airport, Melbourne 129, *212* (*215*)
Etches, Matilda 42–3, 45, *47*
Euston Station, London, Oliviers at *29*, 36
Evatt, Herbert 153
Exhibition Grounds, Brisbane *44*, 184, *186*, *187*

F
fan encounters/ memories 10, 15, 33, 37, 78, 80, 81, 82, 85, 90, 92, 94, 96, *110*, 111, *113*, *124*, 125, 129, 136, 153, 155, 163, *164*, 165, *166*, 171, 173, 174, 180, 182, *194*, 195, 196, 198, 199, 208, 211, *223*, 224, 225, 232, 233
fan frenzy, and 1948 tour 10, 37, 82, 85, 90, 92, 129, 140, 151, 163, *212* (*215*)
Faulkner, Ronald ('Trader') 170, 171, 173, 174, 175, 184
Ffrangcon-Davies, Gwen *59*, 61
Finch, George (Peter's father) 168
Finch, Laura (Peter's grandmother) 168
Finch, Peter: early years 167, 168–9, 170, 175; as actor/ teacher 12, 151, 168, 169, *169*, 170, 171, *172*, 173, 174–5, 221; as poet 175; as talent-spotted by Oliviers 12, 167, 168, 170, 171; affair, significant with Vivien 12, 151, 167–8, 169–70, 174–5; marriages: #1 see Tamara Tchinarova Finch, #2 see Yolande Finch; posthumous honours: Academy Award 174 (see also Mercury Theatre)
Finch, Tamara Tchinarova (Peter's wife #1) 12, 170, 173, 174, 175
Finch, Yolande (Peter's wife #2) 175
Firth, Vincent 173–4
Fitton, Doris 158, *159*
Flinders Naval depot, Melbourne, and Oliviers 120
Flockhart, Trudi 232, 233
Floy, Bell 171, 204
Fontanne, Lynn (also Lynn Lunt) 20
Food for Britain Appeal, and Oliviers *15*, *44*, 46, 48, 94, 118, 162–3, 184, *186*, *187*, 195
Freeman, Carol 136
Fremantle (WA) see Perth (WA)

G
Galloway, Stephen 20, 22
Gardiner, Captain Robert 103
Gascoigne, Clifford 196
Gavin, Tony 35
Gilbert, Olive *59*
Gillan, Sir Angus 28
Gillespie, Graeme 218
Glenn's Newsagency, Melbourne 112, *113*
Goers, Peter 92
Goldwyn, Samuel 33
Gone with the Wind (film) 22, 23, 24, 35, 97
Gooderham, Nan 114
Gordon, Adam Lindsay 103

Government House, Yarralumla (Canberra), and Oliviers 114, *117*, 118
Government House, Old, Brisbane 184, *185*, *186*
Grand Hotel, Auckland 196, 198
Greenberg, Joel 217
Greta Army Camp (NSW), and Oliviers *152*
Guinness, Alec 23
Guthrie, Tyrone 32, 155–6, 225

H
Hamilton, Jamie 52
Hamlet (film) 18, 22, 24, *24*, *25*, 33, 36, 94, 133, 153, 165, 218, 221
Hamlet (play) 23
Harewood Airport, Christchurch 198–9, 204
Hartley, Gertrude (Vivien's mother) 23, 58, 120
Harris, Mrs R.O. *132*
Hayward, Edward 96
Healesville Sanctuary (Vic.), and Oliviers 122
Heathcote, Thomas *157*
Hefti, Mrs R.W. 80
Helpmann, Robert 103, 149, 151, 232, 233
Herbst, Gerard 114
Heysen, Hans *89*, 99, 101; Hans Heysen Trust 101
Heysen, Sallie 99
Hiley, Peter 155, 170–1, 225
His Majesty's Museum of Performing Arts, Perth 218
His Majesty's Theatre, Dunedin 204
Hobart (Tas.) and 1948 tour: city's character/ attractions 128, *129*, 129, *130*, 130, *131*, 131, *135*; company's performances *32*, 130, 133; published booklet *32*, 131, 133; relaxing/ sightseeing *30*, *126* (*129*), *131*, 133, *134*, 136; Oliviers' ambassadorial workload 130–1, *132*
Holman, Leigh (Vivien's husband #1) 22, 58, 192, 201, 229
Hopper, Hedda 49
Hotel St George, Wellington 207
Howes, Sally Ann 24
Humphries, Walter 67
Hunt, Hugh 226
Hunter, Oliver 35

I
Independent Theatre, Sydney 158, *159*, 226

J
Jackson, Sir Barry 182
Jarvis, M.W. 78, 80
Jen's Hotel, Mount Gambier *101*, 101, 103
John Alden's Australian Shakespeare Company 226
Jonah's diner, Whale Beach (Sydney) 161, *162*
Jordan, W.J. 36
Joyce, Eileen *115*
Jumel, Georgina (also Georgina Morgan) 33, *55*, 196, 206, *206*, 207, 208, 215, 221, 228
Jury, C.R. 94

K
Karara (fashion journalist) 46
Kay, John 170, 171
Kennedy, Michalle *194*, 195
Kentish, David *55*, 173
Kerridge Odeon (company) 67, 199
Killara Camellia Flower Show (Sydney) 48, 162–3, *164*
King Lear (play) 22
Kinmont, Joan 94
Kinmont, Meredith (also Meredith Daneman) 94
Knickerbocker, H.R. 70, 73
Koop, Judith 233
Ku-ring-gai Horticultural Society (Sydney) 162–3

L
La Guardia Airport (New York), Oliviers at *16* (*19*), 20, 57
Lady of the Camellias (play) 215, 217
Lake St Clair (Tas.) *126* (*129*), 133, *134*
Las Palmas (Canary Islands), Oliviers in *47*, 54, *55*, *56*, 58
Laurence Olivier Productions (UK company) 170, 171, 225, 228
Laver, Ivy 111
Laver, Richard *110*, 111
Lawrence, Warwick 180
Lawson, Valerie 31
Lee, Vanessa *59*, 61
Legh, Pat 165, 167
Lehrer, Denis 35
Leigh, Vivien (also Lady Vivien Olivier): early years 64, 175, 184; as fashion/ style icon *29*, 36, *38* (*41*), 40, *41*, 42–3, 44, 45–6, *47*, 48–9, 57, 61, 73, 78, *104* (*107*), 114, *115*, 118, *132*, *150*, *164*, 201; as film star 10, 22, 23, 24, 33, 35, 57, 73, 195, 204, 206, 209, 217, 228; as Old Vic's 1948 tour co-leader see Old Vic's 1948 tour; as stage actor

10, 18, 20, 22, 24, 32, 33, 35, 36, *37*, 73, 81, 92, 94, 96, 99, 114, 118, 133, *137*, 153, *154*, 155, 173, *181*, 201, 204, *208*, 211, 215, 217, *222*, 224; as wine connoisseur 97, *98*, 99, 156; affair, significant see Peter Finch; estate auction see Sotheby's Vivien Leigh Estate Auction; estate personal effects and fans 233; feline companions 36, 45, 184, *188*, 189; health issues 12, 18, 20, 22, 23, 24, 57, 58, 119, 122, 148, 158, 167, 175, 178, 189, 214–15, 224, 233; home see Notley Abbey; leisure interests 18, 22, 58, 61, 64, 199; marriages: #1 see Leigh Holman; #2 (Sir Laurence Olivier) see celebrity couple; overwork 20, 22, 24, 58, 75, 119, 148–9, 178, 182, 195, 199, 201, 204, 224; partnership, end-of-life see Jack Merivale; portrait 208, *208*, 209; professional income 33, 228; voice 42, 81

Lennons Hotel, Brisbane 178, *179*
Leonay (Buring home), Nepean River (NSW) 156, *157*
Lewisham Private Hospital, Wellington 209
Light, Colonel William 88
Lodwick, Keith 40
Lorimer, William John (Jack) *79*, 82
Lorking, Diana *95*, 96
Lucas, Betty 94
Lunt, Alfred 20
Lunt, Lynn see Fontanne, Lynn

M

Manzie, F. Keith 108
Marian Street Theatre for Young People, Sydney 163
Marshall, Peggy *157*
Martin, Ray 144, 232
Marx, Chico 120, 122
Maxwell, Meg 35
McGrath, Anne 35
McIntyre, Peter 208–9
McKell, Governor-General William 114
Melbourne (Vic.), and 1948 tour: city's character/ attractions 106, *107*, 108, 109, 111, 112, 161; company's performances 101, 112, 114, 118–19, 120; relaxing/ sightseeing 120, *121*, 122, 161, *223*; ticket sales 112; Oliviers' ambassadorial workload 46, 106, 108–9, *110*, 112, *113*, 114, *115*, *117*, 119, 120, 122, 232; departure 129, *212* (*215*)
Melbourne Cricket Ground 161
Menzies, Robert 65, 225
Menzies Hotel, Melbourne 106, 109, 114, *115*

Mercer family (Melbourne) 111
Mercury Theatre, Sydney 170, 221
Mereford, Bernard 35
Merivale, Jack (Vivien's end-of-life partner) 111, 225, 232, 233
Metcalfe, John 165, *166*
Miller, Tatlock 151
Mills, James 226
Mills, John 35
Mirman, Simone 46
Mitchell, Sir James and Lady 76, 80
Mitchell, Sir William *95*
Moncrieff, Gladys *115*
Moore, Kieron 23–4
SS *Moreton Bay* (ship) 36
Morgan, Georgina see Jumel, Georgina
Morgan, Lyvia Lee 221
Morgan, Terence 33, *55*, 81, 180, 221, 228
Mount Donna Buang (Vic.) 122, (*122*) 123
Mount Gambier (SA) *101*, 101, *102*, 103
Mount Wellington (also Kunanyi), Hobart 128, 133, *134*
Mosca, Bianca 45
Myer, Sidney and Mrs 122

N

Nash, Walter 207–8
National Theatre, push for: and Australian scene 131, 133, 220, 225, 226 (see also Australian Elizabethan Theatre Trust); and British scene 33, 156, 214, 224–5, 228; and New Zealand scene 204, 206
New South Wales, and 1948 tour see Sydney
New York, Oliviers in *16* (*19*), 20, 24, 57, 158
New Zealand (Aotearoa), and 1948 tour: country's character/ attractions 192, 195, 196, *196*, 198, 199, *200*, 201, 202, *203*, 204, 207; welcome to traditional Maori land 201–2; company's performances 195, 198, 201, 204, 206, 208, 209, *210*; relaxing/ sightseeing 201, 202, *202*, 204, *205, 206*; ticket sales 198, 204, 206, 207, 208; Oliviers' ambassadorial workload 49, *194*, 195, 196, *197*, 198, 199, 201, 204, 206, 207–8, 209, 211; arrival/ departure *190* (*193*), *193*, *194*, 206, 211 (see also individual cities)
New Zealand flora/ fauna/ landscape, and Oliviers 14, 192, *203*, 204; and cast members *206*
New Zealand High Commissioner (in London) 29, 36
New Zealand theatre architecture/ heritage, and Oliviers *197*, 198

New Zealand theatre talent/ scene, Oliviers' encouragement of/ impact on 12, 36, 195, 196, 201, 204, 206, 209, 211 (see also National Theatre)
New Zealand/ New Zealanders post-WWII, and Britain 65, 208, 214
Newport (Qld), and Olivier 144, 232
Notley Abbey (Oliviers' Buckinghamshire home, UK) 18, *19*, 20, 22, 58, 97, 189, 225, 233; furnishings and garden cuttings acquired on 1948 tour 99, 101, 201
Novello, Ivor 59, 61

O

O'Brien, Louisa 90
O'Brien's Glass Factory, Sydney (venue) 171, *172*
O'Connor, Dan 28, 75, 109
O'Connor, Garry 14, 15, 75, 78, 106, 119, 128, 140, 155–6, 163, 168, 184, 189, 199, 201, 224, 229,
Oberman, Ray 92
Old Vic Theatre Company: history 31–2; Governors/ Board 12, 32, 35–6, 155–6, 170, 225; directorship by 'triumvirate' (incl. Olivier) 12, 20, 22, 33, 155, 156; triumvirate terminated 12, 155–6, 158, 170, 228
Old Vic's 1945–46 Europe tour (incl. Olivier but not Vivien) 20, 35, 167
Old Vic's 1948 tour to Australasia: genesis 10, 24, 28, 32–3; advance party 36, 75, 111; British Council involvement see British Council; British send-off for *29*, 36, 52; company cast/ crew 30, 33, 35, *60*, *72*, *134*, 165, 167; company celebrating birthdays 120, 122, 133, *134*, 161, *162*, 162, 201, 202, 215, *216*, 232; company relaxing/ sightseeing 14, *30*, 53, *54–6*, 57, 58, *60*, 61, 82, *83*, *84*, 85, *98*, *134*, 136, *138* (*141*), 141–4, 144, *145*, *160*, 161–2, *162*, *181*, 182, 184, 202, *205*, *206*, *216*, *223*, 230; industrial issues for see Actors Equity, Australian; Oliviers as company's leaders 10, 12, 15, *29*, 31, 33, 35, 36, 42, 61, 64, 67, 75–6, 81, 161, 182, 201, 209, *216*, 217, 220, 224, 228 (see also British cultural ambassadors; celebrity couple/ professional partnership; individual cities toured); Oliviers as parent surrogates/ mentors 12, 161, 167, *202*, 215, 229, 232, 233; photographic record 12, 14, 52, 82, 85, 103, 120, 122, 129–30, 133, 165; rehearsals 36, 53, 57, 61, 73, 78, 171, 173, 217, 228; repertoire *34*, 35–6 (see also individual plays); ship travel experience see SS *Corinthic*; ship travel reasons 20, 57, 214–15; souvenir program, official 26 (*29*), 31, 151, *152*; stage performances see cities toured; tour's dimensions: artistic 14; cultural 10, 12, 36, 66; financial 10, 12, 14, 32, 225, 228; political 10, 28, 31, 32, 37, 42, 46, 64–5, 94, 114, 225, 226 (see also British Council; Food for Britain Appeal)
Old Vic's 1961 tour to Australasia (incl. Vivien but not Olivier) 111, 125, 215, 217, 220, 232, 233
Olivier, Sir Laurence: early years 158; as film star/ director 10, 18, 22, 24, *24*, 33, 36, 73, 94, 133, 156, 165, 195, 204, 209, 228; as finest Shakespearean actor of era 10, 24, 35, 92, 94, 153; as an Old Vic 'triumvirate' director 12, 18, 20, 22, 33, 35, 36, 155, 156, 158, 167, 170 (see also Old Vic's 1948 tour); as post-Old Vic director 170, 171, 202, 214, 225, 228; as stage actor/ director 10, 20, 22, 24, 32, 33, 35, 36, *37*, 42, 57–8, 61, 73, 81, 92, 94, 96, 99, 103, 112, 114, 118–19, 120, 133, *137*, 153, 155, 156, *172*, 173, 175, *181*, 201, 204, 208, *210*, 211, *222*, 224; as talent spotter/ actor mentor 33, 94, 167, 168, 170–1, *172*, 173, 218, 221; as wine connoisseur 99, 156; biography draft by sister 158; health issues 12, 18, 20, 57, 75, 78, 80, 82, 119, 140, 155, 158, 170, *172*, 201, 202, 207, 209, *210*, 214, 215, *216*; home see Notley Abbey; honorary degrees 20, *21*; knighthood 23, 24, *25*, 214; leisure interests 18, 58, 61, 199; marriages: #1 see Jill Esmond, #2 (Vivien Leigh) see celebrity couple, #3 see Joan Plowright; overwork 18, 20, 22, 24, 57–8, 61, 78, 119, 148, 178, 182, 184, 195, 199, 201, 204, 209, 214, 224; professional income 22, 33, 228; voice 10, 42, 81, 92, 94, 136, 153, 165
Olivier, Sybille (Olivier's sister) 158
Otago University, Dunedin 204, 206
Otahuna Lodge, Canterbury (NZ) 202, *203*

P

Parafield Airport, Adelaide *89*, 90
Parliament Buildings, Wellington, and Oliviers 207–8
Parliament House, Melbourne, and Oliviers *108*, *117*
Paterson, A.B. ('Banjo') 64
Pavlova, Anna 90, 99
Penley, Derrick 35
Perth (WA), and 1948 tour: city's character/ attractions 70, *71*, 73, 75, 76, 78, 80, 192; company's arrival/ departure 68 (*71*), *72*, 73, 75, 85; performances 80, 81, 85, 94; relaxing/ sightseeing 75, 76, 82, *83*, *84*, 85, 184; ticket sales *77*, 78, 80; Oliviers' ambassadorial workload 45–6, 68 (*71*), *72*, 73, *74*, 75, 76, *77*, 78, *79*, 80–1, 82, 85, 184
Perth Zoo 82

Peterson, Joel 94
Peterson, Ralph 94
Phillips, A.A. 88
Pickworth, John 49
Pissot et Pavy (milliners) 45
Plowright, Joan (Olivier's wife #3) 94, 119
Pound, Reginald 18
Powe, Joan 165, 167
Powell, Alicia 163, 165
Prestige Ltd, Melbourne 114
Pride and Prejudice (film) 204
Prince Charles and Princess Diana, comparison with Oliviers 10, 12, 208, 214
Princess Theatre, Melbourne 76, 112, 118, 119, 122, 125

Q
Queensland: and 1948 tour see Brisbane; Surfers Paradise; and 1977 visit by Olivier see Newport
Quick, Harriet 40
Quinn, John 170

R
Rafferty, Chips 156, 158
Ramsdale, Roger 136, 140
Rank, J. Arthur 22, 67
Redington, Michael 35, 75, 80, 92, 120, 128, 207, 215, 217, 224, 235
Reelers Fraternity (WA) 82, 85
Relph, George 33, *54*, *55*, 58, 153, 180, 224
Relph, Mercia see Swinburne, Mercia
Richard III (play) 32, *34*, 35, 61, 92, 94, 118–19, 153, 155, *172*, 173, 182, 201, 208, *210*, 217, 218, 220, 224
Richardson, Ralph 12, 20, 23, 32, 155, 156, 228
Romano's restaurant, Sydney 162
Royal Queensland Yacht Club 182
royalty of the British screen/ stage, Oliviers as 10, 15, 33, 40, 48, 64, 78, 184, 195
royalty surrogates, Oliviers as 10, 33, 40, 61, 64–5, 195, 208, 214, 226 (see also British cultural ambassadors)

S
Sabina (boat) 82, *83*
St George's Society Ball, Brisbane 182, *183*
St James Theatre, Auckland *197*, 198
St James Theatre, Christchurch 199, 201
St James Theatre, London 92

Sainthill, Loudon 151
Salmon, William 114
Satchwell, Ian 133
Scarborough Beach (WA) *13*, 76, 84, 85
School for Scandal, The (play) 34, 36, *37*, 57–8, 61, 75, 81, 85, 112, 118–19, 130, 153, *154*, 155, 171, 178, 180, *181*, 208, *208*, 209, 217, 220, *222*
Seldon, Haydee 159
Shakespeare, William: and British cultural diplomacy 10, 12, 31, 42, 226; in Australian library collection see State Library of New South Wales; in Australian theatre programs 12, 35, 36, 66, 226
Sharp, Lyn 94
Sherbrooke Forest, Melbourne 233
Shirley, Jane 35
Shmith, Louis Athol 14, 120, 122
Simmons, Jean 22, *24*, 221
Simon, Andre 156
Simpson, Peggy 35, *54*, 58
Sinclair, Julie *164*
Skin of Our Teeth, The (play) 18, 20, 22, 24, 32, *34*, 35–6, 42, 58, *86* (*89*), 94, 96, 119, 120, 155, 173, 217
Sotheby's Vivien Leigh Estate Auction (2017) 14, 40, *89*, 94, 101, 163
South Australia, and 1948 tour see Adelaide
South Australia Hotel, Adelaide 90, *91*
Spicer, Christopher J. 111
State Library of New South Wales (Sydney), Shakespeare's Folios in 165, *166*
Stewart, Hugh 35, 215, 220
Stewart, John McKellar *95*
Stiebel, Victor 45, 59
Stonyfell Vineyard/ Winery (SA) *98*, 99
Strachan, Alan 155, 228
Streetcar Named Desire, A (film) 184, 217
Strutton, Bill 42
Surfers Paradise (Qld), and 1948 tour: location's attraction 136, 140, *144*; Oliviers and friends relaxing/ sightseeing *138* (*141*), 141–3, *144*, 144, *145*, 229, 232
Swinburne, Mercia (also Mercia Relph) 33, *55*, *56*, 58, *98*, *157*, *193*, 221, *223*, 224
Swinburne, Charles 224
Sydney (NSW), and 1948 tour: city's character/ attractions 148, *149*, 149, 151, 156, *157*, 161–2, 163, 165, *166*; company's performances 148, 151, 153, 155, 171, *172*, 173, 178; relaxing/ sightseeing 156, *157*, 158, *160*,

161, *162*, 162; ticket sales 153; Oliviers' ambassadorial workload 146 (*149*), 148, 149, *150*, *152*, 153, *154*, 158, *159*, 162–3, *164*, 165, *166*, 171, *174*
Sydney Harbour Bridge 148, *149*

T
Taieri Airport, Dunedin 206
Tasmania, and 1948 tour see Hobart
Taylor, James Lee 31, 37, 225, 226
Teede, Neville 78
Tennant, Cecil 52, 53, 119, *121*, *126* (*129*), 133, *134*, 136, 140, 158, *162*, 167, 170, 220
(H.M.) Tennent Ltd 220
Theatre Royal, Adelaide *91*, 92
Theatre Royal, Hobart *32*, 130–1, 133, *135*, 136, *137*, 184
Thomas, Marie 163, 165, *166*
Thorne, Ross 76
Thorndike, Dame Sybil 31–2
Tivoli Theatre, Brisbane
Tivoli Theatre, Sydney 66–7, *150*, 151, 153, *154*, 156, 182, *222*
Totterdale, Joseph *74*, 82
Tree, Herbert Beerbohm 66
Trocadero dance hall, Sydney 163, 165, *166*
Tufts College, Boston (USA), Oliviers at 20, *21*
Twenty-One Days Together (film) 209

U
United Services Hotel, Christchurch 199
University of Adelaide (SA) *95*, 96, 97
University of Queensland (QLD) *184-6*
University of Western Australia (Perth) *74*, *77*, 78, *79*, 81, 82
Usher's Hotel, Sydney 146 (*149*)

V
van Sommers, Tess 173
Vickers, Hugo 171, 217, 220
Victoria, and 1948 tour see Melbourne
Vidal, Constance 161
Vivien Leigh Circle (fan club) 174
Vivien Leigh Theatre, Auckland 196
Vizard, Steve 42
Vogue (British), and Vivien 40, *41*, 43, 45, *47*
Vreeland, Diana 40

W
'Waltzing Matilda', and the Oliviers/ other tour members 64, 73
Wardle, Thomas 76
Warlow, John *47*
Waterhouse, Professor E.G. 163
Waterloo Bridge (film) 204
Watney, Dick *121*, 122
Watney, Lorna 122
Welford, Dorothy 52
Wellington (NZ): city's character/ attractions 207; company's performances 208, 209, *210*; ticket sales 207, 208; Oliviers' ambassadorial workload 207–8, 209, 211; arrival/ departure 190 (*193*), 206, 211
West, Laurence 180
Western Australia, and 1948 tour see Perth
Whale Beach, Sydney 161
Whenuapai Airport, Auckland (NZ) 178, *193*, *194*, 195
Wild Duck, The (play) 58
Wilder, Thornton 18, 35, 58, 199, 209, 235
Williams, Air Marshal R. 178
(J.C.) Williamson Ltd 120
Wilmot, Charles 31, 32, 133
Windsor Hotel (Melbourne) 106, *107*, *108*, 109, 111, 112, 125
Woltif, David 226
Wool Board (Australian), and Vivien 114, *115*
Wrest Point, Hobart *131*
Wrest Point Riviera Hotel, Hobart 128, *129*, 129, *130*, 130
Wyngarde, Peter 233

Y
Yarralumla, and Oliviers see Government House, Canberra

Acknowledgements

This book has been a labour of love, born from a need to make an auction win mean something and to share it with Vivien Leigh and Laurence Olivier fans. I initially wanted to write something to add context to the photos in the album that came with that win, but realised the official album held by the National Library of Australia contained photos which could supplement it. Various other collections came to light during the course of research and I thank the owners for allowing me to use their photographs.

I have made every effort to identify persons and locations correctly. If there are inaccuracies, feedback will be most welcome. I have also endeavoured to identify and contact all copyright holders of photos, to give credit to rightful owners and creators where possible, and sincerely regret any omissions. Further, I'd like to emphasise this recount and interpretation of events and characters are purely my own.

For a book to reach publication takes a lot of support, as has this one. It would not have been possible without the encouragement, help, belief and sheer presence of the following people.

First and foremost, Garry O'Connor for paving the way with his meticulously researched book, *Darlings of the Gods*. I hope by adding a visual component from an Australian context, my version has complemented a story he has already told.

My heartfelt gratitude goes to Kendra Bean, who I consider a mentor, for her encouragement, advice and friendship from the start. Access to her vast collection and website was invaluable but most importantly her belief in me kept me going through various set-backs and doubts.

I am indebted to Judith Koop for inviting me to her home and allowing full access to her Aunt Joyce Attwood's collection. Her great-great-grandmother Mary Ann's scrapbook, that she allowed me to keep for months on end, was particularly helpful.

For Lyndsy Spence, thank you for the kinship in magic and the beyond, belief and endorsement.

David Tenenbaum, my publisher, for going with his gut instinct to take this on.

For my editor Sophie Goodin and designer Ellen Cheng at Melbourne Books, thank you both for being an absolute joy to work with.

To Diane Carlyle, thank you for your work and advice along the way.

I am blessed to have Alicia Powell and Carole Anderson as friends and value not only that but their generosity, sharing of information and collections.

I sincerely thank Ron Harper for his professional advice and direction.

Thank you to Greta Ritchie for the moral support, confidence in my writing and access to her amazing Vivien Leigh collection.

To my old-soul children, Christina Scarlett and Sean Patrick, for helping with submissions and technology.

I am humbled by the generosity of Szilvia Perez in sharing all of her personal research at the British Library and Vivien Leigh Archive, amidst life-changing moves and career shifts.

I'd like to thank my first research assistant in London, Lisa Duffy, and Lucy Bolton for introducing her. Thank you Jila Hegan for continuing to travel to the British Library to complete the transcription of Olivier's tour journal that Lisa started.

At the Australian National Library, I'm grateful to Eva Bernroider for her understanding and assistance in getting the photos requested so efficiently.

I am thankful to the following for sharing their memories and other treasures with me; the late Tracer Faulkner, Graeme Gillespie, Lyn Sharp, Barbara Atherton, Margaret O'Meehan, Nola McTavish, Doug Fotheringham.

At Newspix Productions I'd like to thank Jamie Trew for helping me find what photos there were whilst we were in a Covid lockdown.

During my year in Canberra, where I managed to do a lot of writing, I am grateful for befriending Gayle Milne who kept me sane and helped with research. Another Canberran I am thankful for is Vivienne Grey for her company and friendship through what was sometimes a very lonely year away from family.

Special thanks to Irina Gershgorin, Alejandro Franks, Andrew Batt, The Vivien Leigh Circle, Michelle Beck, Peter Goers, Chrystopher Spicer, Kerry B Collison, Marie Pietersz, Hana Dolezalova, Ida Chionh, Rachelle Mosca, David Mosca, Sash Costa, Esperanza Alcastle, Bob Byrne, Sean Hartley, Liz Perritt, Serge Mafioly, Kristen Willenberg, Angela Frodsham, Erica Lorimer, Margarida Araya, Keith Lodwick, Corinne Francois-Deneve, Carol Freeman, Barb Lypka, Rachel Nicholson, and Virosh Perera.

To the talented Victor Mascaro for colourising and restoring two photos.

Merilee Andrews, from Aotearoa, wherever you are, thank you for introducing me to *Gone with the Wind* and thereby Vivien Leigh, many, many moons ago.

Last but not least, all Vivien Leigh and Laurence Olivier fans, I thank you for the support you've given through social media pages, private messages and for keeping their legacies alive. I hope I've been able to give you something in return through this book.

The Author

Shiroma Perera-Nathan is a life-long fan of Vivien Leigh. She has travelled to many places connected with The Old Vic tour and discovered the official tour album held in the National Library collections. She has contributed a chapter to the University of Rennes, Paris, Vivien Leigh conference book, and written several blog entries for classic film websites. With a New Zealand and Australian background, Shiroma has a unique perspective on The Old Vic Tour.

Published by Melbourne Books
Level 9, 100 Collins Street,
Melbourne, VIC 3000
Australia
www.melbournebooks.com.au
info@melbournebooks.com.au

Copyright © Shiroma Perera-Nathan 2024

All rights reserved. No part of this publication may be reproduced, stored in a retrieval system, or transmitted in any form or any means electronic, mechanical, photocopying, recording or otherwise without the prior permission of the publisher.

Title: God and The Angel: Vivien Leigh and Laurence Olivier's Tour De Force of Australia and New Zealand
Author: Shiroma Perera-Nathan
ISBN: 9781922779151

 A catalogue record for this book is available from the National Library of Australia

Photo captions:

Front cover: Credit: Angus McBean Photograph. © Harvard Theatre Collection, Houghton Library, Harvard University.

Back cover: The Oliviers pose for photos at Scarborough Beach, Perth. Colourised by Victor Mascaro. Credit: Author's collection

Page 1: Masses of fans see the Oliviers off at Essendon Airport, Melbourne. Credit: Shmith,Athol. 1948, Australian tour 1948, Laurence Olivier and Vivien Leigh and the Old Vic Company Bib ID 3044576. National Library of Australia

Page 4: In their Brisbane flat with the camera which Olivier presumably used whilst on the tour. Credit: Private collection